Relational Theory

CONCEPTS AND APPLICATION

To Lucille whose devotion to duty has made
our daughters all that they can be

Relational Theory

CONCEPTS AND APPLICATION

Kenmore S. Brathwaite
AKI Group, Inc.
Iselin, New Jersey

ACADEMIC PRESS, INC.
Harcourt Brace Jovanovich, Publishers
San Diego   New York   Boston   London   Sydney   Tokyo   Toronto

005.76

B 824

Academic Press, Inc.
San Diego, California 92101

United Kingdom Edition published by
Academic Press Limited
24–28 Oval Road, London NW1 7DX

Library of Congress Cataloging-in-Publication Data

Brathwaite, Ken S.
    Relational theory : concepts and application / Kenmore S.
    Brathwaite.
        p.   cm.
    Includes bibliographical references and index.
    ISBN 0-12-125881-5
    1. Data base management.   2. Relational data bases.   I. Title.
    QA76.9.D3B696   1991
    005.76--dc20   91-2059
                                                            CIP

PRINTED IN THE UNITED STATES OF AMERICA
91 92 93 94   9 8 7 6 5 4 3 2 1

CONTENTS

PART II

Relational Database Issues

PREFACE

The work reported in this book was developed from notes that I used in courses at the University of Alberta, from research conducted in relational databases since 1979, and from several consulting assignments at major Fortune 500 companies since 1984.

The main objective of this book is to provide information on some important topics in relational databases. In this book, I provide readers with information on traditional topics such as data modeling, logical and physical database design, and normalization; I also cover database-specific topics such as Structured Query Language (SQL), Database 2 (DB2), and Query Management Facility (QMF). The work is intended for data administrators, database administrators, systems designers, and application programmers who want to gain familiarity with the relational database environment. Since the book introduces the topics at a fundamental level, there are no prerequisites.

As the title suggests, the book provides information on interrelated topics in relational databases, but it deals with them independently. Thus, each chapter in the book is intended to stand alone and any congruity between chapters is purely coincidental. Therefore, the reader who is interested only in normalization need not read the chapter on logical and physical database design.

Part I of the book covers the relational database environment. Chapter 1 introduces the database environment and covers topics such as data analysis, functional analysis, data administration, data security, and system development.

Chapter 2 deals with data models, data structures and the role they play in corporate data modeling, business systems planning, and database design. Chapter 3 discusses the logical database design phase of database development. It indicates how this phase fits into the systems development life cycle and discusses the deliverables of the phase. Chapter 4 discusses the normalization process and how it applies to the design of efficient databases.

Chapter 5 discusses the development of a data dictionary that will support the documentational requirements of relational databases. Chapter 6 discusses some of the issues involved in managing and controlling databases. This chapter deals more extensively with external control mechanisms than with internal or software mechanisms design to control the database.

Chapter 7 is perhaps the most intriguing chapter of the book. It highlights how the various departmental units of a management information systems department would support a database environment. The chapter details the support expected from data administration, logical and physical designers, operations, data control, and systems designers.

Part II of the book deals with more specific relational database topics such as DB2 and SQL/DS in Chapter 12, SQL in Chapter 13, and QMF in Chapter 14. The major departure in the last part of the book is in Chapters 16 and 17. In Chapter 16, I devote a large section to detailed discussions of performance issues and standards. The approach here is "this is how DB2 interfaces must be designed and coded to work efficiently." The standards discussed here are a must for any DB2 installation.

Finally, the book ends with a discussion of auditing the database environment. The audit techniques are applied to the DB2 environment, on-line systems, and the controls that must be in place to audit the environment.

I am grateful for comments and suggestions I received from Vic Howard, Stanley Locke, Francis Chin, and Jay Louise Weldon. The initial draft of this manuscript was ably typed by Arlene Bowman, Andrea Drayton, and Earleen Harris. Their efforts are appreciated.

Kenmore S. Brathwaite
Brooklyn, New York
June 1991

PART I

The Relational
Database Environment

CHAPTER 1

Introduction to the Database Environment

Databases are evident in nearly every aspect of data processing today. Database technology was popularized during the 1960s. During that period, the underlying data structures for the databases were based on hierarchies and networks. The relational data structures, the subject that forms the backbone of this book, were popularized during the 1970s.

Databases, or collections of related data, were first marketed as approaches that would allow the greatest amount of data sharing while reducing data dependency and eliminating data redundancy. However, the advent of the database era also heralded new problems with data security, integrity, and privacy and new requirements for developing applications to take advantage of the new technology.

The database era also introduced new tools and management issues into the data processing environment. The remainder of this chapter discusses these tools and issues in greater detail.

1.1 Data Structures and Data Models

Data structures and data models form the underlying structures for the database management systems (DBMS). The data model is primarily a diagrammatical representation of entities and their association. The constraints of the DBMS are then superimposed on the data model to form the distinguishing features of each DBMS. The DBMS and its attendant software are the dominant tools in the database environment. These tools and their different features will be discussed in the next chapter.

Data structures and data models are the primary deliverables of logical database design, business systems planning activities or study, corporate data modeling activities, information engineering efforts, and knowledge-based systems design. During the development of application programs, the data analyst collects information on the user requirements. This information is analyzed on the basis of the entities that interest the user and the data model is then produced.

In business systems planning, the organization seeks to determine what data architecture can be developed to support its long-term data needs and assist it in achieving its goals and objectives. The data architecture is manifested as data models showing all the entities that the corporation will need.

In the information engineering and knowledge-based systems design, the data models become the building blocks. The systems designer uses these building blocks to develop rules-based and data-based systems.

1.2 Data Administration and Database Administration

The database era has witnessed or caused the creation of several new staffing needs. Two of these areas are data administration and database administration.

Data administration (DA) is defined as the establishment and enforcement of policies and procedures for managing the organization's data as a corporate resource. It involves the collection, storage, and dissemination of data as a globally administered and standardized resource.

Database administration (DBA) is a technical function that performs database design and development, provides education on database technology, provides support to users in operational data management-related activities, and may provide technical support for administration.

Before a data administration function can be established, certain conditions are necessary:

- The management must be willing to take a long-range view of the cost structure.
- Data processing and line management must be prepared for the database approach with the associated protocols and standards.
- The entire line management must view data as a resource similar to raw materials, equipment, finance, and personnel.

The initiative for establishing a data administration function can originate anywhere in the data processing organization. However, the most common starting point is with the data processing professional who becomes concerned about the growing demands for the proper administration and management of the organization's data resources.

On the other hand, there are times when top management focuses on the data resource issue before the data processing professionals. This usually occurs when management becomes aware of the need to manage data as a resource or when they experience a lack of information in supporting a planning or decision-making process.

The establishment of the data administration function is fast becoming a critical decision for most organizations. It is a very important area of database management, and once the decision is made to establish the function, everyone charged with that decision should ensure that top management not only supports the decision but becomes involved in the ongoing functioning of the DA department.

1.2.1 The Functions of Data Administration

Data administration provides custody of the organization's data and coordinates data activities with systems developers and users. The data administration functions will include:

- Logical design of database systems
- Liaison to systems personnel during the application development process
- Training all relevant personnel in data administration concepts and techniques
- Setting and monitoring data management standards
- Design of documentation, including data dictionaries
- Promoting and allowing for interdepartmental data sharing
- Resolution of data sharing conflicts
- Setting up facilities to monitor data usage authorization

These functions are achieved by carrying out certain activities. These activities may or may not exist in all DA departments, but those that are classified as successful must undertake to carry out several or all of them. Among these activities, the development and enforcement of policies governing data collection must rank as the most important activity conducted by data administration.

1.2.2 The Function of Database Administration

Database administration is concerned with the technical aspects of managing the data resource within the organization rather than the administrative aspects. Technical aspects include the expertise in a particular database management system and the design of database logical and physical structures. The database administration function will include:

- Physical design of database systems
- Assisting in the negotiation for the acquisition of hardware and software to support the database management system
- Acting as a contact point for users who are experiencing problems with the DBMS and associated software
- Monitoring the performance of the DBMS and the individual transactions against the databases
- Assisting in the development of long-term plans to ensure that adequate hardware capacity and facilities are available to meet the requirements of new systems or the expansions of existing systems

1.3 The Data Dictionary

The data dictionary is the second most important tool in the database environment, with the most important being the database management system. The data dictionary is used to record facts about objects or events in the database environment to facilitate communication and provide a permanent record.

In a database environment, the data dictionary is used to provide information about the database itself, its contents, and its structure. The data dictionary focuses primarily on data-related components, such as data elements or attributes, data groups, rows, or tables, data structures, and databases. The data dictionary should document the following information for the database environment.

- Name/meaning—a unique identifier and descriptive information that convey the full meaning of the component; the name is used for reference and retrieval purposes, while the description is valuable to managers and users
- Physical description—the physical characteristics of the components, such as size of an attribute or the length of a table row
- Edit/authorization criteria—criteria to be used to test the validity of occurrences of the component, such as acceptable range of values (domain) for attributes or passwords for update of a database
- Usage—information on where and by whom or by what a component is used, such as the programs that can reference a given attribute
- Logical description—the characteristics and structure of each user

view of the database, such as logical relationships among tables or
table rows
- Procedures—guidelines for human interaction with the database,
such as for backup, recovery, and system restart
- Responsibility—a record of the individual or organizational unit
responsible for the generation and maintenance of the database
component

The data dictionary is a useful tool for ensuring data security, integrity, and privacy. In the active mode, the dictionary can be used to protect attributes stored in the database, and the DBMS will interrogate the data dictionary regarding the security level of the requestor. If the security level is greater than or equal to that of the requested item, the DBMS retrieves the item as requested.

The data dictionary can also be used in a passive mode to offer protection in the database environment. For example, if a user consults the dictionary to determine whether another user can have access to a particular item and denies or authorizes access on that basis, then the dictionary is being used in a passive mode.

1.3.1   The Data Dictionary and Change Control

Changes are part of the evolutionary process of any database environment. The control of changes is a critical activity in this environment and is necessary for two reasons:

1. To preserve the integrity of the data and maintain existing security standards
2. To ensure that changes are communicated to all affected users and to determine the impact of those changes

The data dictionary can be used to document how these changes are going to be communicated to the affected users and who are the affected users. This can often be accomplished by keeping an inventory of the occurrence of certain items destined for change, the programs that use these items, the data accessed by these programs, and the various users of the data.

1.3.2   The Data Dictionary and Standards

The data dictionary can be used to document the standards that are established in the database environment, which may include data processing standards, system standards, and programming standards.

Data processing standards cover the operation and control of computers, whether they are in a mainframe data center under management control or minicomputers in user locations.

Systems standards cover the various phases of the project life cycle, from the initial business information planning process through the steps of system proposal, functional design, detail design, programming, conversion, and post-audit. The data dictionary must be able to document detailed guidelines and standards for deliverables from the user requirements collection and analysis phase, project-estimating techniques, evaluation of database programs and software, structured design methodology, and documentation standards.

Programming standards must include standard naming conventions, the languages used, program cataloguing procedures, access control methods, JCL standards, and the utilities in use.

Standards that govern the naming of attributes can improve communication among database users and can detect inconsistencies before they become part of the database.

1.4 Data Analysis in the Database Environment

Data analysis is the process of determining the fundamental data resources of an organization. It deals with the collection of the basic entities and the relationship between the entities.

The primary purpose of data analysis is to organize and document all relevant facts concerning the organization's data resource. Data analysis has been used to:

- Determine the fundamental data resources of an organization
- Provide a disciplined approach toward documenting the existing data in terms of the entities and relationships they represent
- Provide the effective means of communicating with non-data processing users by dealing only with aspects that the users are familiar with
- Analyze the inherent structure of the data independently from the details of the applications
- Form a basis for data control, security, and auditing systems
- Organize all relevant facts concerning the organization's data
- Produce a point of reference, the entity model, against which a logical database structure for each of the database management systems can be designed
- Provide a sound basis for database design

Data analysis consists of two dependent parts. First, entity analysis provides a means of understanding and documenting a complex environment in terms of its entities, their attributes, and relationships. Second, functional analysis is concerned with understanding and documenting the basic activities of the organization.

1.4.1 Functional Analysis

Functional analysis is concerned with an understanding and documentation of the basic business activities with which the organization is concerned. Functional analysis has the following objectives:

- Determine how entities are used so as to increase understanding of the entity model
- Provide a firm basis for transaction design
- Gather estimates of data usage for database design

Functional analysis may reveal attribute types of entities that had not been detected during entity analysis. Similarly, relationships between entities that had not been considered meaningful may be found to be required by certain functions.

The basic functions identified in functional analysis would be expected to be translated into transaction types in the data processing system. Estimates of data usage will provide a means for determining which access paths should be made most efficient.

In functional analysis, the data analyst identifies the events and functions. An event may be defined as a stimulus to the organization and functions as tasks that must be carried out as a direct result of the event.

1.5 Structured Systems Design in the Database Environment

The database environment has gained tremendously from the introduction of new structured design methodologies. The gains have been enormous in terms of shorter development times for systems and improved documentation of the design effort.

Database design refers to the process of arranging the data fields needed by one or more applications into an organized structure. That structure must foster the required relationships among the fields, while conforming to the physical constraints of the particular management system in use. There are two parts to the process, namely, logical database design, which is then followed by physical database design.

Logical database design is an implementation-independent exercise that is performed on the fields and the relationships needed for one or more applications. Physical database design is an implementation-dependent exercise that takes the results of logical database design and further refines them according to the characteristics of the particular database management system in use.

Careful database design is essential for a variety of reasons, including data redundancy, application performance, data independence, data security, and ease of programming. All are important factors in the data processing environment, and all can be adversely affected by a poor database design.

The most-used structured database design methodology is currently with the entity–relationship approach. This approach is representative of the class of methods that take entities and relationships as input.

Database design using the entity–relationship model begins with a list of the entity types involved and the relationships among them. The philosophy of assuming that the designer knows what the entity types are at the outset is significantly different from the philosophy behind the other approaches.

The basic components that are necessary to achieve a database design methodology are:

- A structured design process that consists of a series of steps in which one alternative among many is chosen
- A design technique to perform the enumeration required and evaluation criteria to select alternatives at each step
- Information requirements for input to the design process as a whole and to each step of the design process
- A descriptive mechanism to represent the information input and the results at each design step

Achieving a design that results in an acceptable level of database performance for all users has become a complex task. The database designer must be ever conscious of the cost/performance trade-offs when a single integrated database is designed for multiple users. Potential savings of storage space and expanded applicability of databases into corporate decision making should be accomplished by a critical analysis of potential degradation of service to some users. Such degradation is to be avoided if possible. Acceptable performance for all users should be the goal.

Another aspect of database design is flexibility. Databases that are too tightly bound to current applications may have too limited a scope for many corporate enterprises. Rapidly changing requirements and new data elements may result in costly program maintenance, a proliferation of temporary files, and increasingly poor performance. A meaningful overall database design process should account for both integration and flexibility.

1.5.1 Inputs to the Structured Design Process

The major classes of inputs to the database design process are:

- General information requirements
- Processing requirements
- Database management system specifications
- Operating system/hardware configuration
- Application program specifications

The major results from the database design process are:

- Logical database structure or user view
- Physical database structure or storage view

The general information requirements represent various users' descriptions of the organization for which data are to be collected, the objectives of the database, and the users' view of which data should be collected and stored in the database. These requirements are considered to be process-independent because they are not tied to any specific database management system or application. Database design based on these requirements is considered to be advantageous for long-term databases that must be adaptable to changing processing requirements.

Processing requirements consist of three distinguishable components: specific data items required for each application, the data volume and expected growth, and processing frequencies in terms of the number of times each application must be run per unit of time. Each of these components is very important to a particular stage or step of the database design process.

Performance measures and performance constraints are also imposed on the database design. Typical constraints include upper bounds on response times to queries, recovery times from system crashes, or specific data needed to support certain security or integrity requirements. The specific performance measure used to evaluate the final structure might include update, storage, and reorganization costs in addition to response requirements.

The three major outputs of the database design process are the logical database structure, the physical design structure, and the specifications for application programs based on these database structures and processing requirements. As a whole, these results may be considered the specification for the final database implementation.

1.6 Logical and Physical Design

Database development is conducted in two phases: logical database design and physical database design. In logical database design, we take the user requirements, analyze them, and produce a data model. The constructs of the relevant database management system are then superimposed on the data model to form the input to the physical database design process.

The physical database design process is primarily concerned with storing the data as defined in the logical data model and defining access paths to the stored data. Logical and physical database design will be discussed at length in a later chapter.

1.7 Application Prototyping

Prototyping represents a significant departure from traditional development methodologies, which are based on the systems development life cycle framework. In this framework, the application software development process consists of the following discrete, sequential phases:

- Inception—identification of a problem requiring an information system solution
- Feasibility study—analysis of the economic, technical, and organizational feasibility of the proposed system
- Requirements analysis—determination of user needs and specifications of the information system output and of the characteristics required to satisfy those needs
- Systems design—specification of software and hardware components, including processing logic, files, program requirements, and procedures
- Systems development and testing—creation of programs and determination that software is correct
- Conversion and installation—introduction of the system to the user department

● Operation and maintenance—daily use of changes or updates to the application system

The life cycle-based methodologies assume that the user requirements can be completely and correctly determined during the early phases of the application development process.

Prototyping helps developers solve problems and enhances development effectiveness by eliciting and clarifying user requirements and by providing an early opportunity for users to test and experiment with software design and specifications. It is based on the premise that users understand tangible, functional models better than logical, abstract models and are therefore able to evaluate them more effectively.

1.7.1 Prototyping Procedures

The prototyping effort starts with the identification of an initial set of user requirements and specification for the system. The systems designer derives these initial requirements by interviewing users and reviewing the existing procedures and documentation.

As soon as a concrete set of system specifications is identified, the programming team develops a prototype as quickly as possible to meet these requirements. The prototype system is then implemented and operated in context. The users' hands-on operation of the prototype provides a basis for evaluation and learning.

Next, the systems designer solicits user feedback in terms of modification requests and new requirements. The prototype is then quickly modified in response to this feedback. The users again operate and evaluate the revised prototype. The prototype evaluation and revision cycle is repeated as many times as necessary until a satisfactory prototype is obtained.

1.7.2 Prototyping Software

Application software prototyping has become practical because of technological developments in data processing. The following tools are valuable for developing and modifying prototypes:

● Data dictionaries, database management systems, and query languages—These tools provide flexible, interactive, and integrated facilities for data storage and retrieval. A data dictionary provides a single definition, integration, and control point for all system entities. A DBMS facilitates data modeling and the creation and modification of databases and application programs. Query languages support ad hoc queries to databases.

- Interactive programming languages or interactive nonprocedural modeling languages—These powerful programming facilities allow rapid creation of the application and models. Nonprocedural languages enable the user to specify what needs to be done and the form the results should take. The software facilities then translate the requirements into procedural steps that the developers must follow to produce the results.
- Graphics and report generators—These tools provide interactive and flexible data formatting and display capabilities. Graphics generators facilitate the creation of graphics (i.e., pie and bar charts and histograms), and report generators are tools to manipulate and format data for reports.

CHAPTER 2

Data Models and Data Structures

Data models are the basic building blocks for all database design. They provide the underlying structure for the dominant data structures of today's database management systems (DBMS). In addition, data models are used by many large corporations in business systems planning, strategic systems planning, and corporate data modeling.

Data models form the basis for entity–relationship diagrams or entity models, as they are called, and are used to define a conceptual view or real-world view of data and the data requirements of an organization.

2.1 Some Key Terms

A data model is defined as a logical representation of a collection of data elements and the association among these data elements. The data model can be used to represent data usage throughout an organization or can represent a single database structure. A data model is to data what a logical data flow diagram is to a process.

There are three types of data models: conceptual, logical, and internal or physical.

The entity diagram is a representation of the relationship between entity classes. The representation allows us to include only those entities that are required to solve the particular data processing problem. The entity diagram is essentially a real-world view of the organization's data in terms of the entities, attributes, and relationships, and it is an example of a conceptual data model. Figure 2.1 is an example of a data model.

2.2 Entity and Entity Classes

Entity and entity classes are used interchangeably in some of the current literature, whereas some researchers define the entity as an occur-

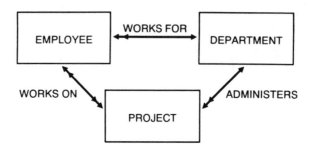

Figure 2.1   Example of a data model.

rence of an entity class. For example, EMPLOYEE is an entity class, whereas P. CAREY, an occurrence of the entity class EMPLOYEE, is an entity.

2.3 Super Entities and Entity Subtypes

An entity may be broken down into smaller subgroups on the basis of the function of each subgroup. These subgroups are often called entity subtypes. The original entity is often referred to as a super entity.

The representation of entity subtypes and super entities is shown in Fig. 2.2, where the large boxes, EMPLOYEE and DEDUCTION, represent super entities, and the small boxes represent entity subtypes.

2.4 Types of Relationships

A relationship is defined as an association between two or more entities. In this section, we will discuss the types of relationships and how they are represented diagrammatically.

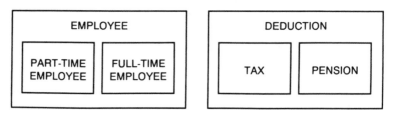

Figure 2.2   Representation of super entity and entity subtype.

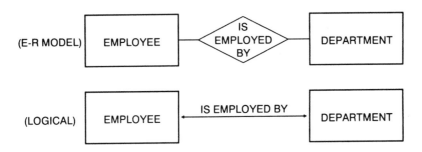

Figure 2.3 Representation of one-to-one relationship.

2.4.1 One-to-One Relationship

At a given time, one EMPLOYEE may be assigned to one DEPART-
MENT. The relationship between EMPLOYEE and DEPARTMENT is
termed one-to-one. This relationship is represented diagrammatically
in Fig. 2.3, where the single-headed arrows denote the one-to-one
relationship.

2.4.2 One-to-Many Relationship

At a given time many EMPLOYEES may be assigned to one DEPART-
MENT. The relationship between EMPLOYEES and DEPARTMENT is
termed one-to-many. The double-headed arrow indicates that many
employees are assigned to one department. This is represented diagrammatically in Fig. 2.4.

2.4.3 Many-to-Many Relationship

At a given time many EMPLOYEES may be assigned to many DEPART-
MENTS. The relationship between EMPLOYEES and DEPARTMENTS

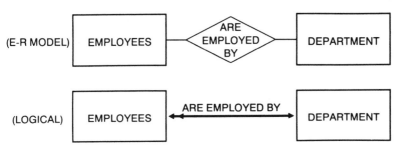

Figure 2.4 Representation of one-to-many relationship.

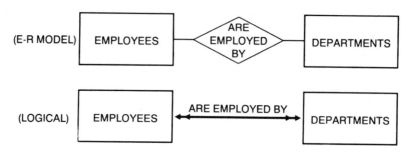

Figure 2.5 Representation of many-to-many relationship.

is termed many-to-many. This is represented diagrammatically in Fig. 2.5.

2.4.4 Mutually Exclusive Relationship

At a given time an EMPLOYEE may be assigned to either DEPART-MENT A or B, but not to both. The relationship between EMPLOYEE and either DEPARTMENT is termed mutually exclusive. This is represented diagrammatically in Fig. 2.6, where the vertical bar in the direction of DEPARTMENT A must always exist in the relationship. The ○ indicates that DEPARTMENT B is optional. We obtain exclusivity by switching the ○ and ▌ around in the relationship.

2.4.5 Mutually Inclusive Relationship

At a given time an EMPLOYEE may be assigned to both DEPARTMENT A and B. The relationship between EMPLOYEE and both DEPART-MENTS is termed mutually inclusive. This is represented diagrammatically in Fig. 2.7. Here the presence of vertical bars in the direction

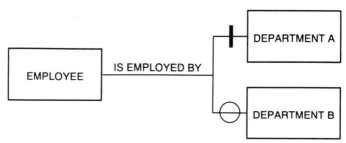

Figure 2.6 Representation of mutually exclusive relationship.

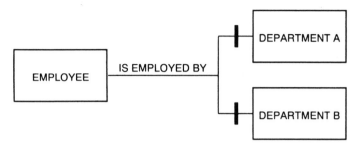

Figure 2.7   Representation of mutually inclusive relationship.

of both departments indicates that both must coexist for the relationship to be completed.

2.4.6 Mandatory Relationship

Sometimes an employer may rule that a DEPARTMENT must exist before the EMPLOYEE is hired. The relationship between EMPLOYEE and DEPARTMENT is termed mandatory. This is represented diagrammatically in Fig. 2.8, where the presence of a vertical bar in the direction of DEPARTMENT indicates that it must exist in the relationship.

2.4.7 Optional Relationship

Sometimes an EMPLOYEE may be hired but not assigned to a DEPARTMENT. The relationship between the EMPLOYEE and DEPARTMENT is termed optional. This is represented diagrammatically in Fig. 2.9, where the presence of the ○ in the direction of DEPARTMENT indicates that DEPARTMENT is not required to exist in the relationship.

2.5 Translation of Entity–Relationship Diagrams to Logical Models

Entity–relationship (E–R) diagrams (models) are sometimes called business entity models since they reflect the business practices of an

Figure 2.8   Representation of a mandatory relationship.

Figure 2.9   Representation of an optional relationship.

organization independently of any requirements for the underlying structure of a database management system. However, for these diagrams to be processed by a computer, they must take on the constructs of the chosen DBMS. This section discusses the translation of E–R diagrams to logical data models.

Let us consider the following problem: A company is heavily project oriented, and each project has one or more employees assigned to it full time, perhaps from different departments. Office space is assigned from time to time. Employees are assigned to an office in the department where they work, and several may share an office. Each department has one employee who is a manager.

The company needs better information on projects, project costs, and utilization of office space and of employees' time.

2.5.1 Identification of Business Entities

When business entities are identified, careful consideration should be given to:

- A generally acceptable *name* for the entity
- A complete definition that makes clear what is included and what is excluded from the members of the entity
- A *business-oriented* entity identified that can be agreed upon across the enterprise

Table 2.1   Examples of Business Entities

Entity name	Abbreviation	Identifier	Description
Department	Dept	Unique ID of DEPT	An organizational unit in the company
Project	Proj	Unique ID of PROJ	A budgeted project now in progress
Employee	Emp	Unique ID of EMP	An active employee of the department; he/she may be full- or part-time
Office	Office	Unique ID of OFFICE	A room allocated to a department

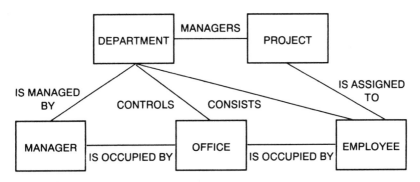

Figure 2.10   E–R diagram for illustrative problem.

The business entities, with their name, abbreviation, identifier, and description for our problem, are shown in Table 2.1.

2.5.2   Determination of E–R Diagram for Problems

The determination of the E–R diagram for the problem may be carried out in a variety of ways. The simplest of these is to take all the nouns in the problem statement and declare them to be entities and to consider the significant verbs as relationships. The diagram resulting from the problem is shown in Fig. 2.10. The degree of the relationships between the entities may be denoted by using 1, M, single-headed, or double-headed arrows.

2.5.3   Conversion of the E–R Diagram to a Logical Data Model

The following steps are taken to convert E–R diagrams to logical data models:

- Convert business entities to data entities
- Represent the degree of the relationship between entities
- Convert many-to-many relationships to associations
- Look for conditional relationships
- Convert repeating groups to characteristic entities

If we apply these steps, we can convert the E–R diagram of Fig. 2.10 to a logical data model as depicted in Fig. 2.11.

In Fig. 2.11, the single-headed arrow in the direction of DEPT and the double-headed arrow in the direction of PROJ indicate that one DEPT may administer many PROJs. The double-headed arrows in the two

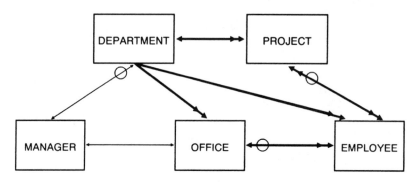

Figure 2.11 Logical data model for problem.

directions PROJ and EMP indicate that many employees may work on many projects. The ○ in the direction of PROJ indicates that there is an optional relationship between PROJ and EMP. In other words, an employee does not have to be assigned to a project to become an employee.

2.5.4 Conversion of Many-to-Many Relationship

Many-to-many relationships are common among business entities but awkward to represent in a logical data model by just two entities, since completeness would require much of the same attribute data to appear in each data entity. However, there is often a need to associate two business entities and, furthermore, to store data about that association. Hence, for each many-to-many relationship, we create a new data entity with the following characteristics:

● The new data entity is called an ASSOCIATION data entity.
● It has a many-to-one relationship with each of the original data entities.

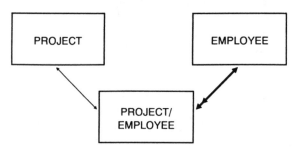

Figure 2.12 Representation of association entity.

● It is a *child* of each of the original data entities.
● The unique identifier of the new data entity will contain the unique identifier of both original data entities.

The new data entities form an association with the two original entities as shown in Fig. 2.12.

2.5.5 Handling of Repeating Groups

A repeating group is a group of one or more attributes of a data entity that may have multiple values for a given value of the unique identifier. Repeating groups are undesirable because:

● There is no way to pick a single occurrence within the group.
● They either impose limitations or cause more complex processing of the physical structure.

To remove repeating groups from the logical model, we must:

● Create a new entity called a CHARACTERISTIC data entity
● Create a one-to-many relationship between the original entity and the new entity
● Use the unique identifier of the original entity as part of the identifier of the new entity

Figure 2.13 illustrates the handling of repeating groups found in the entity PROJ. Let us say that PROJ has the following attributes:

PROJ/(Proj ID, name, address, cost, type)

where cost, address, and type have several values. We can now create a one-to-many relationship with PROJ and a new entity PROJ-TYPE whose attributes are

proj-type ID, type name, cost, and address

The relationship is shown in Fig. 2.13.

2.5.6 Translation of Data Models to Logical Schemas

Logical schemas are defined as data models with the underlying structures of particular database management systems superimposed on

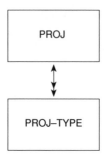

Figure 2.13   Representation of repeating groups.

them. At the present time, there are three main underlying structures for database management systems:

- Relational
- Hierarchical
- Network

2.6 Overview of DBMS Structures

The hierarchical and network structures have been used for database management systems since the 1960s. The relational structure was introduced in the early 1970s.

In the relational model, the entities and their relationships are represented by two-dimensional tables. Every table represents an entity and is made up of rows and columns. Relationships between entities are represented by common columns containing identical values from a domain or range of possible values. Some of the commercially available relational database management systems are:

VENDOR	DBMS
IBM	SQL/DS, DB2
TYMSHARE	MAGMUM
CINCOM	SUPRA
RELATIONAL TECHNOLOGY	INGRES

The hierarchical model is made up of a hierarchy of entity types involving a parent entity type at the higher level and one or more dependent entity types at the lower levels. The relationship established between a parent and a child entity type is one-to-many. At the same time, for a given parent entity occurrence, there can be many occurrences of the child entity type. Some examples of the hierarchical model are:

VENDOR   DBMS
   IBM   IMS
   SAS   SYSTEM 2000

In the network model, the concept of parent and child is expanded in that any child can be subordinate to many different parent entities or owners. In addition, an entity can function as an owner and/or member at the same time. There are several commercially available DBMSs based on the network model:

   VENDOR   DBMS
   CULLINET   IDMS
   HONEYWELL   IDS
   UNIVAC   DMS 1100

2.7 The Relational Data Model

We will use the example discussed in earlier sections of this chapter to illustrate the various relationships between the entities of an organization. The example will also serve to illustrate the various approaches to creating a relational database.

Consider the example shown in Fig. 2.14. These data are represented in a two-dimensional table, which is called a relational model of the data. The data represented in the figure are called a "relation." Each column in the table is an "attribute." The values in the column are drawn from a domain or set of all possible values. The rows of the table are called "tuples."

DEPARTMENT TABLE

DEPARTMENT ID	DEPARTMENT NAME	DEPARTMENT ADDRESS
101	Engineering	Building A
102	Computer Science	Building B
103	Biology	Building C
104	Medical Technology	Building D

Figure 2.14   Representation of data in a relational model.

MANAGER TABLE

MANAGER ID	DEPARTMENT ID	TITLE	NAME
MG101	101	Chief Scientist	Mr. Brown
MG102	102	Systems Designer	Mr. Charles
MG103	103	Sr. Biologist	Dr. Green
MG104	104	Sr. Technologist	Mr. Cave

Figure 2.15   Representation of a relationship in a relational model.

In Fig. 2.14, the DEPARTMENT ID, 101, is the value of the key that uniquely identifies the first row of the table. This key is called the PRIMARY key.

We can now show how the relationship between DEPT and MANAGER in Fig. 2.11 can be represented in the relational model. Let us say that the MANAGER relation is shown as (MGR·ID, TITLE, NAME), where MGR·ID is the PRIMARY key of the relation. We can now represent the relationship as shown in Fig. 2.15.

In Fig. 2.15, column MANAGER ID is called the PRIMARY key and DEPARTMENT ID is called the FOREIGN key. We can also have a column or set of columns identifying the rows of the table. This column is called a CANDIDATE key.

The creation of a table to represent the many-to-many relationship can be accomplished as follows:

● Create the ASSOCIATION entity as outlined earlier
● Create the ASSOCIATION entity table in a similar manner as the preceding MANAGER table

2.7.1 Advantages of a Relational Data Model

1. Simplicity—The end user is presented with a simple data model. His or her requests are formulated in terms of the information content and do not reflect any complexities due to system-oriented aspects. A relational data model is what the user sees, but it is not necessarily what will be implemented physically.
2. Nonprocedural Requests—Because there is no positional dependency between the relations, requests do not have to reflect any preferred structure and therefore can be nonprocedural.
3. Data Independence—This should be one of the major objectives of

any DBMS. The relational data model removes the details of storage structure and access strategy from the user interface. The model provides a relatively higher degree of data independence than do the next two models to be discussed. To be able to make use of this property of the relational data model, however, the design of the relations must be complete and accurate.

2.7.2 Disadvantages of a Relational Data Model

Although some database management systems based on the relational data model are commercially available today, the performance of a relational DBMS has not been comparable with the performance of a DBMS based on a hierarchical or a network data model. As a result, the major question yet to be answered concerns performance. Can a relational data model be used for a DBMS that can provide a complete set of operational capabilities with required efficiency on a large scale? It appears that technological improvements in providing faster and more reliable hardware may answer the question positively.

2.8 Operators in the Relational Data Model

The operators described for the relational data model are those that are found in relational algebra. These operators do not operate on individual rows but rather on entire tables and always produce tables as results. The following sections discuss some of these operators.

2.8.1 The UNION Operator

The UNION operator combines the rows from two similar tables to form new tables. The new table contains the rows that are in either or both of the original tables. Figure 2.16 illustrates the UNION of TABLE A and TABLE B to produce TABLE C. In Fig. 2.16 the "noncommon" rows of the two original tables are combined to form a third table.

2.8.2 The INTERSECTION Operator

The INTERSECTION operator combines the rows from two similar tables to form a new table. The new table contains the rows that are in both of the original tables. Figure 2.17 illustrates the INTERSECTION of TABLE A and TABLE B to produce TABLE C. In this table the "common" rows of the two original tables are combined to form a third table.

TABLE A

STUDENT ID	STUDENT NAME	FACULTY ID
124	FRENCH	A
256	SMITH	B
301	JONES	C

TABLE B

STUDENT ID	STUDENT NAME	FACULTY ID
124	FRENCH	A
125	HARRIS	B
128	SHARP	C

TABLE C

STUDENT ID	STUDENT NAME	FACULTY ID
124	FRENCH	A
256	SMITH	B
301	JONES	C
125	HARRIS	D
128	SHARP	E

Figure 2.16 Example of UNION operator.

2.8.3 The DIFFERENCE Operator

The DIFFERENCE operator combines two tables to produce a third table that contains all rows that are in the first table but not in the second. Figure 2.18 illustrates the DIFFERENCE between TABLE A and TABLE B to produce TABLE C.

TABLE A

STUDENT ID	STUDENT NAME	FACULTY ID
124	FRENCH	A
256	SMITH	B
301	JONES	C

TABLE B

STUDENT ID	STUDENT NAME	FACULTY ID
124	FRENCH	A
125	HARRIS	D
128	SHARP	E

TABLE C

STUDENT ID	STUDENT NAME	FACULTY ID
124	FRENCH	A

Figure 2.17 Example of INTERSECTION operator.

TABLE A

STUDENT ID	STUDENT NAME	FACULTY ID
124	FRENCH	A
256	SMITH	B
301	JONES	C

TABLE B

STUDENT ID	STUDENT NAME	FACULTY ID
124	FRENCH	A
125	HARRIS	D
128	SHARP	E

TABLE C

STUDENT ID	STUDENT NAME	FACULTY ID
256	SMITH	B
301	JONES	C

Figure 2.18   Example of DIFFERENCE operator.

2.8.4   The PRODUCT Operator

The PRODUCT operator combines the rows from two dissimilar tables to form a new table. In this case the third table is formed by concentrating each row of the first table with each row of the second table. Figure 2.19 illustrates the PRODUCT of TABLE A and TABLE B to produce TABLE C. In this table the rows of TABLE A are "multiplied" by each row of TABLE B to form the rows of TABLE C.

2.8.5   The SELECT Operator

The SELECT operator produces a second table from an original table based on a selection criterion. Figure 2.20 illustrates the SELECT operator working on TABLE A to produce TABLE B. Here the SELECT (FACULTY ID = A) produced TABLE B with one row as shown.

2.8.6   The PROJECT Operator

The PROJECT operator produces a new table that contains all the rows from the original table but only a subset of the columns. Figure 2.21 illustrates the PROJECT operator working on TABLE A to produce TABLE B.

In Fig. 2.21 the PROJECT operator is used to produce TABLE B in which the FACULTY NAME column is PROJECT-ed off. This operator is useful in the database environment to exclude from a user view those columns that should not be seen by the particular user.

TABLE A

TABLE B

STUDENT ID	STUDENT NAME	FACULTY ID
124	FRENCH	A
256	SMITH	B
301	JONES	C

CLASS ID	CLASS LOCATION
124	AA
125	AB
126	AC

TABLE C

STUDENT ID	STUDENT NAME	FACULTY ID	CLASS ID	CLASS LOCATION
124	FRENCH	A	101	AA
124	FRENCH	A	102	AB
124	FRENCH	A	103	AC
256	SMITH	B	101	AA
256	SMITH	B	102	AB
256	SMITH	B	103	AC
301	JONES	C	101	AA
301	JONES	C	102	AB
301	JONES	C	103	AC

Figure 2.19 Example of PRODUCT operator.

TABLE A

STUDENT ID	STUDENT NAME	FACULTY ID
124	FRENCH	A
256	SMITH	B
301	JONES	C

TABLE B

STUDENT ID	STUDENT NAME	FACULTY ID

Figure 2.20 Example of SELECT operator.

TABLE A

STUDENT ID	STUDENT NAME	FACULTY ID	FACULTY NAME
124	FRENCH	A	BIOLOGY
256	SMITH	B	HISTORY
301	JONES	C	ART

TABLE B

STUDENT ID	STUDENT NAME	FACULTY ID
124	FRENCH	A
256	SMITH	B
301	JONES	C

Figure 2.21 Example of PROJECT operator.

2.8.7 The JOIN Operator

The JOIN operator combines the rows from two tables to form a third. The resulting table is formed in such a way that in each row, the data values from the columns on which the join is based have the same data

TABLE A

STUDENT ID	STUDENT NAME	FACULTY ID–A
124	FRENCH	A
256	SMITH	B
301	JONES	C

TABLE B

FACULTY ID	CLASS ID	CLASS LOCATION
A	101	AA
B	102	AB
C	103	AC

TABLE C

STUDENT ID	STUDENT NAME	FACULTY ID–A	FACULTY ID–B	CLASS ID	CLASS LOCATION
124	FRENCH	A	A	101	AA
256	SMITH	B	B	102	AB
301	JONES	C	C	103	AC

Figure 2.22 Example of JOIN operator.

TABLE C

STUDENT ID	STUDENT NAME

Figure 2.23   Example of DIVIDE operator.

values. Figure 2.22 illustrates the JOIN operator working on TABLES A and B to form TABLE C.

In Fig. 2.22 the two original tables are joined on columns FACULTY ID-A and FACULTY ID-B when the rows of each column have equal values for the joined columns.

2.8.8   The DIVIDE Operator

The DIVIDE operator compares the data values in columns from the two tables and produces a third table with the columns that have equal volumes eliminated. For example, the DIVIDE operator working on TABLES A and B of Fig. 2.22 will produce TABLE C as shown in Fig. 2.23. Here the empty table is produced since all rows of the two tables had values that matched.

2.9 Summary

This chapter discussed the data models and data structures that form the building blocks of the relational database management system. The fact that relational database management systems are based on solid algebraic theory was emphasized and brought out in the discussion of relational operators.

CHAPTER 3

Logical and Physical Database Design

3.1 Introduction

This chapter discusses the two major phases of database development. In the first phase, logical database design, we take the user requirements as represented by a data model, superimpose the constructs of the database management system, and obtain input to the second phase, physical database design. In the second phase, we are primarily concerned with storing the data as defined in the logical data model and defining access paths to the stored data.

3.2 The Systems Development Life Cycle

In Chapter 1, we discussed two development life cycles for the development of databases. In both cycles, we placed emphasis on the processes and functions that were required to satisfy the user requirements. We want to move away from that approach and adopt an approach in which the data are the driving force behind the database development activities. The phases of this approach are shown in Fig. 3.1.

3.2.1 The User Requirements Phase

The User Requirements phase has been discussed at some length. However, in this section we will concentrate on those areas that are more data related.

During the Initial Survey subphase, the analyst seeks to determine the entities and relationships that are of interest to the users.

In the Data Definition subphase, the analyst obtains descriptions, functions, data characteristics, and editing rules about the entities and all known attributes.

In the Project Scope subphase, the analyst obtains metadata about the

TRADITIONAL	DATA-DRIVEN
1. Identification Phase • Initiation • Initial Survey	1. User Requirements • Initial Survey • Data Definitions • Feasibility Study • Project Scope • Security Plans
2. Systems Study Phase • Feasibility Study • General Systems Study	2. Logical Design • Data Model • Dictionary Population • Process Definitions • Program Specifications • Systems Test Plans • Normalization
3. Systems Development Phase • Detail Systems Design • Data Conversion Plan • Program Specification • System Test Plan • Manual Practices	3. Physical Design • Program Development • Physical DB Design • Database Loading • Testing • Training
4. Systems Implementation • Program Development • Data Conversion • Systems Testing • Training • Parallel Operations	4. Evaluation • Monitoring • Performance Tuning • Reorganization • Auditing
5. Evaluation	

Figure 3.1 The phases of a data-driven systems development life cycle.

boundaries of the data model, the common usage of items in the user views, and information on what should not be included in the project.

In the Security Plans subphase, the analyst obtains information on the security, privacy, and integrity requirements of the data that will be processed by the system. He or she begins to formulate plans and policies for the protection of that data.

3.2.2 The Logical Design Phase

In the Data Model subphase of logical database design, the analyst creates a data model of the entities and relationships that were described in the User Requirements phase. The model is superimposed with the constructs of the relevant database management system. It is during this phase that some attention is paid to key selections and access methods.

In the Usage Statistics subphase, the analyst collects information about the volume of data to be processed, the processing frequencies, the variations in volumes, the volatility of the data, and plans for access to the data other than by unique keys.

In the Normalization subphase, the analyst seeks to ensure that all attributes clearly belong to the entities they best describe. He ensures that existing entities cannot be further collapsed into other entities and that attributes cannot be further grouped into other entities.

In the Data Dictionary Population subphase, the analyst begins to enter all collected metadata about the entities, attributes, relationships, data models, and processes into the corporate data dictionary. This process is usually started in the Data Definitions subphase but must be emphasized in this subphase.

3.2.3 The Physical Design Phase

In the Physical Design phase, the analyst takes the data model from the Logical Design phase as input, selects the best storage and accessing methods, and produces the physical data model. It is during this phase that storage and time estimates for the chosen database management system are calculated.

The analyst may split existing entities in the logical data model or collapse entities to improve performance, to reduce redundancy in storage, or to adhere to access methods requirements. The resulting physical model may differ greatly from the input logical model.

In the Database Loading subphase, the analyst uses a database-specific utility to load data into storage areas on the relevant storage devices.

3.2.4 The Evaluation Phase

During the Evaluation phase, the performance of the database management system is monitored to determine if it meets the user's expectations for response time and throughput. The database is stress-tested for large volumes of data. The pointers and chains are tested to prove ability to return data items from the lowest levels of the hierarchy.

In the Performance Tuning step, utilities are run against the database to repair broken pointers and chains. Transaction rates, mixes, and processing regions are examined to ensure that the system is performing adequately. The analyst must reexamine main storage space, DASD space, channels, and teleprocessing lines to ensure that the database is doing the required work.

In the Reorganization phase, the analyst reorganizes or restructures the database to recapture all unused space between the valid records as a result of the deletion of some records. He also reorganizes the database to prevent fragmentation of space, the creation of long chains, and excessive fetch times. He may also want to rearrange the records so that, for most of them, their physical sequence is the same as their logical sequence. The analyst may also want to reorganize the database so that the frequently accessed records may be stored on a high-speed medium, whereas the rarely accessed records are stored on a slower-speed medium.

In the case of a sequentially organized database, reorganization may take the form of combining the old database records with the transaction log file to form a new database. In an indexed sequentially organized database, reorganization means taking all the database records from the prime and overflow areas and reloading the database without any records going into the overflow area.

In the Auditing phase, the internal auditors examine the audit trails, the transaction log file, the backup and recovery procedures, and all relevant standards and procedures that have been developed during the database development period to determine their adequacy and their ability to ensure the security, privacy, and integrity of the stored data.

3.2.5 Data-Related Activities during the Systems Development Life Cycle

In a data-driven systems development life cycle (SDLC), the analyst, data administrator, database administrator, and system designer carry out activities and produce deliverables, some of which are distinctly data related. These activities and deliverables differ greatly from those that are strictly process-driven or process related. These activities and deliverables are summarized in Fig. 3.2.

3.3 Logical Design of Databases

The logical design of databases is mainly concerned with superimposing the constructs of the database management system on the logical data model. As mentioned earlier, these constructs fall into three categories: hierarchical, relational, and network. In this section, we will develop various logical models of a database using three structures.

TRADITIONAL	*DATA ACTIVITIES*	*DATA DELIVERABLES*

1. Identification
  • Initiation
  • Initial Survey
	1. User Requirement
	  • Define the entities
	    that will be included
	    in project scope
		• Data dictionary
		  containing data
		  items, validation
		  rules, and other
		  definitions

2. Systems Study
  • Feasibility Study
  • Data Conversion
    Plan
  • Program
    Specifications
  • Systems Test Plan
  • Manual Practices
	2. Logical Design
	  • Identify
	    relationships among
	    data items
	  • Normalize user views
	  • Produce logical data
	    model
		• Logical database and
		  data model

3. Systems Development
  • Detail Systems
    Design
  • Data Conversion
    Plan
  • Program
    Specification
  • Systems Test Plan
  • Manual Practices
	3. Physical Design
	  • Develop physical
	    database from
	    logical model
	  • Verify adequacy of
	    physical design
		• Data dictionary with
		  all physical data
		  flows

4. Systems Implementation
  • Program
    Development
  • Data Conversion
  • Systems Testing
  • Training
  • Parallel Operations
	4. Evaluation
	  • Assist DBA in
	    setting procedures
	    for monitoring the
	    database
	  • Assist auditors in
	    setting procedures
	    for auditing the
	    database	

5. Evaluation		

Figure 3.2   Data-related activities and deliverables.

3.3.1   Mapping to a Hierarchical Data Model

The steps to follow in deriving a logical hierarchical database from the logical data model are:

● Derive a hierarchical data model including the constructs of the DBMS

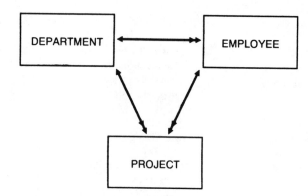

Figure 3.3   Superfluous relationships.

- Refine the data model according to performance requirements
- Select key names
- Add relationships, association, and characteristic entities as required by the particular DBMS

In deriving a hierarchical data model that includes the constructs of the DBMS, we may want to:

- Eliminate superfluous relationships
- Derive all parent–child relationships
- Resolve multiple parentage

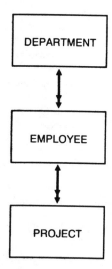

Figure 3.4   Modify relationships.

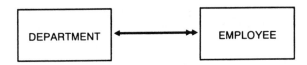

Figure 3.5 Relationship between department and employee.

Let us examine the relationships represented in Figs. 3.3 and 3.4. The relationship between DEPARTMENT and EMPLOYEE is superfluous since it can be derived from the relationship shown in Fig. 3.4.

In deriving relationships, we may want to derive a parent–child relationship from a given relationship. Let us examine the relationships represented in Figs. 3.5. and 3.6. We can derive a new relationship where either DEPARTMENT or EMPLOYEE is the parent.

The significance of creating the parent–child relationship is illustrated as follows. Let us store some information on the date the employee joined the department, the results of performance reviews, promotions within the department, and job functions. We can see that all of these stored attributes do not identify either the DEPARTMENT or EMPLOYEE entity but do identify the relationship between DEPARTMENT and EMPLOYEE. When this situation occurs, the key of the new entity is a combination of the keys of the two original entities.

The resolution of multiple parentage depends on whether some parents are third normal form relations or a created one. Very often, created entities are needed mainly for the physical implementation of the data model. When this is the case, and no data are lost by eliminating the created entity or combining it with another entity, we can safely opt for eliminating the created entity and not the third normal form one.

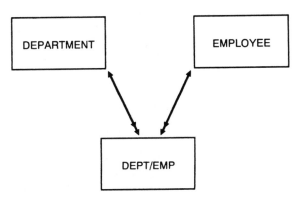

Figure 3.6 Representation of *parent–child* relationship.

Very often, the data model must be modified to conform with the constraints of the DBMS. For example, if the DBMS was an Information Management System (IMS), we would have the following constraints:

- There can be no more than 255 node types or segment types.
- There can be no more than 15 hierarchical levels.
- A child segment type can have no more than two parents, a "physical" parent and a "logical" parent.
- A logical child cannot have a logical child.

On occasion, we may want to add relationships to the data model. The reason may be to add entities that provide better support for the data needs of the organization in the future. These should not be done in a way that would degrade the performance of the system.

3.3.2 Mapping to a Relational Data Model

As we have discussed before, the relational model consists of a number of relations or tables. In mapping the data model onto the constructs of the relational DBMS, we would produce a table for each entity in the model. The relationships between entities would show up as foreign keys in one of the related entities. Mapping into a relational DBMS is a relatively easy process.

3.3.3 Mapping to a Network Data Model

In mapping a data model onto the constructs of the network DBMS, we derive owner–member relationships within set types. We may collapse some of the set types by combining entities or eliminating them after the normalization process.

The logical database designers will have to pay more attention to performance considerations when mapping to a network database than during similar phases of hierarchical or relational database design.

3.4 Physical Design of Databases

The physical model is a framework of the database to be stored on physical devices. The model must be constructed with every regard given to the performance of the resulting database. An analysis of the physical model, the average frequencies of occurrences of the groupings of the data elements, the expected space estimates, and the time estimates for retrieving and maintaining the data should be carried out.

The database designer may find it necessary to have multiple entry points into a database or to access a particular segment type with more than one key. To provide this type of access, it may be necessary to invert the segment on the key, thereby imposing some overhead on space and/or time. This is often the price that must be paid to satisfy this particular business requirement.

The physical designer must have expertise in at least three areas:

- Knowledge of the DBMS functions
- Understanding of the characteristics of direct-access devices
- Knowledge of the applications

The physical designer must know how the DBMS performs its specific functions. For example, in IBM's Information Management System he or she must know the following:

1. That access to all segments, except when using secondary indexing, is through the root segment. Hence, remote segments should be confined to few levels and not spread out from left to right.
2. That retrieval from the database is by segments. This means that a programmer may be presented with more data than are necessary. This often poses security problems for the installation. In this case, the trade-off is between too few and too many segments.
3. That frequently accessed segments should be kept at the top of the hierarchy, since all access is through the root of the hierarchy.
4. That one physical database is based on one root segment. Hence, is one physical database is expected to become too big, he should consider splitting it. However, he must take into consideration the operational issues of backup and recovery for several physical databases.
5. How to provide alternate paths to the data other than through the root segment. For example, we must know that with secondary indexing, IMS database records can be accessed on data elements other than the primary key.

3.5 Selection of Access Methods

We often refer to the way that we store the data for subsequent retrieval as the file organization. How we retrieve the data is called the access method.

The types of access methods vary from manufacturer to manufacturer, and the names also vary from DBMS to DBMS. The physical database designer must be familiar with several access methods. However, because of the author's background with IMS, we will discuss only those that are pertinent to IMS.

IMS allows us to define nine different types of databases. These are:

DATABASE TYPE	GROUP	ACCESS METHOD
HSAM	Sequential	Hierarchical Sequential
SHSAM	Sequential	Simple Hierarchical Sequential
HISAM	Sequential	Hierarchical Indexed Sequential
SHISAM	Sequential	Simple Hierarchical Indexed Sequential
HDAD	Direct	Hierarchical Direct
HIDAM	Direct	Hierarchical Indexed Direct
MSDB	Direct	Main Storage
DEDB	Direct	Data Entry

3.5.1 Hierarchical Sequential Databases

HSAM databases use the sequential method of storing data. All database records and all segments within each database record are physically adjacent in storage.

HSAM data sets are loaded with root segments in ascending key sequence and dependent segments in hierarchical sequence. You do not have to define a key field in root segments, however, you must present segments to the load program in the order in which you want them loaded. HSAM data sets use a fixed-length, unblocked record format (RECFM = F), which means that the logical record length is the same as the physical block size.

HSAM databases can only be updated by rewriting them. They are appropriate primarily for low-use files, for example, audit trails, statistical reports, or files containing historical or archival data.

Segments in an HSAM database are loaded in the order in which you present them to the load program. You should present all segments within a database record in hierarchical sequence. In the data set, a database record is stored in one or more consecutive blocks. If there is not enough space left in the block to store the next segment, the remaining space is filled with zeros and the next segment is stored in the next consecutive block.

Figure 3.7 illustrates the HSAM database records sequence, and Fig. 3.8 illustrates how the HSAM database records are stored.

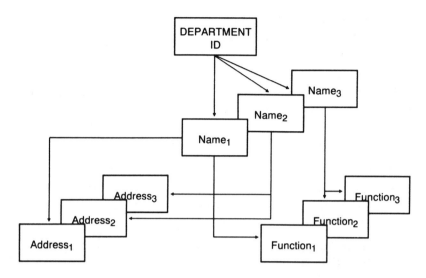

Figure 3.7   Representation of HSAM database in hierarchical sequence.

3.5.2   Hierarchical Indexed Sequential Databases

In a HISAM database, as with HSAM databases, segments in each database record are related through physical adjacency in storage. Unlike in HSAM, however, you must define a unique sequence field in each root segment. These sequence fields are then used to construct an index to root segments in the database.

HISAM is typically used for databases that require direct access to database records and sequential processing of segments in a database record. It is a good candidate for databases with the following characteristics:

- Most database records are about the same size.
- The database does not consist of relatively few root segments and a large number of dependent segments.

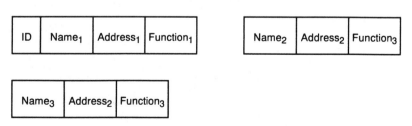

Figure 3.8   Storage of HSAM records.

- Applications do not require a heavy volume of root segments being inserted after the database is initially loaded.
- Deletion of database records is minimal.

HISAM database records are stored in two data sets. The first, called the primary data set, contains an index and all segments in a database record that can fit into one logical record. The index provides direct access to the root segment. The second data set, called the overflow data set, contains all segments in the database record that cannot fit in the primary data set.

Figure 3.9 illustrates the HISAM database records sequence, and Fig. 3.10 illustrates how HISAM database records are stored.

There are several things you need to know about storage of HISAM database records:

- You define the logical record length of both the primary and overflow data set.

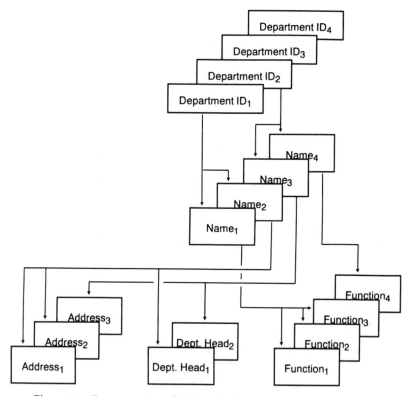

Figure 3.9   Representation of HISAM database in hierarchical sequence.

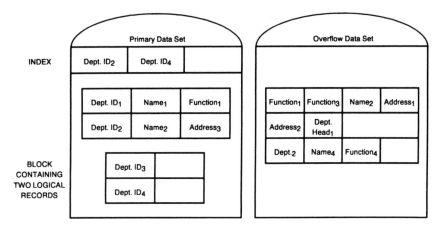

Figure 3.10 Storage of HISAM records.

- You define the size of the control interval or block.
- Each database record starts at the beginning of a logical record in the primary data set.
- Segments in a database record cannot be split and stored across two logical records.

3.5.3 Hierarchical Direct Databases

Hierarchical Direct databases differ from sequentially organized databases in two important ways. First, they use a direct method of storing data, that is, the hierarchical sequence of segments in the database is maintained by having segments point to one another. Except for a few special cases, each segment has one or more direct-address pointers in its prefix. When direct-address pointers are used, database records and segments can be stored anywhere in the database. Their position, once stored, is fixed. Instead, pointers are updated to reflect processing changes.

Hierarchical Direct (HD) databases also differ from sequentially organized ones in that space in HD databases can be reused. If part or all of a database record is deleted, the deleted space can be reused when new database records or segments are inserted.

HDAM databases are used when you need direct access to database records. A randomizing module provides fast access to the root segment.

HIDAM databases are typically used when you need both random and sequential access to database records and random access to paths

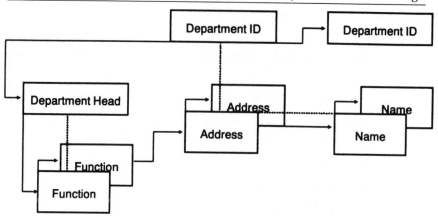

Figure 3.11 Hierarchical forward pointers.

or segments in a database record. Access to root segments is not as fast as with HDAM, because the HIDAM index database has to be searched for a root segment's address. However, because the index keeps the address of root segments stored in key sequence, database records can be processed sequentially.

The next few diagrams illustrate how Hierarchical Direct databases are stored and processed. In hierarchical pointers, each pointer points from one segment to the next in either forward or forward and backward hierarchical sequence (Fig. 3.11).

In physical child first pointers, each pointer points from a parent to the first child or dependent segment (Fig. 3.12). You should notice that no pointers exist to connect occurrences of the same segment type under a parent.

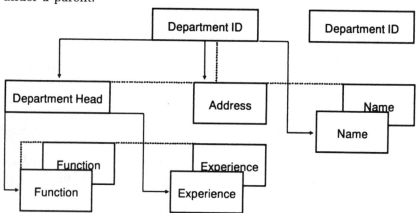

Figure 3.12 Physical *child* first pointers.

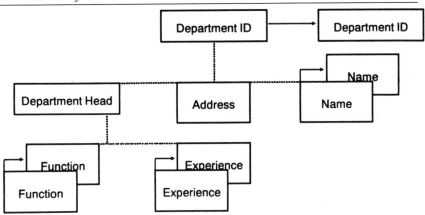

Figure 3.13 Physical twin forward pointers.

In physical twin forward pointers, each segment occurrence of a given segment type under the same parent points forward to the next segment occurrence (Fig. 3.13).

HDAM databases consist of two parts: a root addressable area and an overflow area. The root addressable area contains root segments and is the primary storage area for dependent segments in a database record. The overflow area is for storage of dependent segments that do not fit into the root addressable area. Root segments in HDAM databases must have a key field, although the key field does not have to be unique.

A HIDAM database is actually composed of two databases. One is for storage of the database records and the other is for the HIDAM index. Root segments in HIDAM must have a unique key field, because an index entry exists for each root segment based on the root's key.

3.6 Summary

This chapter dealt with the logical and physical design aspects of database development. In the logical design phase, we discovered that the primary deliverable was a data model with the constructs of the relevant DBMS superimposed. In the physical design phase, we indicated that the important steps were calculating space and time estimates, selecting access methods, and learning the mechanics of the database. The chapter also discussed in some detail the access methods of IMS, an IBM-developed hierarchical DBMS.

CHAPTER 4

Data Normalization

Data normalization is a set of rules and techniques concerned with

- Identifying relationships among attributes,
- Combining attributes to form relations, and
- Combining relations to form a database.

An attribute (also called a field) is a data element. A relation is a group of attributes. For example, a relation called PERSON may contain the attributes NAME, ADDRESS, DATE OF BIRTH, HEIGHT, WEIGHT, SALARY, and so on. A human resources database may contain many relations such as PERSON, DEPENDENTS, and DEPARTMENTS.

4.1 Modification Anomalies

A major objective of data normalization is to avoid modification anomalies which occur when facts within two attributes are lost when a single deletion is made. A few examples will help illustrate modification anomalies. Suppose that the following attributes in a marketing database are grouped together in one record.

CUSTOMER NAME
CUSTOMER NUMBER
CUSTOMER ADDRESS
PRODUCT NUMBER
PRODUCT DESCRIPTION
PRODUCT PRICE

In order to insert information regarding a new product, a fictitious "dummy" customer must be created. Information about an existing product would be lost if all customer information corresponding to that product were deleted.

Grouping together the three attributes EMPLOYEE IDENTIFICATION NUMBER, DEPARTMENT NAME, and DEPARTMENT MANAGER provides a second example. If a department changes managers, then information for every employee in the department must be modified. This problem can be eliminated by forming two groupings of information.

GROUP 1	GROUP 2
EMPLOYEE IDENTIFICATION	DEPARTMENT NAME
NUMBER	DEPARTMENT
DEPARTMENT NAME	MANAGER

Decomposing a set of attributes into smaller groups is one of the techniques used to reduce or eliminate modification anomalies. Suppose that the following attributes are grouped together.

FOOTBALL PLAYERS' UNION IDENTIFICATION NUMBER
NAME OF TEAM
TEAM COACH
TEAM OWNER

Numerous update problems exist with this grouping. For example, if a team obtains a new coach or new owner, then the information for every player belonging in the union must be changed. If all the union players resign from the union, then information concerning the coach and owner is lost. The coach and owner names must be repeated each time a new union player is added. These modification problems are eliminated by forming two groups.

GROUP 1	GROUP 2
FOOTBALL PLAYERS' UNION	NAME OF TEAM
IDENTIFICATION NUMBER	TEACH COACH
NAME OF TEAM	TEAM OWNER

A student new to database design may assume that modification anomalies are rare or unusual. An experienced database designer, however, should have no problem relating to fictitious dummy records that are created to support the insertion of new data. Storage devices contain volumes of data that could be deleted, except for a few fields that may still contain required information.

4.2 Local and Physical Database Design

Data normalization is a useful analytical technique for logical database design. The viewpoints and requirements of the user are considered during the logical database design process. The appropriate attributes and relationships among these attributes are identified and defined. The user's view of the data should not be inhibited by technical hardware and software limitations. Thus hardware and software characteristics are not considered during logical database design.

Eventually the logical database design is implemented physically. Physical implementation is the first stage at which the particular characteristics of the database management system are considered. For example, departures from an ideal logical design may be justified by improved system performance. Data normalization will provide a clear understanding of the relevant attributes and the relationships among these attributes. This knowledge will benefit the technicians who implement the physical database.

4.3 Application Databases and Subject Databases

Database methodology continues to increase in sophistication. Early data processing applications utilized a separate file for each application. The design was generally simple and easy to implement. Such a design, however, resulted in data redundancy and high maintenance costs. Initial database technology was often used to create a separate database for each application. This approach improved data organization and helped reduce data redundancy.

Subject databases provided an additional degree of sophistication. These databases related to organizational subjects (e.g., products, customers, personnel) rather than to conventional computer applications (e.g., order entry, payroll, billing). A subject is data driven rather than application driven. This kind of database is independent of any application and is shared by multiple application. The large, initial investment in analysis (including data normalization) is reduced substantially.

Consider the three application databases in Fig. 4.1: a payroll database, an employment history database, and a medical claims database. Each database is comprised of data common to all the applications. The data must be stored and maintained by all the applications.

Data redundancy increases physical storage requirements and the likelihood of update errors. For example, a change of address must be entered in three different databases. Inconsistencies may result if the definition of an attribute changes within the various application databases. For example, a "home address" may differ from a "mailing

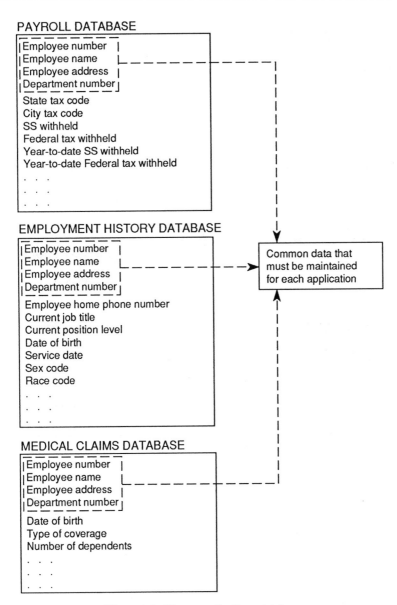

Figure 4.1   Three applications databases.

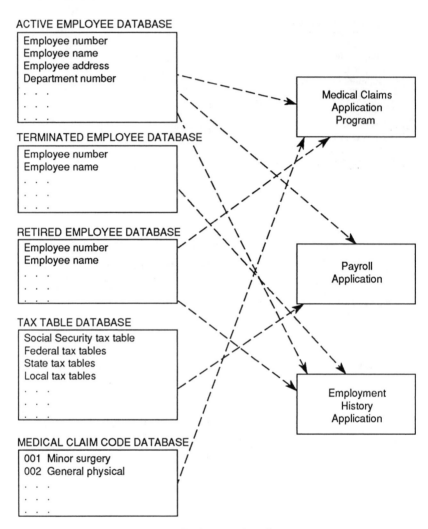

Figure 4.2 Subject databases and applications programs.

address." Multiple application databases may also cause other incompatibilities (e.g., different computer languages or different formats).

The combination of subject databases and application programs is illustrated in Fig. 4.2. Each application program uses data that are stored and maintained in one database. Ad hoc inquiries will use the same data. Thus consistency is maintained among various applications.

Successful design of subject databases and comprehensive information systems usually incorporates both strategic data planning (to identify the required databases) and logical database design (to specify the
logical record structure of those databases). Data normalization should
be included as an integral part of the logical design process.

4.4 Database Models

Databases are often classified as hierarchical, network, or relational.
Hierarchical models are also called tree structures (see Fig. 4.3a). A
typical corporate organizational chart is an example of a hierarchical

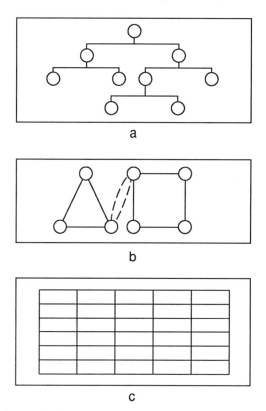

a

b

c

Figure 4.3 Database models: (a) a hierarchical database model, (b) a network database
model, and (c) a relational database model.

model. The president of the company is at the top of the structure. Several vice presidents may report to the president. Director-level executives may report to the vice presidents. This reporting structure may continue for several additional levels of management.

The terms *parent* and *child* are often used in describing a hierarchical model. The president is the *parent* of the vice presidents, and each vice president may be the *parent* of several directors. A vice president is also a *child* of the president, while a director is a *child* of a vice president.

An important characteristic of the hierarchical model is that a *child* is associated with only one *parent*. The relationship between *parent* and *child* is one-to-many. A hierarchical business organization implies that an employee must report to only one supervisor.

A network model allows a *child* to be associated with more than one *parent* (see Fig. 4.3b). The relationship between students and classes is an example of a network structure. A student may enroll in more than one class, and most classes contain more than one student. A tree structure can be considered a special case of a network model.

The distinction between hierarchical and network models is rapidly becoming obsolete. Software enhancements allow network models to be represented in the major hierarchical database systems. Consequently the database designer in a hierarchical environment has considerable flexibility.

The relational model is a significant departure from the hierarchical or network models. Relationships among attributes are represented in a tabular format using rows and columns (see Fig. 4.3c). The model is conceptually easier to understand than either the hierarchical or the network model. However, the hardware and software required to implement the relational model efficiently are limited.

Data normalization is a valuable logical design technique in hierarchical, network, or relational database environments, although the normalization process is most often associated with relational databases, since data normalization was defined in the context of the relational model. Also, during the initial implementation of hierarchical and network designs, the distinction between logical and physical design was not as prevalent. Techniques used in the logical design process (such as data normalization) were not emphasized in these earlier implementations. Data normalization will increase in importance as the relational structure gains acceptance and as the distinction between logical and physical design is incorporated in the database design process.

4.5 Benefits of Data Normalization

The major benefits of a correctly normalized database from the management informations systems (MIS) perspective include:

- Development of a strategy for constructing relations and selecting keys.
- Improved interfaces with end-user computing activities (e.g., ability to accommodate unplanned inquiries).
- Reduced problems associated with inserting and deleting data.
- Reduced enhancement and modification time associated with changing the data structure (e.g., adding or deleting attributes).
- Improved information for decisions relating to physical database design.
- Identification of potential problems that may require additional analysis and documentation.

From the end-user's perspective, a correctly normalized database translates into improved response time from the MIS organization as well as improved capabilities for end-user computing activities.

A database contains facts and figures. Information is the knowledge derived from this data. Intelligent planning and decision making require accurate, reliable information. Data normalization is a major component used to transform data into information.

4.6 Structure of a Relation

The definitions and descriptions presented in this section are fundamental to understanding data normalization. Included are a discussion of the basic relational structure, a definition of functional dependence, a discussion of repeating groups, and an introduction to relational operators. This material will be used throughout the text to define, describe, and illustrate the data normalization process.

4.6.1 The Properties of a Relation

A set of two-dimensional tables called relations is required in the normalization process. Relations are developed using the 14 structural properties presented in Fig. 4.4.

1. Columns (also called attributes) represent fields. Each column has a unique name.
2. Each column is homogenous. Thus the entries in any column are all of the same type (e.g., age, name, employee number, etc.).
3. Each column has a domain; the set of possible values that can appear in the column.
4. Rows (also called tuples) represent records. If a relation has n columns, each row is an n-tuple.
5. The order of the row and columns is not important.
6. No duplicate rows are allowed.
7. Repeating groups (collections of logically related attributes that occur multiple times within one record occurrence) are not allowed.
8. A candidate key is an attribute (or set of attributes) that uniquely identifies a row. A candidate key must possess the following properties:
   • Unique identification: For every row, the value of the key must uniquely identify that row.
   • Nonredundancy: No attribute in the key can be discarded without destroying the property of unique identification.
9. A primary key is a candidate key selected as the unique identifier. Every relation must contain a primary key. The primary key is usually the key selected to identify a row when the database is physically implemented. For example, a part number is selected instead of a part description.
10. A superkey is any set of attributes that uniquely identifies a row. A superkey differs from a candidate key in that the superkey does not require the nonredundancy property.
11. A foreign key is an attribute that appears as a nonkey attribute in one relation and as a primary key attribute (or part of a primary key) in another relation.
12. A composite key is a key that contains more than one attribute.
13. A relational schema is a set of attributes, dependencies, and other constraints that characterize a relation. Various types of dependencies and constraints are discussed throughout the book.
14. An instance of a relation is a set of rows that populate the relation. Updates to the database will change the instance of a relation over time. An instance is valid if all the dependencies and other constraints specified in the relational schema are satisfied.

Figure 4.4   The structural properties of a relation.

4.6.2 Other Definitions

The following definitions are also helpful in discussing data normalization.

The union of relations R and S is the set of all attributes contained in either R or S or in both. RS is used to denote the union of relations R and S.

The intersection of relations R and S is the set of all attributes contained in both R and R. R ∩ S is used to denote the intersection of relations R and S.

The difference of relations R and S is the set of all attributes contained in relation R but not in relation S. R–S is used to denote the difference of relations R and S.

A decomposition of a relation R is a set of relations R such that the union of relations R is the relation R.

4.7 Functional Dependence

The following table represents the annual sales of a corporation over a 16 year period.

Year	Sales (billions of dollars)	Year	Sales (billions of dollars)
16	3.0	8	2.0
15	3.2	7	1.7
14	3.1	6	1.4
13	3.0	5	1.2
12	2.6	4	1.1
11	2.4	3	1.1
10	2.0	2	1.1
9	1.9	1	0.9

This data is in relational form. Each row contains two attributes (YEAR and SALES). The primary key attribute is YEAR. This relation (called SALESDATA) is represented using the following notation.

SALESDATA (YEAR SALES)

In this format, the relation is named first. Each attribute is then identified; the primary key attribute(s) are underlined.

Only one sales value exists for a specific year. More than one year, however, may be associated with the same values of sales. For example, the sales value 3.0 is associated with both year 16 and year 13. Thus YEAR determines SALES but SALES does not determine YEAR. SALES is a function of YEAR (i.e., SALES depends on YEAR). If SALES is represented as y and YEAR as x, the familiar mathematical expression $y = f(x)$ represents the functional relationship between y and x. Thus a discrete mathematical function may be displayed as a relation.

The 16 values in the SALES attribute are a subset of the domain SALES. Understanding the domain of an attribute is important both in determining the size of the corresponding field and in checking the validity of data. Knowledge of the domain is also used in advanced normalization theory.

Functional dependence in relational terminology can be defined formally as follows. For any R, attribute A is functionally dependent on attribute B if, for every valid instance, the value of B determines the value of A.

The phrase "for every valid instance" ensures that the functional dependency is valid irrespective of any insertions or deletions. The functional dependence of A on B is represented by an arrow as follows: $B \rightarrow A$. Thus YEAR $\rightarrow$ SALES. The notation $B \nrightarrow A$ is used to denote that A is not functionally dependent on B.

An instance does not imply a dependency. However, dependencies imply valid instances. An instance cannot be used to show that a dependency is true but can be used to demonstrate that a dependency is false.

An attribute can be functionally dependent on a group of attributes rather than on a single attribute. An attribute (or group of attributes) X is fully functionally dependent on another collection of attributes Y, if X is functionally dependent on the whole of Y but not on any subset of Y.

Functional dependence is limited to numerical data. For example, consider the relation AIRPORT (NAME, CITY) with the following instance.

NAME	CITY
LaGuardia	New York
Hopkins	Cleveland
J. F. Kennedy	New York
Logan	Boston
Burke Lakefront	Cleveland
L.A. International	Los Angeles

Each airport name is unique, but more than one airport can be associated with a given city. Thus CITY is functionally dependent on NAME but NAME is not functionally dependent on CITY. These facts are expressed in the following ways:

CITY = f(NAME)   NAME = f(CITY)
NAME $\rightarrow$ CITY   CITY $\nrightarrow$ NAME

4.8 Inference Axioms for Functional Dependencies

A given set of functional dependencies will usually generate additional, implied functional dependencies. For example, $X \rightarrow Z$ can be inferred from the dependencies $X \rightarrow Y$ and $Y \rightarrow Z$. Sets of inference axioms associated with functional dependencies were developed by W. W. Armstrong ("Dependency Structures of Database Relationship." Proceedings, IFIP Congress, 1974) and by C. Berri, R. Fagin, and J. H. Howard ("A Complete Axiomatization for Functional and Multivalued Dependencies in Database Relations," Proceedings, 1977 ACM SIG-MOD International Conference on Management of Data, Toronto, August 1977). These axioms are presented in Fig. 4.5. All possible functional dependencies implied by a given set can be generated using these axioms.

Suppose that A, B, C, D and E are attributes with the following dependencies:

$A \rightarrow B$
$CD \rightarrow A$

Let X, Y, Z, and W represent subsets of the attributes that comprise the database then:

1. Reflexive rule $X \rightarrow X$
2. Augmentation rule if $X \rightarrow Y$, then $XZ \rightarrow Y$
3. Union rule if $X \rightarrow Y$ and $X \rightarrow Z$ then $X \rightarrow YZ$
4. Decomposition rule if $X \rightarrow Y$, then $X \rightarrow Z$ where Z is a subset of Y
5. Transitivity rule if $X \rightarrow Y$ and $Y \rightarrow Z$, then $X \rightarrow Z$
6. Pseudotransitivity rule if $X \rightarrow YZ \rightarrow W$, then $XZ \rightarrow W$

Figure 4.5   Inference axioms for functional dependencies.

$C \rightarrow E$
$E \rightarrow C$
$BD \rightarrow C$

Some of the dependencies implied by the inference axioms are:

$A \rightarrow A$ (axiom 1)
$AC \rightarrow B$ (axiom 2)
$CD \rightarrow AE$ (axioms 2 and 3)
$AD \rightarrow C$ (axiom 6)
$DE \rightarrow A$ (axiom 6)
$CD \rightarrow B$ (axiom 5)
$BD \rightarrow E$ (axiom 5)
$ED \rightarrow A$ (axiom 6)
$AD \rightarrow E$ (axioms 5 and 6)
$DE \rightarrow B$ (axioms 5 and 6)

Functional dependencies also exist that are trivially true. Trivial functional dependencies occur when a set of attributes implies a subset of the same set (e.g., $XY \rightarrow X$). A trivial dependency is always true for every instance. The dependency is trivial because duplicate rows in XY will also be duplicate rows in X and Y individually.

4.9 Repeating Groups

A repeating group is a collection of logically related attributes that occur multiple times within one row.

Examples of repeating groups include names of employee dependents, products associated with an invoice, and employee's career interest designations. A repeating group is often characterized by an OCCURS clause in COBOL, an array in FORTRAN, or a structure in C.

For example, consider the following attributes that relate to an employee benefit program.

ESSNUM	employee number
ENAME	employee name
PCODE	code for benefit plan type
DNAME	dependent name
DBIRTHD	dependent birth date
DSEX	dependent sex

The attributes DNAME, DBIRTHD, and DSEX comprise a repeating group that is duplicated for each dependent. The repeating group can be represented in COBOL with an OCCURS clause.

```
01 Employee Dependents Record
   03 ESSNUM
   03 ENAME
   03 PCODE
03 DEPENDENT DATA OCCURS 10 TIMES
   05 DNAME
   05 DBIRTHD
   05 DSEX
```

The repeating group can be represented in FORTRAN using an array. For example,

(ESSNUM (I), ENAME(I), PCODE(I), M(I), (DNAME(I,J), DBIRTHD(I,J), DSEX(I,J), J-1,M(I)))

where M(I) represents the number of dependents associated with the Ith employee and DNAME(I,J) represents the name of the Jth dependent for the Ith employee.

The representation of the repeating group in C can be accomplished with the following structure.

```
struct employee
{
        int essnum;
        char ename [30];
        char pcode;
        struct dep_rec
        {
                char dname [30];
                char dbirthd [6];
                char dsex;
        } emp_deps [10];
},
```

A relational representation begins with a grouping of attributes as follows:

BENEFITS (ESSNUM, ENAME, PCODE, DNAME, DBIRTHD, DSEX)

The repeating group is eliminated by creating two relations.

BENEFITS (ESSNUM, ENAME, PCODE)
DEPENDENTS (ESSNUM, DNAME, DBIRTHD, DSEX)

An employee number, name, and plan code are entered once for each employee. The dependent data is entered in separate relations. DNAME is used to identify a particular dependent. The ESSNUM attribute is used to connect the BENEFITS and DEPENDENTS relations.

4.10 Relational Operators

Relational operators are used to manipulate relations in a manner similar to the way arithmetic operators (plus, minus, multiply, and divide) are used to manipulate numbers. The relational operators, projection and join, are especially important in data normalization.

A relation can be decomposed into new relations that consist of subsets of the attributes in the original relation. This is accomplished by using the projection operator. Consider the following instance of the relation EMPLOYEE (NUM, NAME, DEPT, SALARY).

NUM	NAME	DEPT	SALARY
101	Charles Miller	Accounting	35,000
102	Fawaz Ghumrawi	Accounting	40,000
103	Shelly Knight	Marketing	40,000
104	Michael Rodriquez	Human Relations	38,000
105	Clair Schler	Accounting	40,000

The projection of this instance onto the attributes DEPT and SALARY will result in the following instance of a new relation.

DEPT	SALARY
Accounting	35,000
Accounting	40,000
Marketing	40,000
Human Relations	38,000

The new relation contains the two attributes specified (DEPT and SALARY). Note that the number of rows is reduced since the duplicate row (Accounting 40,000) was eliminated from the new instance. This projection answers the question "How many unique DEPT and SAL-ARY combinations exist?" but is inappropriate for responding to commands such as "List all the salaries for employees in the Marketing Department."

The projection operator is concerned with the attributes in a relation. A similar operator, selection, is concerned with the rows in a relation.

4.11 First, Second, and Third Normal Forms

A major objective of data normalization is to eliminate update anomalies. The first three normal forms progress in a systematic manner toward achieving this objective. More subtle types of anomalies, however, continue to be discovered. Thus the first three normal forms provide an excellent way to begin to learn the normalization process. Advanced normal forms that address more subtle anomalies are introduced in later chapters.

4.11.1 First Normal Form

A relation is in first normal form if it contains no repeating groups. Relations only in first normal form suffer serious problems associated with insertions and deletions. For example, the following relation might be used by a university in developing a student and class database.

SCL (SNUM, CNUM, SNAME, SMAJ, TIME, BLDG)

where

SNUM = student number
CNUM = class number
SNAME = student name
SMAJ = student major
TIME = class time
BLDG = class building location

All the data concerning a student will be deleted if the student withdraws from all of his or her classes. Thus data regarding student number, name, and major will be lost. Insertions are also a problem. Data regarding class time and building location cannot be entered until a student enrolls in the class.

A problem with the SCL relation is that nonkey attributes are dependent on various parts of the primary key but not on the entire key. For example,

SNUM $\rightarrow$ SNAME but CNUM $\nrightarrow$ SNAME
SNUM $\rightarrow$ SMAJ but CNUM $\nrightarrow$ SMAJ
CNUM $\rightarrow$ TIME but SNUM $\nrightarrow$ TIME
CNUM $\rightarrow$ BLDG but SNUM $\nrightarrow$ BLDG

The normalization process must continue beyond first normal form in order to eliminate undesirable insertion and deletion problems.

4.11.2 Second Normal Form

A relation is in second normal form if the relation is in first normal form and every nonkey attribute is fully functionally dependent upon the primary key. Thus no nonkey attribute can be functionally dependent on part of the primary key.

A relation in first normal form will be in second normal form if any one of the following applies:

1. The primary key is composed of only one attribute.
2. No nonkey attribute exists.
3. Every nonkey attribute is dependent on the entire set of primary key attributes.

The SCL relation can be decomposed into three new relations as follows:

SINFO (<u>SNUM</u>, SNAME, SMAJ)
CINFO (<u>CNUM</u>, TIME, BLDG)
STUCLASS (<u>SNUM</u>, <u>OCNUMO</u>)

The primary keys for both the SINFO and CINFO relations consist of just one attribute. The STUCLASS relation contains no nonkey attributes. Thus the relations are in second normal form. Student data can be entered into the SINFO relation before the student enrolls in a class. Class data can be entered into the CINFO relation before any student enrolls in the class. Deletion of all students in a particular class in the STUCLASS relation will not result in either class or student data being deleted. Deletion of all classes for a particular student will result in the loss of student data.

Elimination of the insertion and deletion problems is not entirely due to second normal form. Actually the relations are also in third normal form. The differences between second and third normal form can be illustrated by considering another potential relation in the student and class database.

MAJOR (SNUM, MAJDEPT, COLLEGE)

The primary key consists of a single attribute, and thus this relation must be in second normal form. A typical instance is:

SNUM	MAJDEPT	COLLEGE
91001	Statistics	Science
81062	English	Liberal Arts
83719	Music	Liberal Arts
94201	Statistics	Science
86319	Music	Liberal Arts
97001	Statistics	Science

Note the following:

● If student 81062 is deleted, the fact that the English department is in the liberal arts college is lost.
● Several rows must be changed if the statistics department moves to the engineering college.
● The fact that the electrical engineering department is in the engineering college cannot be entered until a student with that major is added.

These problems appear similar to those encountered with relations only in first normal form. Actually the problems are caused by a different type of dependency. The difficulty is that a dependency exists (MAJDEPT → COLLEGE) that does not involve the primary key. This dependency allows the attribute to determine COLLEGE in two ways:

1. SNUM → COLLEGE
2. SNUM → MAJDEPT → COLLEGE

The second structure creates the insertion and deletion problems. For example, if a student drops all classes, the deletion of SNUM could result in a loss of data regarding the MAJDEPT and COLLEGE relationship. Thus the normalization process must continue in order to eliminate these undesirable dependencies.

4.11.3 Third Normal Form

A relation is in third normal form if, for every nontrivial functional dependency $X \to A$, either

- Attribute X is a superkey, or
- Attribute A is a member of a candidate key

Third normal form is often described as a situation in which an attribute is "a function of the key, the whole key, and nothing but the key." This description captures the essence of third normal form but is difficult to define precisely and is also partially incorrect.

An attribute is a "function of the key, the whole key and nothing but the key" if the following two conditions are true:

1. Every nonkey attribute depends on the entire primary key.
2. No nonkey attribute is functionally dependent on another nonkey attribute.

These conditions, however, are too restrictive. A relation can be in third normal form even if a dependency exists among nonkey attributes. This occurs if all possible values of the implying attribute are unique (e.g., the implying attribute is a candidate key). For example, the relation

R (SSNUM, NAME, DEPTNUM)

is in third normal form if NAME → DEPTNUM and NAME is guaranteed never to contain duplicate values.

The second condition also becomes somewhat complicated if sets of attributes are considered. The condition should actually be stated as "no nonkey attribute is functionally dependent on a set of attributes that does not contain a key."

Third normal form is often described by introducing a concept called transitive dependencies. Consider the relation R (A, B, C). Attribute C is transitively dependent on attribute A if attribute B satisfies

$A \to B$
$B \to C$
$B \to A$

A relation in second normal form is in third normal form if no transitive dependencies exist. The dependency $B \rightarrow C$ represents the potential problem in the relation (i.e, functional dependence among nonkey attributes). Attribute B is not a candidate key since $B \rightarrow A$, and thus the relation is not in third normal form.

Eliminating transitive dependencies will eliminate anomalies of the following nature: If $A \rightarrow B \rightarrow C$, then a B value cannot be associated with an A value unless a C value is also associated with a B value. Thus an $A \rightarrow B$ association cannot be inserted unless a $B \rightarrow C$ association is also inserted. Conversely, if a C value associated with a B value is deleted, then corresponding $A \rightarrow B$ association may be lost.

The relation MAJOR (SNUM, MAJDEPT, COLLEGE), discussed in the previous section, can be decomposed into two new relations that are both in third normal form.

SMAJ (SNUM, MAJDEPT)
MDEPT (MAJDEPT, COLLEGE)

Transitive dependencies may also occur between sets of attributes. For example, consider the relation

SHIPMENT (NUM, ORIGIN, DESTINATION, DISTANCE)

which might be used by a transportation company to record shipment order numbers and origin, destination, and distance data. An instance of this relation is

NUM	ORIGIN	DESTINATION	DISTANCE
101	Atlanta	Boston	1088
102	Atlanta	Boston	1088
103	St. Louis	Chicago	288
104	Cleveland	Dallas	1187
105	Los Angeles	San Francisco	403
106	Kansas City	Memphis	459

Note that ORIGIN, DESTINATION, and DISTANCE are not functionally dependent on each other when the attributes are considered in a pairwise manner. However, the combination of ORIGIN and DESTINATION determines DISTANCE. Since this dependency exists, the rows that contain duplicates of the ORIGIN, DESTINATION combination also contain duplicates of DISTANCE.

The SHIPMENT relation can be decomposed into two relations (each in third normal form) as follows:

SHIPMENT (NUM, ORIGIN, DESTINATION)
DISTANCE (ORIGIN, DESTINATION, DISTANCE)

The fact that the distance between New Orleans and Pittsburgh is 1093 miles can then be added to the database even though a corresponding shipment order does not exist. This flexibility is desirable when analyzing "what-if" questions. SHIPMENT can also be deleted without loss of the distance data. The distance between reoccurring origin and destination combinations need not be entered with each shipment.

4.11.4 Examples

Three examples are presented in this section to illustrate how relations in third normal form are constructed. The chapter concludes with some general guidelines for developing relations in third normal form.

Example 4.1   Credit History for Consumer Loans

This example involves enhancing an existing database used to record consumer loan history by individual. The current database allows space for a maximum of three loans per individual. A major objective is to expand the historical capabilities so that a complete loan record is available for each individual. The attributes associated with this example are illustrated in Fig. 4.6

A repeating group associated with amount, date, and payment rating must be eliminated. The attributes DL1, DL2, and DL3 can be replaced by the attribute DATE. Similarly, RL1, RL2, and RL3 can be replaced by AMOUNT.

The functional dependencies are:

SSNUM, DATE → AMOUNT
SSNUM, DATE → PAYMENT RATING
SSNUM   → NAME
SSNUM   → ADDRESS
SSNUM   → CITY
SSNUM   → ZIP
ZIP   → STATE

Three relations, each in third normal form, can be developed.

R1 (SSNUM, DATE, AMOUNT, PAYMENT RATING)
R2 (SSNUM, NAME, ADDRESS, CITY, ZIP)
R3 (ZIP, STATE)

NAME	Name of person
SNNUM	Social security number of person
ADDRESS	Address where person resides
CITY	City where person resides
STATE	State where person resides
ZIP	Zip code where person resides
AMTL1	Amount of most recent loan
DL1	Date of most recent loan
RL1	Payment rating most recent loan
AMTL2	Amount of second most recent loan
DL2	Date of second most recent loan
RL2	Payment rating for second most recent loan
AMTL3	Amount of third most recent loan
DL3	Date of third most recent loan
RL3	Payment rating for third most recent loan

Figure 4.6   Attributes associated with *Example 4.1.*

The loan information is no longer restricted to a maximum of three loans per individual. However, relation R1 assumes that at most one loan per day can be granted to any one individual.

Example 4.2   Manufacturing Specifications

The example involves the machines, setup times, production times, and name and amount of each ingredient used in manufacturing a specific product. The number of machines and ingredients varies depending on the individual product. At most three machines and two ingredients are used in any one product. The attributes identified by a systems analyst are presented in Fig. 4.7.

Two repeating groups must be eliminated.

1. Number, setup time, and production time for each machine.
2. Number and amount of each ingredient.

The attribute names should be simplified as follows:

1. Replace MACNUM1, MACNUM2, and MACNUM3 with MACNUM.
2. Replace SETUP1, SETUP2, and SETUP3 with SETUP.

NUM	Product number
DES	Product description

MACNUM1	Number of first machine used
SETUP1	Setup time for first machine
PRORATE1	Production time for first machine

MACNUM2	Number of second machine used
SETUP2	Setup time for second machine
PRORATE2	Production time for second machine

MACNUM3	Number of third machine used
SETUP3	Setup time for third machine
PRORATE3	Production time for third machine

IGD1	Number of first ingredient used
AMT1	Amount of first ingredient used

IGD2	Number of second ingredient used
AMT2	Amount of second ingredient used

Figure 4.7 Attributes associated with Example 4.2.

3. Replace PRORATE1, PRORATE2, and PRORATE3 with PRORATE.
4. Replace IGD1 and IGD2 with IGD.
5. Replace AMT1 and AMT2 with AMT.

The functional dependencies are

NUM, MACNUM $\rightarrow$ SETUP
NUM, MACNUM $\rightarrow$ PRORATE
NUM $\rightarrow$ DES
NUM, IGD $\rightarrow$ AMT

The following relations are each in third normal form.

R1 (<u>NUM</u>, <u>MACNUM</u>, SETUP, PRORATE)
R2 (<u>NUM</u>, <u>IGD</u>, AMT)
R3 (<u>NUM</u>, DES)

Note that setup time is dependent on both machine and product but not on the previously produced product on a particular machine. The

UFN	User's first name
ULN	User's last name
UDIX	User's work division number
UEXT	User's telephone extension
ULOC	User's work location
CPER	Contact person (individual knowledgeable about the software)
CEXT	Contact person's telephone extension
CLOC	Contact person's work location
HPU	Date hardware was purchased
HTYPE	Type of hardware (e.g., XT, AT, PS/2)
SNAME	Name of software (e.g., Lotus 1-2-3)
SPUR	Date software was purchased
SRATE	Software rating (opinion of contact person)
STYPE	Type of software (e.g., spreadsheet, database)
SVER	Version number of software

Figure 4.8   Attributes associated with *Example 4.3*.

database also does not capture any information relating to the order in which the machines or ingredients are used.

Example 4.3   An Inventory of Personal Computer Hardware and Software

This example involves a database to store information concerning personal computer hardware and software used by employees. An expert "contact" person for each software product is included along with the expert's rating of the software. The attributes associated with this example are presented in Fig. 4.8.

The functional dependencies are:

$$\begin{array}{rcl}
\text{UFN, ULN} & \rightarrow & \text{ULOC} \\
\text{UFN, ULN} & \rightarrow & \text{UDIV} \\
\text{UFN, ULN} & \rightarrow & \text{UEXT} \\
\text{CPER} & \rightarrow & \text{CEXT} \\
\text{CPER} & \rightarrow & \text{CLOC} \\
\text{SNAME} & \rightarrow & \text{STYPE} \\
\text{CPER, SNAME, SVER} & \rightarrow & \text{STRATE} \\
\text{UFN, ULN, HPUR, SNAME, SVER} & \rightarrow & \text{SPUR} \\
\text{SNAME, SVER} & \rightarrow & \text{CPER}
\end{array}$$

Note that HTYPE was not included in the functional dependencies and thus must be included in a relation containing all key attributes. Two repeating groups must be eliminated.

1. Hardware type and date of purchase.
2. Software information (SNAME, SPUR, SRATE, STYPE, and SVER).

Elimination of the repeating groups is accomplished with the following two relations.

R1   (UFN, ULN, HTYPE, HPUR)
R2   (UFN, ULN, HPUR, SNAME, SVER, STYPE, SPUR, SRATE, CPER, CEXT, CLOC)

Relation R1 assumes that an employee purchases no more than one given hardware type on a given day. If HPUR was not included in the primary key, the assumption would be that an individual will purchase at most one given hardware type. R1 also assumes that an individual is uniquely identified by first and last name.

Relation R2 assumes that only one version of a particular software product is installed on any one machine. This relation must be further decomposed since CPER $\rightarrow$ CEXT and CPER $\rightarrow$ CLOC. Thus R2 is decomposed into

R3   (UFN, ULN, HPUR, SNAME, SVER, SPUR, CPER)
R8   (CPER, SNAME, SVER, SRATE)

The contact person provides a software rating independently of any hardware. Thus R7 is further decomposed into

R9   (*UFN, ULN, HPUR, SNAME, SVER, SPUR*)
R10   (*SNAME, SVER, CPER*)

Information about the user can be incorporated in the following relation:

R11   (UFN, ULN, ULOC, UDIV, UEXT)

The database now contains seven relations.

R1   (UFN, ULN, HTYPE, HPUR)
R4   (CPER, CEXT, CLOC)

R6 (SNAME, STYPE)
R8 (CPER, SNAME, SVER, SRATE)
R9 (UFN, ULN, HPUR, SNAME, SVER, SPUR)
R10 (SNAME, SVER, CPER)
R11 (UPN, ULN, ULOC, UDIV, UEXT)

Another modification to the database is required. The attribute CPER is not necessary in the key or relation R8; SNAME and SVER are the only attributes needed since SNAME, SVER → CPER. The original dependency CPER, SNAME, SVER → SRATE should be replaced by SNAME, SVER → SRATE since the inclusion of CPER creates a trivial dependency. Relations R8 and R10 can then be combined. The revised database contains the following six relations.

R1 (UFN, ULN, HTYPE, HPUR)
R4 (CPER CEXT, CLOC)
R6 (SNAME, STYPE)
R8 (SNAME, SVER, CPER, SRATE)
R9 (UFN, ULN, ULOC, UDIV, UEXT)

Suppose that a software vendor introduces a new version of a spreadsheet package. The new version is an integrated package that also contains database, word processing, and graphics capabilities. The dependency SNAME → STYPE is no longer valid since STYPE is determined by both SNAME and SVER. Relation R6 should be modified as follows.

R12 (SNAME, SVER STYPE)

The database now appears as follows:

R1 (UFN, ULN, HPUR, HTYPE)
R4 (CPER, CLOC, CEXT)
R9 (UFN, ULN, HPUR, SNAME, SVER, SPUR)
R11 (UFN, ULN, ULOC, UDIV, UEXT)
R13 (SNAME, SVER, STYPE, SRATE, CPER)

One other modification may be desirable. To simplify physical implementation, the two key attributes UFN and ULN can be replaced by a single attribute, such as UPER. Key attributes SNAME and SVER can also be replaced by a single attribute SNV. These modifications require the following changes.

Change R11 to R15 (UPER, ULOC, UDIV, UEXT)
Change R13 to R16 (SNV, STYPE, SRATE, CPER)
Change R1 to R17 (UPER, HPUR, HTYPE)
Change R9 to R18 (UPER, SNV, HPUR, SPUR)

The final database contains R4, R15, R17, and R18. Two additional relations could be created to capture the detailed SNV and HPER information.

R19 (SNV, SNAME, SVER)
R20 (UPER, UFN, ULN)

4.12 Guidelines for Developing Relations in Third Normal Form

Relations in third normal form can be developed by following the guidelines presented in Fig. 4.9. Experienced database designers may

1. Define the attributes.
2. Group logically related attributes into relations.
3. Identify candidate keys for each relation.
4. Select a primary key for each relation.
5. Identify and remove repeating groups.
6. Combine relations with identical keys (first normal form).
7. Identify all functional dependencies.
8. Decompose relations such that each nonkey attribute is dependent on all the attributes in the key.
9. Combine relations with identical primary keys (second normal form).
10. Identify all transitive dependencies.
    a. Check relations for dependencies of one nonkey attribute with another nonkey attribute.
    b. Check for dependencies within each primary key (i.e., dependence of one attribute in the key on other attributes within the key).
11. Decompose relations such that there are no transitive dependencies.
12. Combine relations with identical primary keys (third normal) if no transitive dependencies occur.

Figure 4.9 Guidelines for developing third normal form.

find that the problems associated with first or second normal form are obvious. Thus the actual design process may not follow a sequential consideration of all three normal forms; an experienced designer may develop initial relations in third normal form.

CHAPTER 5

Data Dictionaries and Relational Databases

5.1 Introduction

The role of the data dictionary in the design, implementation, and maintenance of database systems has been well documented in the current literature.

The growing awareness of data as a corporate resource, resulting in data-driven rather than process-driven systems, has led to recognition of the impact of data on departments outside of data processing. In this way, the system development life cycle has evolved from the focus of concern being on highly localized data processing problems. It is now recognized that the efficiency of a given system usually depends on its end-user orientation and how well it represents and serves the organization as a whole. Current methodologies are becoming less process-oriented and more data-oriented.

Because of this new awareness the data dictionary can play a significant part in supporting the SDLC. It provides a wealth of detail on which early research work can be based, and it then becomes an invaluable communications tool between the different departments that are involved in the SDLC. For these reasons the succeeding sections discuss the role of the data dictionary in the SDLC.

5.2 What Is a Data Dictionary?

The data dictionary can be defined as an organized reference to the data content of an organization's programs, systems, databases, collections of all files, or manual records.

The data dictionary may be maintained manually or by computer. Sometimes the term "data dictionary" refers to a software product that is utilized to maintain a dictionary database. The data dictionary will contain names, descriptions, and definitions of the organization's data resources.

5.3 The Concept of Metadata

In the broadest sense, a data dictionary is *any* organized collection of information about data. In the real world, any information system, whether or not it is computerized, exists to store and process data about objects (entities). We then create data records to represent occurrences of these entities. We define specific record types to represent specific entity types. Frequently we also assign keys or identifiers, such as customer names and invoice numbers, to differentiate one record occurrence from another. A data dictionary can then be designed that contains data about those customer and invoice record types.

The customer and invoice records in the database contain ordinary data. The record in the data dictionary contains metadata, or data about the data. For example, the record in the data dictionary may contain the name, the record length, the data characteristics, and the recording mode of the record in the database.

5.4 Active versus Passive Data Dictionaries

Data dictionaries are often categorized as active or passive, which refers to the extent of their integration with the database management system. If the data dictionary and the DBMS are integrated to the extent that the DBMS uses the definitions in the dictionary at run time, the dictionary is active. If the dictionary is freestanding or independent of the DBMS, it is passive.

An active dictionary must contain an accurate, up-to-date description of the physical database in order for the database management system to access the data.

In a passive dictionary environment, more effort is required to keep two copies of the same data, and great care must be taken to ensure that the two copies are actually identical.

5.5 The Role of the Data Dictionary in the SDLC

The role of the data dictionary in the system development life cycle is best exemplified in Fig. 5.1. Any analysis of Fig. 5.1 will show that the

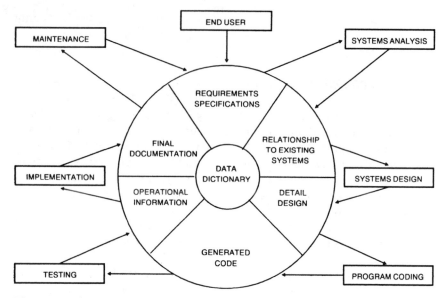

Figure 5.1   The SDLC showing the data dictionary as a communication and documentation tool.

data dictionary is at the core of systems design and development. The metadata collected in the dictionary about the different phases of the SDLC are demonstrated in the second layer of the diagram. The third layer depicts the various interfaces to the different phases of the SDLC. The directions of the arrows indicate that the interfaces act as input to the phases and also extract design information from the phases.

As we move in a clockwise direction around the second layer, we notice, starting with the input from the end users, that the following types of metadata are collected:

- Requirements Specifications
- Relationships to Existing Systems
- Detail Design
- Generated Code
- Operational Information
- Final Documentation

5.5.1   Requirements Specifications

As indicated in Chapter 1, the systems analyst or the data analyst collects data from the end user on the entities in which he has a particular interest. He or she may collect definitions and descriptions about the entities, data characteristics, security requirements, attribute content, and the processes involved in moving the data across interfaces and manipulating that data.

The analyst synthesizes these data and then enters as much of it into the data dictionary as the constructs of the dictionary allow. For example, in the DATAMANAGER data dictionary marketed by Manager Software Products (MSP), the analyst can enter data about the system, file, groups of data, and data items that will constitute a solution to the user's requirements.

5.5.2 Relationship to Existing Systems

In arriving at what may be the optimum solution to the user's requirements, the analyst must seek to determine from the dictionary if:

- A system already exists that can solve the problem
- No system exists, what portions of the existing systems can be used in the solution
- Alternate solutions can be obtained

5.5.3 Detail Design

During detail system design, the analyst will enter data about the data models, the process flows, the programming specifications, the file layouts, and report formats. If the current design has any relationship to designs already existing in the data dictionary, the analyst can extract that portion and implement it with the new metadata.

5.5.4 Generated Code

The data dictionary may contain copy books (source statements) or pointers to source statement libraries that may be extracted to use for program testing.

It is now possible to generate code from process definitions and programming specifications stored in the data dictionary. Current CASE tools can generate this code for several languages and several different platforms, for example, PC or mainframe.

5.5.5 Operational Information

The data dictionary may contain information that will enable the data processing staff to execute the programs. This information may include

run instructions, job control language (JCL) setup, distribution information, test plans and requirements, and processing exceptions.

5.5.6 Final Documentation

The final documentation information stored in the data dictionary may
include user-manual instructions, impact analysis information, acceptance testing and sign-off information, change control information, and
job control language information.

5.6 Interfaces to the Data Dictionary

The interfaces with the data dictionary are many and varied. They act
in two directions: those that provide the deliverables to the dictionary
and those that extract information from the dictionary. These interfaces
include:

- End User
- Systems Analysis
- Systems Design
- Program Coding
- Testing
- Implementation
- Maintenance

5.6.1 The End User

The end user is the primary source of input to the requirements specifications phase of systems development. It is during this phase that data
are collected on the objectives and scope of the project, the data and
processing requirements, the operating environment, alternative processing, data security, and the input and output formats.

The advent of database management systems, structured design
methodologies, and new development tools has signaled a larger role
for the end user in systems development. The end user is now as much
a part of the systems development team as the data analyst or systems
analyst. The success or failure of the system depends, to a large degree,
on the quality of the data collected regarding the user requirements.

5.6.2 The Systems Analysis Phase

During the systems analysis phase, data are obtained from the end user
and the user requirements specifications and are fed into the systems

design phase. The relationship to existing systems data is stored in the data dictionary.

During this phase, the data and systems analyst will iteratively extract data from the requirements specifications already stored in the data dictionary and augment it with that from the end user and any obtained from existing systems to come up with data and process models that form the primary deliverables of the systems design phase.

If, during the systems analysis phase, no data are found in the data dictionary that connects the current system with other systems, the analyst enters any existing relationships into the data dictonary.

5.6.3 The Systems Design Phase

During the systems design phase, the data analyst extracts information from the analysis phase and relationship to existing systems stored in the data dictionary and develops a data model. In turn, this model is stored in the data dictionary as detail design metadata. Meanwhile, the systems (process) analyst develops a process model with information from the data dictionary and the systems analysis phase. The data collected during this phase are stored in the detail design section of the data dictionary and used as input, through programming specifications, to the program coding phase.

5.6.4 The Program Coding Phase

During the program coding phase, the programmer/analyst takes specifications from the systems design phase and couples it with metadata from the detail design information stored in the data dictionary to produce program code for the testing phase and to be stored as metadata and sometimes source data in the data dictionary.

5.6.5 The Testing Phase

During this phase, the analyst takes program code from the program coding phase and generated code stored in the data dictionary and tests it to obtain operational metadata to be stored in the data dictionary and use as program code for the implementation phase.

5.6.6 The Implementation Phase

During this phase, operational information metadata stored in the data dictionary are coupled with the tested program code to produce implementable systems. The results from the phase are stored in the data

dictionary as a final document and are used as input to the maintenance phase.

5.6.7 The Maintenance Phase

During this phase, metadata from the final document stored in the data
dictionary and input from the implementation phase are used to maintain the production systems. This phase also encompasses the updating
of requirements specifications stored in the data dictionary and the
constant reporting to the user of the results of these changes.

5.7 The Data Dictionary as a Documentation Tool

As was mentioned earlier, the data dictionary plays a significant role in
the systems development life cycle. One major role is documenting the
results of each phase of the SDLC. This section describes some of the
entries that are documented in the data dictionary for the major phases
of the SDLC.

5.7.1 Documenting the System Design Phase

The data dictionary can offer substantial assistance to the designer
during the system design phase by providing the source and storage for
the inputs and outputs of the design step.

The inputs to data design are full descriptions of the business processes and the data required by these processes. The outputs are the
logical views and the logical database (also known as logical schemes).
A logical database refers to a structuring of entities and relations between entities supporting the business processes of the application.

There are many different methods of transforming the business processes and their required data into a logical database. One is a top-
down data design method identifying entities and the relationships
between the entities before defining the attributes of each entity. Alter-
natively, there are bottom-up data design techniques that encourage the
description of entities, and the attributes identifying the entities, before
identifying relationships between entities.

There are five basic steps in top-down data design:

1. Identifying the business functions of the application
2. Identifying the data required by each function and the procedure
   by which data are collected

3. Identifying the entities of the application
4. Defining the relationships between the entities
5. Ascribing attributes to their entities

Nowhere is the importance of the data dictionary more obvious than in the building of the function's logical model. As the keeper of the "who," "what," and "how" of the organizational information system, the data dictionary provides full descriptions of:

- The business functions
- The data generated by and used by the business functions
- The application entities
- The relationships of the application's entities to one another
- The attributes of the entities

Frequently, even data go through an evolutionary process, with its definition becoming more and more refined until it can finally be set. Data also can be perceived simultaneously from several user points of view. A data dictionary that has facilities for multiple logical dictionaries can document the history of a data item or process as well as hold these varied points of view. This can be a most valuable aid during the design stage.

5.7.2 Documenting the Detailed Design Phase

In a Business System Plan (BSP) the design phase is composed of two levels, the General Design and the Detailed Design, in which business activities, data, entities, relationships, and attributes are described, not just on the application level, but from a higher level providing a corporate, transfunctional perspective. In BSP, the methodology is the same as with SDLC; it is simply engineered on a higher plane. Once these elements are plugged in, they remain in documented form on the data dictionary and can be accessed for future systems development as well. Another feature of the data dictionary that can prove to be most useful at this point in the SDLC is its facility for providing implicit, as well as explicit, relationships. The systems designer, who might otherwise overlook these implicit relationships, is spared one more trap to fall into.

5.7.3 Documenting the Physical Design Phase

The details of physical design depend very much on the characteristics of the DBMS chosen for the database design.

In an IMS environment, the physical design includes the following selections:

- Physical databases and types of logical relationships, whether unidirectionally or bidirectionally physically paired
- Access methods, whether HISAM, HIDAM, or HDAM
- Segments and hierarchical structures and data representation, including type and size
- Secondary indices
- Types of pointers in relationships

The data dictionary is a very useful tool to document these selections. In addition, volume and usage statistics necessary for the ordering of database segments and for determination of storage estimates can be documented in the data dictionary.

5.7.4 Documenting the Implementation Phase

The implementation phase is very often not considered a part of the SDLC because by that point, the system has been installed and consequently has entered a separate, operational period.

This stage has enormous impact not just on the system, but on the entire organization as well. Maintenance is also a task that is especially well served by the data dictionary, which can provide:

- Complete up-to-date documentation of the system
- A historical and multiuser perspective view of the development of the definitions of the systems entities, process entities, and the relationships among them
- Enforcement of the use of definitions in a logical manner
- Security of the integrity of these definitions
- The means of assessing the impact of system changes

Consequently, the maintenance staff is provided with a comprehensive and logically consistent picture of the system, its functions, processes, and data components. The staff is thus properly prepared to respond in ways that will minimize error and save time, money, and frustration.

The maintenance stage is also the point at which the use of the data dictionary as a systems development tool is most easily validated. Systems founded on data dictionary resources are the most likely to be spared the unnecessary and yet most typical function of maintenance, namely, rectification of bad systems planning and specifications. Consequently, these systems are the ones most likely to free the maintenance stage for its proper function of adapting the system to the organization's changing environment. Obviously, this frees up the staff for the development of new systems and reduces many of the external pressures that are otherwise imposed on all systems.

5.7.5 Documenting the Structured Maintenance Phase

Structured maintenance deals with the procedures and guidelines to achieve system change or evolution through the definition of data structure change to accommodate the requirements of system change. The inputs to structured maintenance are user change requests and the current system design information, including database design and systems design. These are included in the data dictionary. Ideally, the output from structured maintenance is a system reflecting the user change request.

There are five steps in structured maintenance:

- The identification of the changes to the data structures required to accommodate the user request.
- The identification of the program functions that currently process the data structures. These functions are reviewed and systems changes are identified.
- The determination of the cost of the change. One of the benefits of this method is that it quickly indicates significant costly changes, which are seen when the data structures required to accommodate the change are very different from the current data structures.
- Perform the implementation if the cost is acceptable.
- Test the results.

Structured maintenance thus goes through all the steps of the structured system development methodology as defined here. This is an effective way to minimize the need to recover from past mistakes of the system, whether they are the result of unstructured or structured methodologies.

A systems development life cycle is used to produce the means by which the organizational data are to be manipulated. Before it may be manipulated, however, it must be managed, and that is the function of the data dictionary.

5.8 The Data Dictionary and Data Security

The data dictionary can be used in the database environment to protect the organization's data. Entries can indicate who has access rights to what data and who can update or alter that data. The dictionary can also be used to indicate who has responsibility for creating and changing definitions.

Current data dictionaries utilize several different protection mechanisms to effect data security in an environment. Data dictionaries can have pointers in an "authorization" section to various data security software packages. Some of these are:

- Access Management
- Privacy Transformations
- Cryptographic Controls
- Security Kernels
- Access Matrix

Because of space constraints, we will not discuss all of these mechanisms at length but will instead refer you to some of the current literature on data security. However, the following sections briefly discuss four of the mechanisms.

5.8.1 Access Management

Access management techniques are aimed at preventing unauthorized users from obtaining services from the system or gaining access to its files. The procedures involved are authorization, identification, and authentication. Authorization is given for certain users to enter the database and request certain types of information. Users attempting to enter the system must first identify themselves and their locations, and then authenticate the identification.

5.8.2 Privacy Transformations

Privacy transformations are techniques for concealing information by coding the data in user–processor communications or in files. Privacy transformations consist of sets of logical operations on the individual characters of the data and are of two general types—irreversible and reversible. Irreversible privacy transformations include aggregation and random modification. In this case, valid statistics can be obtained from such data, but individual values cannot be obtained.

Reversible privacy transformations are:

- Coding—replacement of a group of words in one language by a word in another language
- Compression—removal of redundancies and blanks from transmitted data
- Substitution—replacement of letters in one or more items
- Transposition—distortion of the sequence of letters in the ciphered text; all letters in the original text are retained in this technique
- Composite transformation—combinations of the preceding methods

5.8.3 Cryptographic Controls

Cryptographic transformations were recognized long ago as an effective protection mechanism in communication systems. In the past, they were used mainly to protect information that was transferred through communication lines.

There is still much debate about the cost/benefit ratio of encrypting large databases. The author's experience with encryption indicates that the cost of producing clear text from large encrypted databases is prohibitive.

5.8.4 Security Kernels

Security kernels, as the name suggests, are extra layers of protection surrounding operating systems. The kernels are usually software programs that are used to test for authenticity and to either authorize or deny all user requests to the operating system.

A request to the operating system to execute a task or retrieve data from the database is routed to the security kernel, where the request is examined to determine if the user is authorized to access the requested data. If all checks are passed, the request is transmitted to the operating system, which then executes the request.

5.9 Data Dictionary Standards

There are two types of data-related standards for data dictionaries: data definition standards and data format conformance.

"Data definition" refers to a standard way of describing data. One example is the naming of data, in which the naming standard may be in the form of rigid rules or established conventions for assigning names to data entities. All user areas within the enterprise will know that, for instance, the data element "customer name"—used in files, programs, and reports—means the same throughout the enterprise.

"Data format conformance" is content related. It means that a data element, in addition to having the same name throughout the enterprise, also must conform to a common set of format rules for the data element to retain the same meaning. For example, all data elements involving "data" should have the same format throughout the enterprise—and only that format should be assigned. Similarly, if codes are to be used throughout the enterprise, these must be uniform. If an acceptable "state" code uses two letters then that must be the universally accepted code in the enterprise, and no other code should be used.

5.9.1 Standard Formats for Data Dictionary Entries

Standards are required for the format and content used in defining and describing meta-entities of the data dictionary. This requires setting standards for the type of information that must be collected for each entry type and, most important, for the conventions that must be observed in defining these attributes. In effect, this amounts to defining a set of standards for methods of preparing attribute, entity, and relationship descriptions.

Data Element	Definition
Identification number	A 7-character unique identifier beginning with ELXXXXX.
Designator	A short name composed of the keywords of the DESCRIPTION.
Programming name	An abbreviated form of the DESIGNATOR using only approved abbreviations. Example: LEGL-CUST-NAME.
Description	A narrative explanation of the data element; the first sentence must identify the real-world entity being described. The second sentence may expand on usage characteristics. Example: The name of a customer, which is the legal name. It may not be the commonly used name. It is usually derived from legal papers.

Figure 5.2 Sample standard for data element description.

There are a number of general guidelines for establishing a standard. Several standard entries are available in commercially produced dictionaries, however, a typical standard entry for a data element is illustrated in Fig. 5.2. A data element may be described in terms of the attributes in this figure.

5.9.2 Standards for Programs Interfacing with a Data Dictionary

Data dictionary standards for programming interfaces basically fall into the area of the structure of the "call" statement from the programming language to the dictionary package.

Other standards in this area will indicate how high-level languages will use the data dictionary to build file structures and record layouts from "copy" books. They will also indicate how these languages will access the dictionary itself.

5.9.3 Security Standards

Standards for access rules and controls will indicate who can access the dictionary, how the dictionary will be accessed, and whether the contents will be accessed in their original form or as copies.

Standards in the area of security will cover the use of the data dictionary as a protection mechanism and the entries that must be made in the data dictionary to achieve those standards.

5.10 The Repository

The repository is defined as a place for storing information about items and activities of importance to your enterprise; it is an organized, shared collection of information that supports business and data processing activities.

The repository is clearly more than a data dictionary and more than a project management database; in effect a complete repository combines the functions of a project database, a data dictionary, and a process dictionary. It stores the deliverables of the software development process, as well as information about those deliverables.

The repository concept also encompasses the common notion of an encyclopedia, which is a database that includes all design information for an integrated CASE toolkit in an abstract, internally consistent form that is independent of any particular tool or representational style.

5.10.1   Repository Data Management and Protection

A repository provides services to help manage the large amount of design data generated by a full CASE environment. It provides operations to input, organize, and select data, to produce reports, to manage multiple versions, and to recover in the event of system failures. While most interaction with the repository will be via specific CASE tools, a direct repository user interface is also a useful facility for making ad hoc queries.

5.10.2   Data Integrity

A repository provides facilities to validate data on input and to ensure consistency among related data elements. This includes mechanisms to check data types and value ranges, to flag incomplete objects, to automatically initiate cascading deletes when required, and to perform specific tests specified by the repository administrator.

5.10.3   Information Sharing

The repository makes it much easier to share information among developers. It provides standardized, multiuser access controls and keeps track of synchronization requirements and change dependencies.

5.10.4   Tool Integration

The repository provides a set of data manipulation services and a semantic model to enable individual CASE tools to share information. This becomes particularly important for environments supporting the full life cycle, since tool-to-tool "pipes" become very unwieldy over many development phases, especially when prototyping and other interactive approaches are used. In addition, code generation typically requires input from multiple tools, and it is much easier if the task of synchronizing the input is left to the repository. The repository also acts as a place to store information about existing programs generated by reverse engineering tools.

5.10.5   Methodology Enforcement

Besides ensuring that the design data are valid, the repository plays a role in helping developers follow the organization's methodology. The repository can store a blueprint of the system development process and compare this to the actual status of the project, since it also has knowledge about the specific deliverables for an application.

5.10.6 Extensibility

In some integrated CASE workbenches, the methodology is "hardwired" into the tools and their accompanying dictionary. The repository provides an opportunity to extend the definition of representations, design rules, process tasks, and deliverables, thus allowing the user to define a methodology that is unique to the organization.

5.10.7 Documentation Standardization

The repository defines a standard schema for design information and provides mechanisms to generate reports in standardized formats. If a repository is used across the development organization, the documentation of each project and application will be more complete and understandable to anyone having to interface with a new system.

5.10.8 Consolidation of an Information Architecture

Once an organization has come to grips with the need to understand and optimize its own information architecture, it needs a secure place to store the definition of that architecture and to maintain it over time. The repository not only provides such a storage facility, but provides the lineage to the system development architecture that builds applications that operate against the information architecture.

CHAPTER 6

Management and Control of the Database Environment

6.1 Introduction

The advent of minicomputers and microcomputers meant that organizations could begin to establish distributed processing database environments. Management information systems (MIS)-driven distributed processing usually resulted in a centralized distributed environment, whereas user-driven distributed processing led a decentralized distributed environment. In either situation, an organization may need to share some of the data that have been either distributed across or decentralized to various locations and departments. Sharing data can be difficult, especially in a decentralized distributed environment in which each department is responsible for the systems that automate its functions.

Problems of autonomy, or decentralized control, are particularly acute in a database environment. The architecture of the DBMS may dictate its usefulness primarily in one type of control environment. If a DBMS is selected solely on the basis of one application's needs, it may prove inappropriate for the desired control environment. In such cases, management control decisions may be made unwisely on the basis of previous technical decisions.

Unfortunately, many organizations select a DBMS without a long-term objective. When problems arise, the DBMS may be discarded and replaced with another. In some cases, the organization may become dependent on the DBMS because of the amount of data and systems that have been committed to it. The organization may then continue to use the inappropriate DBMS and acquire another for future development. If a new database management system is acquired, however, problems may occur when data must be shared among DBMSs. If a desired database environment has not been specified, the MIS manager may want to consider a strategy that will avoid commitment to a specific environment.

This chapter examines several alternative database environments from a management control perspective and explores the impact of the DBMS selection on the ability to achieve the desired management control.

6.2 Centralized versus Decentralized Control

The terms centralized and decentralized refer to the organizational level at which control and decision making are exercised. Absolute centralization or decentralization cannot be achieved. Absolute centralization would imply that only one person could decide anything, whereas absolute decentralization would imply that a manager delegated all authority.

Figure 6.1 illustrates decentralization and centralization of database authority in an organization. In the decentralized example, each function is responsible for its own database. Function 1 makes all decisions concerning Database A, and Function 2 makes those concerning Database B. Such authority is delegated by the manager to whom the function reports. In a centralized environment, the manager usually delegates authority to one functional area—in this case, the database administration function. The manager may choose not to delegate the authority, but may elect to retain some authority or delegate some to the

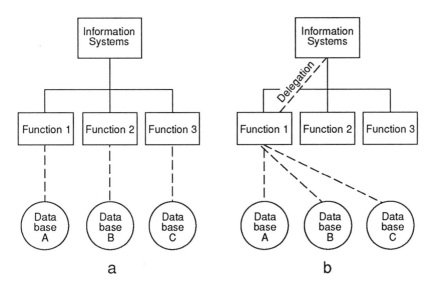

Figure 6.1   (a) Centralized and (b) decentralized authority.

other functional areas. Centralization and decentralization imply tendencies to delegate or to not delegate; the two extremes encompass a broad spectrum of possibilities.

6.3 Distributed versus Nondistributed Location

The terms distributed and nondistributed refer to location. Distributed and nondistributed database environments are illustrated in Fig. 6.2. In the distributed environment, each location—ABC, DEF, and GHI—has

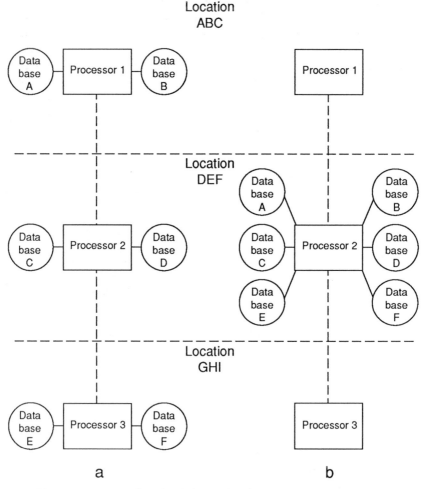

Figure 6.2   (a) Distributed and (b) nondistributed database environments.

its own processor and databases. The databases are distributed to the location at which they are primarily ruled. The nondistributed environment shows the same three locations. Each has its own processor, but all the databases are concentrated on processor 2 at location DEF—a case of nondistributed data and distributed processing.

6.4 Alternative Database Environments

Centralized or decentralized and distributed or nondistributed databases can be combined in the same environment. The following sections describe four possible environments: centralized and nondistributed, centralized and distributed, decentralized and nondistributed, and decentralized and distributed.

6.4.1 Centralized and Nondistributed

In this environment, the data are located in one place and management retains control or delegates it to a single entity. A typical example is a mainframe environment with a strong data or database administration function.

6.4.2 Centralized and Distributed

In this environment, management retains control or delegates control to a single entity, and the data are physically located in many places. The metadata, or data about the data, are usually located in one place with the controlling organization unless required by the distributed data. A typical example is a bank machine network with customer and account data stored at the branch that owns the data.

6.4.3 Decentralized and Nondistributed

In this environment, the data are located in one place, and management delegates control of the data to many lower-level entities. A typical example is a mainframe environment in which each user organization has its own systems and programming staff.

6.4.4 Decentralized and Distributed

In this environment, management delegates control of the data to many lower-level entities. The data are physically located in many places, and the metadata are likely to be distributed with the data. A typical example is an organization with many minicomputers located at and under the control of the using department.

6.5 DBMS Characteristics and Control

The characteristics of a DBMS can affect an organization's ability to establish a particular control environment. With some DBMSs, for example, it is very difficult to relate a diversity of data for the purpose of sharing. If sharing data on the physical level is one of the organization's goals, the manager should beware of selecting a DBMS with characteristics that make this relating of data difficult. Other DBMSs require central management because they can be used economically only if applications share physical facilities.

6.5.1 Characteristics Requiring Central Control

DBMS characteristics that require an organization to adopt centralized operational control of the data include the sharing of physical resources by applications, a large number of optional functions, and any characteristic that requires expertise in a particular area. Many well-known mainframe DBMSs have such characteristics.

Some DBMSs require all applications, or at least major subsets of them, to share physical resources, including databases and files, program libraries, dictionaries, and operating system regions. In some cases, resource limitations, rather than the software, necessitate sharing. For example, an organization with 15 on-line DB2 database applications would not want 15 copies of the communications handler up and running at the same time. This would require extraordinary machine resources and management. If the organization required all 15 applications to be running simultaneously, they would have to share the physical resources of one or perhaps a few DB2 control regions. Such systems as DB2, IMS, ADABAS, and IDMS were designed to share control regions, as noted in Fig. 6.3.

Another DBMS characteristic that requires an organization to adopt central control is a large number of optional functions. The more functions a system has, the more complex it is; many decisions must be made for configuring the systems to meet the organization's needs, and many trade-offs must be evaluated. Because such decisions require

Programs

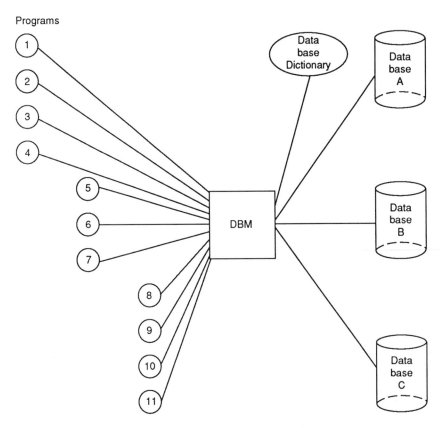

Figure 6.3 Example of sharing of control regions.

scarce expertise, the formation of a central group that can share its expertise with others is recommended.

In fact, any characteristic of a DBMS that required expertise should make the system a candidate for central control. Many functions and characteristics of a DBMS fall into this category. Unfortunately they are not always discovered during the selection process or with the implementation of the first few applications. One such characteristic is a limit on the number of files or databases that a DBMS will support from one control region. Such a limit may seem unimportant until an organization approaches it. At that time, it may be too late to prevent the purchase of an additional machine and the partitioning of the databases into unrelated systems. Intelligent central control of the physical resources can prevent such a situation.

Control		Data	Systems and Programs	
Level	Type		Data-oriented	Compute-oriented
Strategic Planning and Management Control	Centralized	1	2	A
	Decentralized	3	4	B
Operational Control	Centralized	5	6	C
	Decentralized	7	8	D

Figure 6.4   Example of central operational control of programs.

6.5.2   Characteristics Hindering Central Control

When central physical control is unnecessary, centralized planning and control are often difficult to establish. DBMS characteristics that render central control of the physical facilities unnecessary include ease of use, lack of shared resources, and a limited ability to share and relate data.

If a DBMS is easy to use, justifying the formation of a special group to provide centralized operational control is difficult. When database definitions are embedded with the data, each database is self-contained. In these cases, it is usually unnecessary to share other resources of significance from a control point of view. The lack of shared resources reduces the requirements for central operational control. Figure 6.4 illustrates this type of environment.

Finally, if a DBMS does not allow for logically relating separate physical databases, the ability to share and relate data is significantly diminished, thus substantially limiting the ability to gain the benefits that a centralized control environment can offer.

6.5.3   Characteristics Hindering Decentralized Control

Many DBMSs that are marketed as easy to use may enable end users to easily retrieve and report data in the desired format, but may also require considerable effort on the part of the database administrator. An organization seeking decentralized operational control in the database environment must be assured that no special requirements lurk behind the ease of use offered by the vendor.

6.6 Administrative Controls

Administrative controls may be defined as management policies formulated to ensure adequate maintenance of a selective access program, whether it be selective authorization to databases or to physical areas. The controls may include the development and implementation of security policies, guidelines, standards, and procedures. Effective administrative controls can go a long way in helping to ensure that an organization has a secure operating database environment. These controls certainly will assist in reducing or eliminating both deliberate and accidental threats. Once an intruder realizes that the chances of being detected are good, he or she may be deterred from attempting to breach the security. This determination of the probability of being detected can be made from the intruder's knowledge of the existing administrative controls. For example, if the intruder knows that there is a requirement for the user's name and terminal log-on times to be recorded, then he will very likely not use the terminal.

The probability of accidental threats succeeding decreases with an increase in the user's knowledge of the operating environment and requirements. Clear and precise administrative procedures and assertions help to increase that knowledge and, in turn, decrease the probability of successful accidental threats.

Administrative controls, and security features in particular, should be developed parallel to the actual systems and programs development. A group consisting of internal auditors, development team, and users should be assigned to develop these controls and standards.

Administrative controls can be defined in the following areas:

- Top-level management decisions—decisions pertaining to the selection and evaluation of safeguards
- Security risk assessment studies to identify and rank the events that would compromise the security of the database and the information stored in it
- Personnel management—decisions pertaining to employee hiring and firing procedures, employee rules of conduct, and enforcement
- Data-handling techniques—a well-defined set of rules describing

the precautions to be used and the obligations of personnel during the handling of all data

- Data processing practices—the methods to control accountability for data, verification of the accuracy of data, and inventories of storage media
- Programming practices—they pertain to the discipline employed in the specification, design, implementation, program coding, and debugging of the system
- Assignment of responsibilities—assign each individual a specific set of responsibilities toward carrying out certain security functions for which he or she is held responsible
- Procedure auditing—an independent examination of established security procedures to determine their ongoing effectiveness

6.7 Auditing and Monitoring the Database

Auditing and monitoring are integral features of database management and control. Should a violation be attempted, the system must be able to detect it and react effectively to it. Detection then implies that the system has a threat-monitoring capability. Threat monitoring requires the following actions:

- Monitoring the events of the systems as related to security
- Recognizing a potential compromise to the security system
- Diagnosing the nature of the threat
- Performing compensatory actions
- Reporting and recording the event

Whereas threat monitoring is an active form of surveillance, an equally important but more passive form is auditability of the database. A security audit should be able to cover the past events of the system and, in particular, cover all security-related transactions.

Audit trails that can lead to the identity of users, terminals, and authorizing bodies should be a feature of all applications. The monitoring process within an organization should include the ability to determine whether:

- The controls over the database administration function are effective.
- The process by which sensitive data are determined is adequate.

- The procedure by which security violations are detected is in place and effective.
- The extent to which data access is restricted to only authorized individuals is workable.
- The ability to restrict access by a program to the database, other programs, and catalogs exists.
- Terminal security features, such as log on, log off, and re-start, are adequate and effective.
- The procedures to follow during processing interruptions are effective.

The importance of keeping records and logs of events that affect the database and its environment cannot be overemphasized. The events recorded should include performance data, all error or abnormal events, all transactions related to sensitive information, and all overrides of established system's control.

Several DBMSs provide logging capabilities as part of their package. These logs should be examined for their adequacy and ability to meet the auditing requirements of the environment. Organizations should not be hesitant to design and implement their own in-house logging facilities if the vendor's prove inadequate.

Any security effort in an organization should eventually involve internal auditors. This involvement becomes mandatory because of the changing requirements for evaluating and verifying controls in a secure database environment. Personnel responsible for security can offer considerable assistance to the auditors in determining the accuracy, integrity, and completeness of systems.

Researchers are now suggesting that internal auditors become involved in the development phases of system design and not only in the postimplementation evaluation. The auditor's experience should provide the development teams with insight into the various methods they can use to approach their responsibilities in controlling and auditing the total information processing systems.

Because of the rapidly changing database technology, internal auditors need to consistently upgrade their skills. System development teams with current knowledge should assist the auditors in filling the gaps in their knowledge of techniques and concepts of integrated database systems design. The development teams should strive to increase management's awareness of changes in the database environment as they affect internal audit and the controls governing data processing.

Finally, the following list of management activities should enhance the internal auditing capabilities within an organization and especially how they affect the database environment.

- Ensure that all staff realize the importance of internal auditing in the database environment
- Ensure a clearly defined internal audit mandate that specifies the responsibility of internal audit as it relates to all phases of the security of the database environment
- Clearly define the working relationship among users, internal auditors, and development teams responsible for database management and control
- Encourage the development of new techniques and internal audit approaches to ensure the security, privacy, and integrity of the database
- Require the development of security control guidelines
- Ensure that internal auditors participate in the security effort

6.8 Protection Mechanisms in the Database Environment

Protection mechanisms can be defined in as the techniques and methods used to ensure security, integrity, and privacy in the database environment. There are two types of protection mechanisms: those built into the computer operating system, also known as internal mechanisms, and those not linked to the operating system or external mechanisms. This section discusses two protection mechanisms.

6.8.1 Resource Access Control Facility (RACF)

RACF is a program product of IBM that is designed to identify system users and control their access to protected resources. RACF's authorization structure can be contrasted with a data-set password mechanism. With typical password protection, a password is assigned to a specific data set. The system ensures that the data set can be accessed only when that password is supplied.

Protected data sets can be accessed by anyone who knows the password. Obviously, there are control problems associated with restricting knowledge of the passwords. There are also problems in withdrawing access to data sets. If three people know the password for a particular data set and an administrator wants to take away one person's access rights, the password must be changed and the new password communicated to the users.

RACF authorization structure is based on principles that are different from password protection. RACF eliminates the need for data-set passwords. With RACF, an administrator can tell which users are authorized to access which data sets. A user's right to access data sets can be withdrawn by changing the profile.

RACF authorization structure contains three kinds of elements: users, groups of users, and protected resources. It stores descriptions of users, groups, and resources in profiles contained in a special data set called the RACF data set.

RACF interfaces with the operating system in three main areas:

- Identification and verification of users
- Authorization checking for access to protect resources
- Monitoring to provide both immediate notification of security problems and a log for post de facto analysis

6.8.2 The Access Matrix or Authorization Table

The access matrix or authorization table is an internal mechanism built into the operating system. It is essentially a set of tables that indicate who has access to what data. The access matrix consists of the following components:

- Objects that are to be protected
- Subjects seeking access to these objects
- Different protection levels for each object
- Rules that determine how the subjects access each object
- A monitor that mediates all access of a subject to an object
- Directories containing information about the objects and subjects.

The interaction between objects and subjects can be represented by an access matrix (see Fig. 6.5). The protectable objects are the new-components of the matrix, and the subjects seeking access to the objects are the column-components of the matrix. Each entry in the access matrix determines the access rights of the subject to the object and is defined as the access attribute in the model. The access matrix is dynamic enough to include any class of objects or subjects within the database environment. It can provide a high level of protection for any object irrespective of whatever application the organization's personnel develops and runs against the integrated database.

Each object will be placed in a class determined by the level of protection for that object. For example, an object may be placed in a

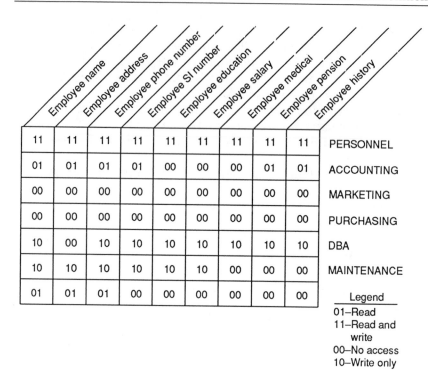

Figure 6.5 Example of access matrix.

READ only protection class. Each subject will be a member of a hierarchy. The hierarchical classifying of the subjects will allow subjects to create object subjects while ensuring that the created subject will not have more privileges then the creator. Figure 6.5 illustrates the access matrix.

In Fig. 6.5, each entry in the access matrix represents the access rights of the subject to the objects. For example, the 01 in the first column and the second row indicates that the accounting department can READ the employee name; the 11 in the first column and row indicates that the personnel department can both READ and WRITE to the employee name on the employee database; the 00 in the fifth column and second row indicates that the accounting department can neither READ nor WRITE to the employee education information; and the 10 in the first column and sixth row indicates that the maintenance department can only WRITE to the employee name on the employee database.

The matrix can accommodate several other access attributes, such as EXECUTE, DELETE, UPDATE, APPEND, SORT, and CREATE.

CHAPTER 7

Infrastructure Support for the Database Environment

7.1 Introduction

The introduction of a database management system into an enterprise has an enormous effect on the environment and the way things are traditionally done. Many organizations fail in their efforts to introduce database technology not because of the failure of the software, but because of the failure of personnel to offer the infrastructure support necessary for the success of the database environment.

For database technology to succeed in an organization, there must be management support for the environment as well as the MIS infrastructure support. The infrastructure support consists of all efforts by MIS personnel to ensure a smooth and efficient running database operation. It ensures that there is adequately trained personnel not only to operate the environment, but to respond to and solve problems as they occur. This support will come from the following areas:

- Data administration
- Database administration
- Technical support
- Physical database designers
- Logical database designers
- Application programmers
- Computer operations
- Input/output data control
- System analysts/designers

7.2 Data Administration Support

The infrastructure support for the database environment, which is given by the data administration function, consists of, but is not limited to, offering assistance to all functional MIS groups and users in a variety of areas, including:

- Database design methodologies
- Database security and integrity
- Database access
- Data dictionary support
- Logical database design
- Database audit
- Database performance and maintenance
- Database standards
- Database education and training

7.2.1   Database Design Methodologies

Database administration will provide assistance in the selection of a structured design methodology for the MIS environment. Present design methodologies fall into two main categories: data-driven and process-driven.

The primary deliverable from a data-driven design effort is a data model. There are several approaches to producing data models, the most often being the entity–relationship approach.

The primary deliverable from a process-driven design effort is a process model or a set of processes that are decomposed into programming specifications. Data-flow diagrams are very often classified as deliverable from a process-driven design effort. In several instances, data-driven and process-driven designs are done in parallel during the development life cycle. In other instances either one or the other is done.

7.2.2   Database Security and Integrity

The issue of database security and integrity becomes more relevant and important in a database environment. In a database environment, the primary objective is to expose the data to the widest audience of users (data sharing) while maintaining the integrity of the data and avoiding abuse of the database (data security).

Data administration will assist in conducting threat analyses and risk assessments to determine the level of protection that will be needed. It will assist in the evaluation and selection of any required protection mechanisms. Data administration will also establish data security standards for password protection, database accessing, and program interfacing with the database.

7.2.3 Database Access

Data administration will assist in determining who will access the database, what functions can be performed by authorized users of the database, what terminals can update the database, and whether dedicated terminals should be used in the database environment.

7.2.4 Data Dictionary Support

In a database environment, the data dictionary is a very important tool for systems design, documentation, data management, and data security. The data dictionary can be used as a repository to collect the user requirements that are used as the primary input to the logical design phase of database development. Characteristics of the data model can also be stored in the data dictionary as well as the input to the physical design phase.

The dictionary can be used to carry out maintenance on the various databases, once they are installed. In the database environment, the data dictionary as it is currently constituted cannot support a data-driven design environment as outlined in the foregoing. However, applications that access the database are adequately supported.

7.2.5 Logical Database Design

Data administration will assist system developers in the logical database design phase of database development. During this phase, the system developers produce a data model from the user requirements.

Data administration will assist in synthesizing the data model to ensure that it meets the needs of the users. It will assist in documenting the entities, attributes, and relationships; the normalization of the entities and tables (in a relational environment); and population of the entities and data dictionary.

7.2.6 Database Audit

Data administration will assist internal auditors, external auditors, and application programmers in developing and maintaining audit trails, audit software, and audit standards. It will also provide education and training to auditors and users in database technology and the needs for auditing the database.

7.2.7 Database Performance and Maintenance

Database monitoring and tuning are very important activities in the database environment. Database monitoring involves the periodic appraisal of the performance of the database management software. Database tuning involves the adjusting and reorganizing of the database and access methods parameters.

Data administration does not have the primary responsibility for database monitoring and tuning, but generally assists the database administrators, technical support staff, and physical designers in providing guidelines for performing these tasks.

7.2.8 Database Standards

Data administration will assist in developing standards for accessing the database, naming of tables and table columns, selection of primary and foreign keys, and the use of utilities in the database environment, especially in the area of backup and recovery.

7.2.9 Database Education and Training

Data administration will provide input regarding the education and training needs of the various functional units in the database environment. The immediate needs for an MIS department are in the following areas:

- Data analysis techniques
- Data modeling
- Introduction to SQL
- SQL/DS and DB2 internals
- QMF and other reporting packages
- Introduction to VM/CMS
- Introduction to MVS
- MVS internals
- MVS operating and console messages
- Performance monitoring and database tuning

7.3 Database Administration Support

The infrastructure support given to the database environment by database administration consists of offering assistance to system designers in a variety of areas. These areas include but are not limited to:

- Loading the database
- Reorganizing the database
- Maintenance of the database
- Data storage calculations
- Selection of access paths
- Performance monitoring
- Normalization

The support that data administration (DA) offers should not be confused with that offered by database administration (DBA). DA offers overall data management support to the database environment, whereas DBA offers technical support as dictated by the database management system. That is, the support offered by DA is the same irrespective of the DBMS. The same is not true for DBA. In the database environment, DBA support may be offered by the current Technical Support staff.

7.3.1 Loading the Database

DBA will load both test and production versions of the database. There are several utilities available in both the SQL/DS and DB2 environments for loading the database. The DBA must certainly become familiar with the operation and operational requirements of these utilities.

7.3.2 Reorganizing the Database

It may become necessary because of the database performance or changes in systems design to reorganize the database (i.e., alter the physical storage of data within the database). DBA will accept requests for database reorganization from systems development teams, analyze those requests, and reorganize the database, if necessary.

7.3.3 Maintenance of the Database

DBA has the primary responsibility for maintaining all application database and corporate databases where applicable. The database maintenance includes but is not limited to:

- Restoration or modification of access paths
- Modification to primary and foreign keys
- Reorganizing the database
- Modification to tables and table contents

7.3.4 Data Storage Calculations

DBA will be responsible for advising all relevant personnel about space and storage requirements for all databases. That function will do the calculations related to space and storage estimates and will also advise about the best access methods to select for each application database.

7.3.5 Selection of Access Paths

DBA will assist the systems development teams in determining, on an application by application basis, which columns of a particular row will be used to access the database. The function will also assist in the determination of the frequency in which these columns will be accessed. DBA will also determine what columns are used in joining tables, ORDER BY clauses, and WHERE predicates.

7.3.6 Performance Monitoring

DBA will be responsible for monitoring the performance of application and corporate databases. The function will establish measures to calculate database performance. One such measure will be response time for on-line access of the database.

7.3.7 Normalization

DBA will assist systems developers in ensuring that the relationships between entities, association of attributes within entities, and the data model itself are optimized. The function will assist with the normalization process, which is conducted to reduce data redundancy and problems with inserting, updating, and deleting data from the database.

7.4 Technical Support

The infrastructure support for the database environment, which is given by Technical Support, consists of, but is not limited to, offering assistance in the following areas:

- Software installation, including DB gens
- Application of PTFs
- Software maintenance
- Performance tuning

- Backup and recovery
- Utilities maintenance

7.4.1 Software Installation

Technical Support staff is primarily responsible for installing all the database management system and relevant software. The installation will include database, gens, utilities, operating system interfaces, communication handlers, and editors.

7.4.2 Application of PTFs

The DBMS vendor will, from time to time, send PTFs to database to apply to the various software programs. It will be the sole responsibility of Technical Support to apply these fixes as they come in.

7.4.3 Software Maintenance

Technical Support will be responsible for ongoing maintenance of database software. The maintenance requirements, to a large extent, may be confined to software upgrades, changes in versions or levels, installation of new releases, and addition of utilities.

7.4.4 Performance Tuning

Data administration, database administration, and Technical Support will share responsibility for monitoring the performance of the database and taking steps to tune it wherever necessary.

Performance tuning in the database environment must begin during the design process. It will be reflected in the way queries are structured and will be taken into consideration during application and utility processing.

Some performance tuning considerations that must be taken into account are:

- Applications using DDL commands for tablespaces, tables, and indexes should have their own databases.
- Unless very small tables are being developed, use the guideline of only one table per tablespace.
- Attempt to keep all the data in a tablespace within its primary location.
- Keep table row length to less than 4K byte of storage.

- Minimize the use of variable-length columns, unless you are saving an average of 20 bytes per row.
- Do not select columns that you do not need.
- Avoid using subroutines for I/O, if possible.

7.4.5 Backup and Recovery

The vendor provides several utilities that can be used to back-up and recover the database. The following utilities will be used for backup and recovery:

- LOAD   Loads data into tables from data sets
- COPY   Creates copies of tables for recovery purposes
- MERGE COPY   Combines partial and full image copies
- MODIFY   Removes recovery information from CATALOG
- RECOVER   Recovers a table or index
- REORG   Resequences rows of tables
- REPAIR   Fixes bad data or pointers
- RUNSTATS   Records information about data in tables and indexes in CATALOG
- STOSPACE   Records space information in the CATALOG

Technical Support must become familiar with the use of these utilities, the JCL required to run each utility, and the occasions when they will be used. They must also become involved in the management and judicious use by others of these utilities.

7.4.6 Utilities Maintenance

The management and maintenance of utilities in a database environment are very critical issues. Technical Support will be responsible for making changes to the utilities, adjusting the JCL required to run the utilities, and maintaining correct and up-to-date versions of each utility.

The management of database utilities requires that only authorized users have access to them. Technical Support must ensure that there is no illegal use of these utilities.

7.5 Physical Database Designers

In a database environment, physical database designers may often perform the duties of application database administrators or may even be called application DBAs.

In the database environment, the role of the physical database designers may be more appropriately given to the senior systems analyst who demonstrates a fondness for the technical aspects of database design. The duties of the physical database designer include several of the tasks outlined for the database administrator in addition to the following:

- Development of storage formats
- Normalization
- Table creation
- Key selection
- Input to programming specifications
- Data integrity considerations
- Data security considerations
- Useful physical design knowledge

7.5.1 Development of Storage Formats

The physical database designer is responsible for determining how the database will be physically stored and how many tables will occupy a tablespace, for building storage groups, and for determining whether indexes should be built.

The physical designer will determine what data will be stored in the primary area of the direct access storage device (DASD) and what data will be stored in the overflow area. He must be/become familiar with the fundamentals of disk structures and the storage requirements of the database.

Disk space calculations are very often carried out by the DBA, however, sometimes the physical designer may be called on to do space calculations.

7.5.2 Normalization

Normalization is an activity that is generally done during the logical data design phase of systems development. However, because of performance considerations and storage requirements, the physical designer may be asked to contribute to normalizing and synthesizing of databases and also to denormalizing of normalized data.

7.5.3 Table Creation

Physical database designers will be responsible for all table and index creation in the environment. This activity will be carried out on an application by application basis.

During table creation, the physical designer will take several performance considerations into account, including:

- Whenever it is practical, create one table per tablespace.
- Limit the table to less than 300 columns.
- Unique indexes should be created based on columns that are not updated frequently.
- Table names may be up to 18 characters in length.
- Unique indexes should not be created from columns whose data type is specified as VARCHAR since the software will reserve spaces for the longest occurrence of the data irrespective of actual length.
- Create composite indexes for columns that are frequently used together in a WHERE clause.

7.5.4 Key Selection

The physical database designer along with the logical database designer will select the primary and foreign keys for the databases. The key selection should be based not only on performance and integrity considerations but also on the business function usage and requirements of the access methods.

7.5.5 Input to Programming Specifications

The primary input to programming specifications will still come from the systems designers, who consist of project leaders, systems analysts, and programmer analysts. However, the physical designers will still have some input to the specifications, which will include recommendations to:

- Store keys and attributes in related tables.
- Store derived data.
- Use partitioned table spaces for very large tables.
- Minimize the number of tables with rows whose defined length is greater than 4056 bytes.
- Only use VARCHAR when the field is at least 18 bytes in length and there is a 30% savings per row length.
- Use numeric data types if a column's data are restricted to numeric data.
- Eliminate duplicate key rows before creating a unique index on an existing table.
- Avoid indexes on VARCHAR columns.

The reader can easily determine from these recommendations that the input to programming specifications from physical designers will mainly concern performance issues.

7.5.6 Data Integrity Considerations

Data integrity issues for physical designers will be limited to ensuring that whenever a query is made to the database, the results obtained from the database are always the same as long as no modifications have been made to the database.

The physical designers will ensure data integrity through the judicious selection of unique indexes and access paths.

7.5.7 Data Security Considerations

Physical designers will advise the users of the database about the various protection mechanisms available in relational databases to ensure that threats against the data will not succeed. They will advise the users about the various locking mechanisms and view creating that are available to protect the data from illegal use.

7.5.8 Useful Physical Design Knowledge

The physical designers must be willing to educate users on various topics that are pertinent to the effective operations of the database, including:

● Referential integrity
● Fundamentals of disk structures
● Primary and secondary access methods
● Indexing for performance and integrity
● Indexing, B-trees, and hashing
● Data clustering
● Locking mechanisms

7.6 Logical Database Designers

The logical database design phase of database development includes all activities that produce a data model from the user requirements. In the database environment, the role of the logical database designers may be more appropriately given to the senior systems analyst who demonstrates a fondness for understanding and interpreting the business functions of the organization.

The duties of the logical database designer include several of the tasks outlined for the data administrator in addition to the following:

- Analysis of formulated user requirements
- Development of data model
- Mapping the data model to a relational model
- Normalization of the relational model

7.6.1 Analysis of Formulated User Requirements

The logical database designers will analyze the user requirements collected by the systems development team for relevant entities and relationships. The known entities and relationships will be represented in the form of a data model (E–R diagram).

7.6.2 Development of the Data Model

The data model that results from the analysis of the user requirements is revised several times until it adequately represents the user's needs. The logical database designers will assist in the selection of unique identifiers for the entities and establishing definitions for the attributes, entities, and relationships.

7.6.3 Mapping the Data Model to a Relational Model

The logical database designers will convert the entities of the data model into tables. They will analyze the table columns for uniqueness and establish which columns will be used for primary keys and which will be used as foreign keys. The logical database designers will assist the systems developers in selecting column names that can be referenced in queries by all users.

7.6.4 Normalization of the Relational Model

The logical database designers will assist systems developers in the three major steps involved in the normalization process.

7.7 Application Programmers

Application programmers are responsible for developing the programs that access the database. They work from specifications developed by the systems designers to produce the reports requested by the various users. Application programmers support the database environment by:

- Prototyping for specification debugging
- Testing the interfaces to the database
- Assisting in the development of programming standards and naming conventions
- Testing the application software
- Educating the environment about specific application requirements

7.7.1 Prototyping for Specification Debugging

Application programmers will support the environment through prototyping applications at an early stage of systems development to ensure correctness and adequacy of the systems design.

7.7.2 Testing the Interfaces to the Database

Application programmers will support the environment by testing applications that access the database. The test will include CALLS to the database from COBOL, queries to the database through QMF, and access through utilities.

7.8 Operations Support

Operations support is very critical to the success of the database environment. The support includes but is not limited to:

- Generation of activity logs
- Generation of operating procedures and manuals
- Administration of the operating environment and software
- Maintenance of hardware manuals
- Creation of operating/override logs, for example, SYSLOG, SMF, and JOB scheduling
- Running of utilities to monitor integrity, for example, LOAD, Reorg, Repair, and Check

The database environment has little impact on the way operations is run in a traditional data processing environment. The additional requirements and activities of the database environment are usually transparent to the operations staff. Therefore, with this proviso, these activities will not be discussed.

7.9 Input/Output Data Control Support

As with Operations, the activities and requirements of data control in a database environment do not differ to any significant degree to those in a traditional data processing environment. Therefore, these activities will not be discussed any further.

7.10 System Designers Support

In a database environment, the system designers role parallels that of the systems analyst in the traditional data processing environment. However, the designers role may be divided into logical design and physical design in larger organizations. With this in mind, the author would like to refer the readers to the sections on logical and physical database designers in earlier sections of this chapter for coverage of system designers' activities in a database environment.

CHAPTER 8

Administration of the Database Environment

In an earlier chapter, we established the premise that data are a resource in much the same way as employees, products, natural resources, finances, and other material products or resources. In the same chapter, we defined Information Resource Management (IRM) as a discipline that deals with planning for, allocating, maintaining and conserving, prudently exploiting, effectively employing, and integrating the data resource.

This chapter deals with three aspects of IRM. First, we address the effective management of the data resource. Second, we emphasize that to effectively manage data, it is necessary to obtain as much data about the data resource as possible. Third, we focus on planning for the data resource, during which we emphasize the strategic, tactical, and operational aspects of IRM planning. Regarding control of the data resource, we discuss how to establish lines of authority and responsibility for the data, by emphasizing the importance of having common procedures for collecting, updating, and maintaining the data. Finally, we establish that in order to control the data resource, the organization must evaluate, mediate, and reconcile the conflicting needs and prerogatives of its functional departments.

8.1 Management of the Data Resource

To manage data effectively as a resource, it is necessary to obtain as much data about the data resource as possible. There must be stringent procedures for collecting, maintaining, and using the resource. The next several sections of this chapter will discuss various tools that can be used in the effective management of the data resource.

8.1.1 The Data Dictionary

The data dictionary may be defined as an organized reference to the data content of an organization's programs, systems, databases, collections of all files, or manual records.

The data dictionary may be maintained manually or by a computer. Sometimes, the term "data dictionary" may refer to a software product that is utilized to maintain a dictionary database. The data dictionary will contain names, descriptions, and definitions of the organization's data resource.

8.1.2 The Data Dictionary as a Management Tool

The data dictionary is perhaps the most important tool that information resource managers have at their disposal. It allows management to document and support application development and assists in designing and controlling the database environment. It also allows managers to set standards and monitor adherence to those standards.

In the database environment, the data dictionary can be used to document the single user view of the organization's data or several integrated views. It can document the related data models of those views, the logical databases that result from those views, and the physical representation of those logical models.

The organization can store complete representations of its data architecture in the data dictionary. This data architecture can be used to indicate how adequately the data resource supports the business functions of the organization and also show what data the company will need to support its long-range plans for expansion.

The dictionary allows information managers to respond quickly to upper-level management's needs for data in a decision support environment. It supports the organization's need for consistent data definitions and usage.

The data dictionary can be used to indicate management's desire to control access to the organization's data resource. Managers can now state who can access the data and the level of access assigned to the individual. They can use the data dictionary, in consort with the operating system, to deny access to unauthorized individuals.

The data dictionary can also provide managers and other users with concise definitions of entities and data items that are important to the organization. It can indicate where data are used, what uses it, how data are used, and other dependencies on those data.

Management can indicate, via the dictionary, who is responsible for changing the characteristics of the data resource and the procedures for effecting the change. On the other hand, managers can use the dictionary to control changes to the data resource and readily assess the effect on systems, programs, and user operations when such changes are made.

8.1.3   The Database as a Management Tool

Today's highly competitive business climate, characterized by more educated consumers and shorter product cycles, forces companies to be information driven. Corporate decision makers derive information by analyzing raw data, gathered internally or externally, in a particular business context. Therefore, to be successful, a company must ensure that these raw data are captured and readily available for analysis in various forms. If such data are easily accessible, various levels of support must be built before meaningful information can be obtained.

Various tools have evolved over the past two decades to facilitate data resource management. When first introduced, database management systems (DBMS) were thought to offer a panacea to the growing lack of control over the company data resources.

The database can be defined as a collection of interrelated data items processable by one or more application systems. The database permits common data to be integrated and shared between corporate functional units and provides flexibility of data organization. It facilitates the addition of data to an existing database without modification of existing application programs. This data independence is achieved by removing the direct association between the application program and physical storage of data. The advantages of the database are:

- Consistency through use of the same data by all corporate parts
- Application program independence from data sequence and structure
- Reduction and control of redundant data
- Reduction in application development costs, storage costs, and processing costs

Database technology has permitted information resource managers to organize data around subjects that interest the company. It has allowed for data sharing among divergent parts of the organization and has introduced new methods of managing data, as well as new and sophisticated logical and physical design methodologies. By having a central pool of data, the organization can now secure the resource more efficiently and in more cost-effective ways. Access to the data can be more readily controlled while making it available to a wider audience of diverse users.

The technology has allowed management, through Decision Support Systems (DSS), to more readily adjust to the changing environment of their respective businesses and to reduce the impact of these changes on the organization's economy.

8.1.4 Managing the Corporate Database

Effective management of the corporate database requires that the following activities be addressed consistently and logically:

(a) Planning—The corporate database must be planned according to the specific needs of the company.
(b) Organization—A data-driven company requires new organizational entities.
(c) Acquisition—Once the corporate database has been planned, the needed data must be acquired.
(d) Maintenance and Control—The data in the corporate database must be securely, accurately, and completely maintained. In addition, proper control must be exercised over access to the database. Data ownership, use, and custodianship issues must also be addressed.
(e) Usage—The corporate database must be available to all authorized users in the company.

Planning   Planning entails the preparation of all corporate data models. This is best achieved through interviews with the department heads of each functional area in the company. These managers should be asked to determine what data influence their functional areas and what information is required to successfully operate and manage their departments. After all the interviews are completed, the collection of data items must be analyzed and distilled into a model that can be understood, presented, and accepted by corporate management. This analysis should include a determination of the source of the data as well as its characteristics and interrelationships with other data items. This corporate data model must then be compared with currently held and maintained data. The difference between what is currently available and what is ultimately required determines what data must be collected.

Organization   There are two distinct aspects of organizing the corporate database. The first is the business aspect: identifying what data are relevant to the company, its source and method of capture, and the interrelationships among the data items. The second is the technical aspect: storing data on computer-readable media in a form readily accessible by the corporate decision makers.

The business tasks of organizing the corporate database often requires the creation of the relatively new Chief Information Officer (CIO) and the more traditional data administration function. The CIO is the executive in charge of the information systems department and is responsible for formulating an information strategy that includes all systems development, computer operations, and communications planning and operation.

The data administration function links computer systems and the business functions that they are designed to serve. The group responsible for data administration builds and maintains the corporate data model. A properly constructed data model places the system to be developed into a proper business perspective. This model is instrumental in the preparation of the information systems department's strategic plan.

Acquisition   In a data-driven organization, information strategy is derived from the corporate data model. Systems planned for development should provide information or a level of service that was previously unavailable. In a typical systems development project, a major part of the effort is spent in acquiring and storing the data that are used to produce the required information.

Although data analysis and design is defined as a separate activity in the definition of data resource management, application programs to collect and validate data items and add them to the appropriate database must still be written. The interactions among systems development, data administration, and database administration must be in place to ensure that the corporate database effectively acquires data.

Maintenance and control   Maintenance tasks include making changes to the corporate data model, reflecting these changes in the data dictionary, and properly communicating changes to all users who must know the model's current status. Given the degree of data independence that can be achieved in today's DBMSs, changes to the database should not necessitate changes to application programs. However, the addition of new data items and changes or deletions to existing data items must be controlled as vigorously as changes to application systems. That is, the change control principles applied to application programs must be applied to changes in data definitions used by these programs.

Data security issues are critical in data-driven organizations. The data are used and relied on by all corporate users, including high-level decision makers. Procedures must be established that define what level of access each individual should be granted. Unauthorized access must be detected and reported. The cause of the infraction also must be determined, and action taken to prevent its reoccurrence.

The distinction must be made between data owners—those with update authority—and data users—those with read-only access or limited update authority.

The computer operations group is the custodian of all data. This group must ensure that proper monitoring is performed and that back-up and recovery procedures are in place and functioning. The data administrator should also have sufficient authority to arbitrate any ownership disputes between rival users.

Maintenance and control activities should also monitor systems performance and the time required to access needed data items. The database administration group should monitor system performance and take whatever corrective action is needed to provide an adequate level of response to users or systems requiring access to particular data items.

Usage Procedures that clearly define how to use the database must be established. First, potential users must know what data exist. Then, tools must be provided to enable users to easily access selected data items. For example, query languages that provide flexible database access and allow what-if questions to be presented and answered are implemented in many companies. Another area of great potential is the ability to interface selected data items with business software tools. These interfaces provide users with more meaningful presentations of the extracted information.

The delivery vehicle used to bring the data to the users must also be considered. Many companies have established information centers to provide a user-friendly environment for data access. This access may be provided through interactive query languages that enable users to view results on-line or through batch report generators that enable users to obtain preformatted printed reports.

Downloading segments of the database to a microcomputer is another method of information delivery that is becoming more common. The microcomputer environment typically provides the user with interactive access to the data as well as easy-to-use and powerful software. With the continuing emergence of local-area networks (LANs), more and more data will be downloaded to microcomputers for use by the end-user community.

8.1.5 The Data Model as a Management Tool

A data model is defined as a logical representation of a collection of data elements and the associations among those data elements. It can be used to represent data usage throughout an organization or can represent a single database structure. A data model is to data what a logical data flow diagram is to a process.

The data model can be used by management to:

(a) Develop new systems
(b) Maintain existing systems
(c) Develop data structures for the entire organization
(d) Prioritize the data needs of the organization
(e) Assist in planning for expansion into new markets or business areas
(f) Delegate authority for data usage
(g) Classify data by data areas or business functions
(h) Determine security needs of the data and implement protection mechanisms

Develop new systems Data models are fast becoming a very important tool in the development of new systems in an organization. The advent of new structured design methodologies, especially data-driven methodologies, saw the birth of data models as tools for systems development. The traditional approach to developing computer systems focuses on the processes to be performed, particularly with operational-type systems. However, process-oriented system designs generally do not fulfill subsequent tactical or strategic information needs. In many cases, information requests go unanswered because either the source data do not exist or the necessary custom-built software that supports ad hoc inquiries is too costly and time-consuming. This accurate information is a major disadvantage of many conventional systems.

The data resource management approach overcomes this limitation by focusing on data and information requirements during systems planning and building. The data model now becomes the vehicle by which application systems are built while addressing these limitations.

Maintain existing systems It is now determined that 80% of an organization's programming resources are expended during maintenance on existing systems. This expenditure is consumed by programmers trying to determine where changes should be made to existing systems and what data are best suited to test the modified programs. The expenditure may even occur before the changes are made. Programmers may spend, depending on their experience, a considerable amount of time determining how the application meets the requirements of the business function. This expenditure in time and financial resources can be minimized if there are data models of all existing systems in place.

The programmers can determine from the data model the section or user view that must be modified. Then, with the data model section or user view as a guide, the parts of the application programs that must be changed will be more readily identified and programming maintenance expenditure would be less costly.

Develop data structures for the organization   The organization, by undertaking a Business System Plan (BSP), can identify the business processes and data classes that are required to design databases for its informational needs. Various charts showing the relationship between business processes and classes of data can be prepared. This relationship is the backbone of the data architecture for the organization. The data architecture, in turn, is obtained through a single data model or set of data models.

Prioritize the data needs of the organization   In most organizations it is impossible to implement systems to satisfy their data needs all at once. Priorities must be set and phased implementation of these systems undertaken. The data model can show what data are available, where they are available, and where they are needed. Data managers can use this information to determine the cost and complexity of implementation of systems and hence prioritize the implementation of these systems.

Assist in planning for expansion of business   Whenever an organization expands its business into new markets or business areas, data are needed to aid or even implement the expansion. Data models are very useful tools that management can use to determine what data are needed and where it can be obtained for the expansion program.

Delegate authority for data usage   Data models can indicate to an organization what business function uses what data. They can also be used to indicate the common uses and functions of corporate data. Corporate management can use this information to delegate authority for data usage throughout the organization. Managers can also use this information to control access, on a need to know basis, to the corporate data.

Classify data by data areas   Data are very often classified by the business function they serve. For example, data that serve an accounting function are very often classified as accounting data. Data models that show the relationship between business functions and business entities (data) can assist in the proper classification of corporate data.

Determine the security needs of data   Data models allow an organization to determine what data are available, who uses it, and where data are being used. They allow the organization to determine the common usage of data and the parameters that are needed to allow data usage across organizational boundaries. Armed with this knowledge, an organization can now plan for its data security needs. It can determine what protection mechanisms are needed to control access to the data and the level of authorization to be given to users of corporate data.

8.1.6   Data-Flow Diagrams as a Management Tool

Data-flow diagrams assist the systems analysts in determining where data are being held from one transaction to the next, or stored permanently, because they describe some aspect of the world outside the system. They indicate how the data flow from process to process and assist the analysts in determining what immediate accesses to each data store will be needed by the user.

Data-flow diagrams are powerful tools that can be used by organizations to develop process-flow architectures for their environment. Management can use this tool to determine where data are created, where data are being used, and who uses the informational contents.

Management can use the data-flow diagrams to build complete databases to store the required data for users' needs. They can use the processes to transform flows of data. The processes can be decomposed into functions and activities from which programs can be coded to manipulate the data stores.

Data-flow diagrams are currently being used on a worldwide basis as the major deliverable from process-driven structured systems analysis and development. Several organizations are using data-flow diagrams as a deliverable of a basic Business Systems Plan. Data-flow diagrams are also being used by several organizations to demonstrate and illustrate their corporate data needs.

Management can use the ability to break down processes into several levels to determine the operational processing requirements of each data store in the process architecture. For example, one organization is currently using data-flow diagrams to determine whether operational processing, such as sorting, dumping to other storage media, deleting of files, and creating of backup files, is consuming too much of the corporation's operational budgets and time. This same organization is using data-flow diagrams to illustrate where various reports are distributed to other users, whether current users should have access to the reports, and where reports are produced but never distributed.

Management can use existing data-flow diagrams to audit the corporate data dictionary for completeness and currency. For example, a complete data dictionary should have data about all the processes and data stores that exist in the organization. By checking the data dictionary content against existing data-flow diagrams, the completeness of the data dictionary can be determined. The assumption here is that the data-flow diagrams are in themselves complete and represent the entire information and process architecture of the corporation.

Data-flow diagrams can be used to create functional specifications for systems development. The data-flow diagram shows the sources and distinctions of data and hence indicates the boundaries of the system. It identifies and names the logical functions, names of the data elements that connect the function to another, and the data stores that each function accesses. Each data flow is analyzed, and its structures and the definitions of its component data elements are stored in the data dictionary. Each logical function may be broken down into a more detailed data-flow diagram. The contents of each data store are analyzed and stored in the data dictionary.

These documents make up a comprehensive account of a system that can be used by management to build systems or prioritize the building of systems. The documents and the data-flow diagrams may also prove very useful in the maintenance of existing systems.

Finally, data-flow diagrams can be used by systems designers to prepare functional specifications that are:

- Well understood and fully agreed to by users
- Used to set out the logical requirements of the system without dictating a physical implementation
- Useful in expressing preferences and trade-offs

Several organizations attest to the fact that data-flow diagrams can prevent very costly errors in systems development. Figure 8.1 is an example of a data-flow diagram.

8.1.7 Managing Information through CASE Tools

More and more organizations are looking to CASE tools to improve the effectiveness of analysts and designers, increase the role of end users in systems design, reduce programming and maintenance time, and manage data more effectively.

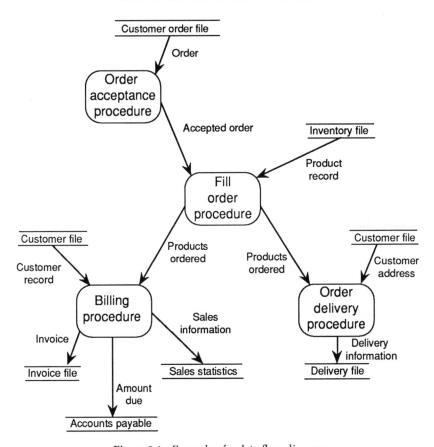

SALES DISTRIBUTION SYSTEM

Figure 8.1   Example of a data flow diagram.

Computer-aided software engineering (CASE) is the automation of software development. CASE is a combination of software tools and systems development methodologies. It is different from earlier software technologies because it focuses on the entire software productivity problem, not just on implementation solutions. CASE attacks software productivity problems at both ends of the life cycle by automating many analysis and design tasks, as well as program implementation and maintenance tasks.

CASE offers full support for the systems development life cycle. At the analysis phase, CASE allows the designer to collect user requirements whether through conventional interview methods or by the use of Structure English. The collected user requirements are entered into a

CASE repository or data dictionary and become the input to the design phase. The deliverables from the design phase can be data models, such as entity–relationship diagrams or data-flow diagrams. The tools have the ability to explode the data-flow diagrams down to several levels and balance the data stores at each level. The deliverables are checked against the data dictionary entries for accuracy, consistency, and completeness.

Most of the CASE tools have a prototyping capability and can create screens of the user requirements and models of the systems so that users can review the design at a very early stage of systems development. During prototyping, simulated reports can be produced that reflect the actual reports required by the users.

CASE tools can use the entries in the data dictionary and the processes from the design phase to develop programming specifications for application programmers, and some tools can even generate the actual program code that is compatible with standards for several programming languages.

At the moment, the major weakness of CASE tools is in their inability to maintain program code and changes to existing systems over the life of the system. Several manufacturers of CASE tools are now developing solutions to this problem and the answers may not be too far off.

CASE tools have become very important tools for managers to use in their efforts to manage data more effectively and to prudently exploit the data resource. They now represent the most rapidly growing sector of the software industry. CASE tools—what they are and how they should be selected—is the topic of a subsequent chapter.

8.1.8 Managing Information through Reverse Engineering

Reverse Engineering is defined as the act of taking unstructured programs or systems not designed using one of the current structured design methodologies and either structuring the programs or producing deliverables that are more appropriate to the structured systems development life cycle (SDLC).

Reverse engineering accomplishes the following:

- Produces programs that are structured and are less costly, in both time and money, to maintain
- Enhances the quality of programs, program documentation, and informational content
- Increases the useful life of program code and identifies sections of programs that can be reused as subroutines.

- Removes or identifies unreachable or unexecutable codes in programs
- Indicates problem areas in unstructured programs that could be responsible for seemingly inexplicable processing behavior

Although most of the effort of reverse engineering is now centered on producing structured program code from unstructured code, a considerable amount of effort is now being expended in producing deliverables that are more appropriate with a structured SDLC. For example, efforts are being undertaken to produce entity–relationship (E–R) diagrams from the Data Division of COBOL programs. These E–R diagrams are then used along with the major processes defined by the COBOL programs to populate data dictionaries, produce logical and physical design schemas, provide better documentation for programming specifications and maintenance, and build relevant databases. Managers can now use the data dictionary content, the documentation, and the databases to more effectively manage the data resource.

8.1.9 Project Management Tools and Management of Data

Several automated project management tools are now on the market that seek to aid in the development of systems and indirectly in the management of data. Project management tools are used in the following areas:

- Project planning
- Project duration
- Costing
- Manpower scheduling
- Manpower allocation
- Project reporting

8.2 Planning for the Data Resource

Planning for the data resource is done at three levels: strategic, tactical, and operational.

1. Strategic Planning defines the data environment's mission and objective in achieving the goals of the organization. The strategic plan is driven by the current and future information needs of the business. Strategic planning helps businesses share the data resource.

The strategic data plan defines the organization's data requirements and states the benefits of data resource management and how it differs from database technology management. The strategic plan serves as the baseline for data resource management and directs all subsequent data-related activities.

The strategic plan defines the target toward which all subsequent data-related activity is directed.

2. Tactical Planning identifies a resource and directs how it will be managed to achieve goals set forth in the strategic plan. Because each resource is to be managed in its own life cycle, each should ideally be governed by its own plan. The tactical planning window is 12 to 18 months, with a review cycle of 9 to 12 months.

3. Operational Planning describes the details of the tactical plan and identifies the tasks to be carried out in a scheduled time frame, the expected deliverables, and the assigned responsibilities. The window operational planning is 3 to 9 months, depending on the size of the project.

8.2.1 Contents of the Strategic Plan

The strategic plan should address the broadest context under which data sharing will exist and should contain the following sections:

(a) The purpose of the data resource
(b) Goals for supporting the information strategies of the organization
(c) Strategies that pursue the goals
(d) Factors critical to achieving the goals successfully
(e) Constraints imposed on the data environment
(f) The concepts of data resource management
(g) The resources needed to manage data

Mission statement   The mission statement reflects an overall direction for data resource management from a single, high-level perspective. It defines the scope of the data environment. For example, a mission statement may read as follows: To provide data about shared corporate entities to all regional offices in a timely and controlled manner.

Goals   Goals identify expected results to be gained in that domain. For example, a goal of data resource management may be to build a strategic data architecture that will ensure the integrity of data as they are integrated across application systems.

Strategies   Strategies are general statements of direction for achieving data resource management goals. Strategies are generally applied across goals to identify how the goals will be achieved. For example, a strategy for data resource management may be to train systems staff and end users in data-oriented systems design and database development or to provide effective data security with minimal interruption to end-user service.

Critical success factors Critical success factors are broad statements of achievements in data resource management. For example, a critical success factor may be the management of data through a data dictionary. Success is achieved with the implementation and effective use of the data dictionary.

Constraints Data resource management may be constrained by the evolution of the business, the state of the technology in the environment, and the availability of staff. Current business operations and the role of information in the organization's planning may force constraints on the scope of data resource management.

Conceptual planning Conceptual planning for the data resource must include acquisition of data through application systems, employment and exploitation of data through end-user reports, maintenance of data through the technology tools, and disposition of the data depending on the life cycle of the business subject matter. The deletion of the data element is determined by its relationship to other elements.

Resources to manage data Planning for the data resource must identify the tools to manage the data resource, including database management systems; data dictionaries; data modeling tools; CASE tools; and database auditing, journaling, and recovery tools.

8.3 Controlling the Data Resource

The third component of information resource management is the control of the data resource. Although the other two components, management and planning, were discussed first, this is no indication of their relative importance in the triumvirate.

Management control of the data resource includes:

- Common procedures for access control to the data
- Establishing lines of authority and responsibility for the data
- Common procedures for collecting, updating, and maintaining the data
- Common formats and procedures for data definition
- Identifying entities that are important to the enterprise

- Evaluating, mediating, and reconciling the conflicting needs and prerogatives of functional departments
- Ensuring the auditability of the data and all transactions against the data
- Control the data in order to measure and evaluate the corporation and predict its reaction to change in its environment and its own internal organization

This list, although quite extensive, is by no means all-inclusive. We will leave the readers to expand on this list and also to research the various activities that must be performed to materialize each item in the list.

PART II

Relational Database Issues

CHAPTER 9

Coexistence of Relational and Nonrelational Databases

9.1 Introduction

Because of the financial investment that an organization may have in an older database management system, it may be necessary for that organization to have dual DBMSs, one of which is the relational DBMS. Furthermore, an application that is running well, is already paid for, and has little or no need to exchange information with a relational database may never be rewritten to a relational database structure. This again points up the necessity for dual DBMSs.

This chapter discusses the coexistence of relational and nonrelational databases and the issues involved in operating and maintaining these two environments.

9.2 The Dual DBMS

The application of dual databases to DBMS software centers on performance, usually on-line performance. That is, can a single piece of DBMS software satisfy the need for high-performance on-line processing as well as the need for flexibility and rapid development all within the structure of a single DBMS technology? Aside from the specifics of teleprocessing monitors and database management software, much controversy exists regarding whether or not high-performance and high-flexibility capabilities can cohabit in the same DBMS technology.

Undoubtedly, a single DBMS is desirable for both performance and flexibility. Every new technology, DBMS or otherwise, requires its own support training period and costs. Having multiple technologies in one environment is a manager's nightmare. For many reasons, the fewer technologies a company has, the stabler and more streamlined the organization. DBMS technology is no exception to this rule. A single DBMS technology that serves both performance and flexibility objectives is much more desirable than a separate set of DBMS technologies.

9.2.1 The Dual Database

For a dual database, the first issue is whether any DBMS technology will suffice to secure both performance and flexibility. Even if a DBMS technology exists that can serve both needs, the next issue is whether it can be done simultaneously for the same data on the same processor. A DBMS technology may well be able to be used for both performance and flexibility needs but not for the same data at the same time. For example, one group of end users may be using the technology for decision support system (DSS) processing and another group for performance systems, but not on the same processor on the same data at the same time.

When using a single DBMS to handle both performance and flexibility needs, it is necessary to separate data—one collection of data to serve the need for flexibility and another to serve the need for performance.

The primary division of data in the dual database environment is along the lines of on-line, operational database systems and flexible, easy-to-build DSS. This split of data appears to be a result of the performance conflict between the operational and DSS environment.

It is unreasonable to expect that the same data can or should be so widely accessed in many different ways at the same time. Even if the same DBMS technology could be used, or even if the nature of the basic input/output operation—the main impediment to performance—were fundamentally changed to be able to accommodate some degree of performance for simultaneous set-at-a-time and record-at-a-time data use, the differences in data use are so diverse and so severe that there must be a separation of data under even a limited amount of processing.

In light of these very fundamental differences in data use and processing, it is not surprising that the world is evolving to the dual database approach. Given the nature of I/O operation as it is currently known, the performance needs for access and control over any given data element are such that no processor can keep up with the totality of demand. However, the performance differences are only the forerunner of many deeper differences in the use of data.

9.2.2 The Historical Orientation of DBMS Software

Ideally, a single DBMS technology would be malleable enough to provide adequate facilities for both operational and DSS processing, however, software has traditionally been designed to service one function or the other. Considering the fundamental differences in operational and DSS environments and the limitations of traditional software, the direction for traditional software is duplicate databases—one serving the operational needs of a company and one serving the DSS needs.

With dual databases the issue of data redundancy must be addressed. The redundancy that exists in the dual database environment is across the operational and DSS environments. The summarized, historical nature of DSS processing does not mandate the use of up-to-the-second data. Indeed, most forms of DSS processing, for example, trend analysis, projections, and demographic analysis, require that detailed data be frozen as of some time. The implication is that redundancy across the DSS/operational environment is not only acceptable but desirable, and for some types of DSS processing it is absolutely mandatory.

Redundancy within the DSS environment is a different matter. On the one hand, redundancy within the DSS environment is necessary if the end user is to have the flexibility of processing that is inherent to the end-user computing environment. On the other hand, uncontrolled redundancy in the DSS–end-user computing environment leads to inconsistent results, which potentially undermine its original purpose.

Despite the deep differences between operational and DSS data, there is always a temptation to assume that a more effective use of technology can bridge the gap.

9.2.3 System Performance and the Dual Database

The primary performance issue of the dual database centers on data use. In particular, end-user computing access and use of data usually operate on indeterminate or large amounts of data in an unstructured fashion. Operational processing typically accesses limited, determinate amounts of data, and data use is generally structured. This difference in use is perhaps the main performance difference between the on-line operational and DSS–end-user computing systems using conventional I/O operations.

DSS systems typically access data one set at a time. Set-at-a-time use of data results in the consumption of an indeterminate amount of resources. Accessing a small database would consume few resources; however, for large databases, set-at-a-time processing can consume a huge amount of resources using conventional inboard I/O operations.

Unlike DSS processing, rapid on-line processing usually accesses data one record at a time. Unquestionably, record-at-a-time processing is more difficult and time-consuming to encode and develop. Resource consumption can be contained, however, when records are processed under the current standard operation of I/O. In addition, when resource consumption can be measured and contained, effective on-line performance is the result.

For optional performance, longer-running processes, that is, set-at-a-time processes, are not mixed with short-running processes, that is, record-at-a-time processes. In this case, performance can be consistently maintained at a high level. Managers will still conflict, however, with software developers who seek to mix long- and short-running processes in the same jobstream, when there is a fair load on the processor on which conventional I/O is being run and efficient performance is still the objective.

9.3 Comparison of Relational and Nonrelational Models

In comparing relational databases and nonrelational databases, we must differentiate between two types of database languages: high-level languages that operate on sets of records and low-level languages that operate on a single record at a time.

Most high-level database languages are associated with the relational model, whereas the network and hierarchical models are associated with record-at-a-time low-level languages. Several high-level query languages have recently been proposed for the E–R model, and an E–R algebra has been specified, but we will not discuss these languages because they are not available commercially and are not well established yet.

The relational model has several high-level languages. The formal operations of the relational algebra apply to sets of tuples, so they are high-level operations. A query is specified by a sequence of relational algebra operations on relations. In relational calculus, a single expression—rather than a sequence of operations—specifies a query, so we specify what we want to retrieve but not how to retrieve it. The relational calculus is considered to be at even a higher level than the relational algebra because in the latter, we specify a certain order among the high-level operations. This order specifies how the system should retrieve the desired information. The formal basis of the relational calculus is provided by a branch of mathematical logic called predicate calculus. The basic set of relational algebra operations has been shown to have expressive power equivalent to that of the relational calculus.

Commercial languages for the relational model—such as SQL, QUEL, and QBE—are based primarily on the relational calculus. QUEL is based on tuple relational calculus, as is SQL to a lesser degree. Both languages introduce some operations and order resembling some aspects of relational algebra. They also incorporate facilities for aggregate functions, grouping, sorting, keeping duplicate tuples, and arithmetic, which are outside the realm of basic, relational algebra of calculus. QBE is based on domain relational calculus. These are high-level languages that retrieve a set of tuples by a single query.

The network and hierarchical DML commands are low-level because they search for and retrieve single records. We must use a general-purpose programming language and embed the database commands in the program. In both of these languages, the concept of current record is crucial in the interpretation of the meaning of DML commands, because the effect of a command depends on the current record.

The network model DML uses additional currency indicators such as current of set types and current of record types, which also affect the outcome of DML commands. Although these currency concepts facilitate record-at-a-time access, the programmer must be thoroughly familiar with how the different commands have their origin in traditional file processing commands.

For the network model, the user must understand the effect of the various variations of the FIND command for record and set access. The effect of the FIND command depends on the current values of the various currency indicators and will also change the values of any affected currency indicators.

For the hierarchical model, the programmer must understand the concept of hierarchical sequence of records. Records are generally accessed in that sequence forward from the current record. Therefore, records of different types in the hierarchy must be processed along hierarchical paths from left to right within the tree. Again, exceptions do occur, for example, IMS allows stepping back within one hierarchical occurrence tree and then proceeding forward again within the tree.

From this discussion, it is clear that the relational model has a distinct advantage as far as languages are concerned. Both the formal and commercial languages associated with the relational model are quite powerful and are high level. In fact, several network and hierarchical DBMSs, such as IDMS/R and IMS, have implemented high-level query languages that are similar to the relational languages for use with their systems along with the traditional DML commands. Both high-level query language interfaces and traditional embedded DML commands are available in the systems.

Table 9.1   Comparison of Terminology

E–R model	Relational	Network	Hierarchical
E–R schema	Table	Record type	Record type
Entity type	Table	Record type	Record type
Entity instance	Row	Record occurrence	Record occurrence
1: N relationship		Set type	Parent–child relationship
Attribute	Column	Field	Data item
Value set	Data type	Data type	Data type
Key	Candidate key		
	Primary	Key	Sequence key
Multivalued			
Attribute		Repeating group	

Table 9.1 contains a comparison of the terminology used by each of the data models. Table 9.2 contains a summary of the modeling power of the various data models.

9.4 Comparison of Storage Structures

For the relational model, the general technique is to implement each base relation as a separate file. If the user does not specify any storage

Table 9.2   Summary of Modeling Power

E–R model	Relationship	Network	Hierarchical
Weak entity type	As a relation but include the primary key of the identifying relation	As a record type that is a member in a set with record type as owner	As a record that is a child of the record type
1: N relationship type	Include the primary key of the "1-Side" relation as foreign key in the "N-Side" relation	Use a set type	Use a parent–child relationship
M: N relationship type	Set up a new relation that includes as foreign keys the primary keys of the participating relations	Set up a linking record type and make it a member in set types owned by the record types	Use a single hierarchy and duplicate records

structure, most relational DBMSs will store the tuples as unordered records in a file. Many relational DBMSs will allow the user to specify dynamically on each file a single primary or clustering index and any number of secondary indexes.

The network model is usually implemented by using pointers and ring files. This file structure is suitable for implementing sets. Most network DBMSs will also present the option of implementing some sets by clustering, that is, the owner record is followed by the member records in physical contiguity for each set instance.

The hierarchical model is usually implemented using hierarchical files, which preserve the hierarchical sequence of the database. In addition, a variety of options, including hashing, indexing, and pointers, are available, so we can have efficient access to individual records and to related records.

9.5 Comparison of Integrity Constraints

The relational model is generally considered weak on integrity constraints. Two standard constraints are now considered to be part of the model: entity integrity and referential integrity. Commercial DBMSs implement entity integrity via the key constraint by disallowing null values on a key attribute. Unfortunately, many relational DBMSs combine the specification of a key with that of a physical index. Referential integrity has not been generally available in relational DBMSs. However, some of the newer DBMSs, like DB2, are allowing the specification of this integrity.

The hierarchical model has the built-in hierarchical constraints that a record type can have at most one real parent in a hierarchy. Other constraints exist in each individual DBMS; for example, IMS allows only one virtual parent for a record type. There is no provision for enforcing consistency among duplicate records; this must be enforced by the application programs that update the database. The implicit constraint that a child record must be related to a parent record is enforced. Also, child records are automatically deleted when their parent or ancestor is deleted.

The network model is the richest among the three implementation models in the types of constraints it specifies and enforces. The set retention option specifies constraints on the behavior of member records in a set with respect to the owner record, such as whether every record must have an owner or not. Automatic set types with SET SELECTION BY STRUCTURAL match the key field of an owner with a field in the member record. The CHECK option can be used to specify a similar constraint for MANUAL nonautomatic set types. Key constraints are specified by a DUPLICATES NOT ALLOWED clause. Hence, many structural constraints on relationship types can be specified to a network DBMS.

9.6 Advantages and Disadvantages of the Models

From the preceding discussions, it is clear that the relational model has a more formal mathematical foundation than the other two—both in the description of its structures and in the languages specified for it. The network and hierarchical models were developed originally as representation of specific commercial systems. Hence, it is understandable that their record-at-a-time languages are close to traditional file system commands.

The relational DBMSs generally provide more flexibility. Most relational DBMSs make it easy to expand a schema by adding new relations or by adding new attributes to a relation. In addition, it is usually quite easy to add or drop indexes dynamically as needed. Another advantage of relational DBMSs is that most provide high-level query language interfaces as well as a programming interface. For these reasons, a relational DBMS is more suitable for many small- and medium-sized database applications where flexibility and quick system development are important.

However, for large databases that have well-defined applications, relational DBMSs sometimes do not provide the high performance that may be required. This is because the access to the database is always through the query language and DBMS system optimizer. Hence, programmers often do not have the capability to access the data using the method that they know is most efficient.

Network and hierarchical systems are good for designing and implementing large databases with well-defined queries, transactions, and applications. The database designers and users should spend enough time during system implementation to choose appropriate storage structures and ensure that their applications are programmed in the most efficient way. However, unforeseen future applications may cause very expensive system reorganization.

CHAPTER 10

Distributed Relational Database Management System

10.1 Introduction

Since the early 1980s, centralizing an organization's data in a large and expensive computer has been the single approach to data processing. Recent development in these areas of database technology, computer networks, minicomputers, and microcomputers has made the distributed database approach a practical alternative. A distributed database is a collection of logically related data distributed across several machines interconnected by a computer network. An application program operating on a distributed database may access data stored at more than one machine.

A distributed database has four main advantages. First, each group having a computer has direct control over its local data, resulting in increased data integrity and more efficient data processing. Second, compared to the centralized approach in which the data must be transferred from each group to the central computer, the communication overhead is reduced. Third, the distributed approach is the natural solution to data processing in a geographically dispersed organization. Fourth, performance and reliability may be increased by exploiting the parallel processing and redundancy capabilities of multiple machines.

The need to integrate and share the data located and managed on different computers is the basis for a distributed database. Such data sharing requires the interconnections of the various computers through a local or general network and specific software support to manage and process distributed data. Such software must provide high independence from the distributed environment. Relational database technology has been successful at providing data independence, making transparent to the application programs any change in the physical or logical data structure. Therefore it has been the natural support to distributed data sharing. As a result, most relational database systems today offer a solution to sharing distributed data.

10.2 Distributed Database Capabilities

The distributed database capabilities offered by current database systems range from remote database access to a heterogeneous distributed database. A more recent use of the distributed database approach is to distribute the data across the modes of a multiprocessor computer so that performance and reliability are increased.

A remote database is a database located on a computer other than where the user is executing. In general, the user is aware of the remote database location, which must be specified to access the data. A data communication component is necessary for accessing the remote database.

A local database may also reside on the computer where the user is running. The user can then download remote database data to the local database. Recent development in microcomputers technology has favored the workstation, or server organization, in which the remote database is managed on a mainframe server by a DBMS and private databases are managed on workstations by a microversion of the same DBMS. The interconnection server/workstation is typically handled by a local network. The remote database approach provides little functionality and thus does not face the problems of distributed databases.

A distributed database is a set of cooperating databases residing on different machines, called sites, and interconnected by a computer network. A user at any site can then access the data at any site.

The main difference from a remote database is that the user is not aware of data distribution and perceives the distributed database as a nondistributed database. The management of a distributed database requires the following system components at each site: a data communication component, a local DBMS, and a distributed DBMS. The main functions of the distributed DBMS are:

- Management of a global data dictionary to store information about distributed data
- Distributed data definition
- Distributed semantic data control
- Distributed query processing, including distributed query optimization and remote database access

• Distributed transaction management, including distributed concurrency control, recovery, and commit protocol

A distinguishing property of a distributed database is that it can be homogeneous or heterogeneous. A homogeneous distributed database is one where all local databases are managed by the same DBMS. This approach is the simplest one and provides incremental growth, which makes the addition of a new site in the network easy, and increased performance, by exploiting the parallel processing capability of multiple sites. A good example of homogeneous distributed databases is illustrated by the R* system.

A heterogeneous distributed database is one where the local databases need not be managed by the same DBMS. For example, one DBMS can be a relational system while another can be a hierarchical system. This approach is far more complex than the homogeneous one but enables the integration of existing independent databases without requiring the creation of a completely new distributed database. In addition to the main functions, the distributed DBMS must provide interfaces between the different DBMSs. An example of a heterogeneous distributed database is illustrated by the INGRES/STAR system.

10.3 Objectives of Distributed Systems

A distributed database may provide various levels of transparency. However, each level of transparency participates in the same goal: making the use of the distributed database equivalent to that of a centralized database. All the following objectives are rarely met by a single system. Rather, depending on the targeted applications, a distributed DBMS will meet only a subset of these objectives. For example, a homogeneous distributed DBMS will provide DBMS transparency.

10.3.1 Site Autonomy

Site autonomy is an important objective that enables any operational site to control and process its local data independent of any other site. Therefore each site must store all data dictionary information necessary to be autonomous, without relying on a centralized global data dictionary and a global database administrator. The immediate advantage of site autonomy is that the administration of the distributed database need not be centralized. Each local database may be independently

controlled by a local database administrator. Intersite cooperation requires coordination among the local database administrators using specific capabilities by the distributed DBMS. The support of site autonomy can range from no autonomy to full site autonomy (decentralized
control).

10.3.2 Location Transparency

Location transparency is the primary objective of a distributed database
and hides the fact that the data may not be stored at the user site. The
database user does not need to know the location, and therefore queries
involving relations stored at different sites need not specify the relation
locations. Location transparency provides physical independence from
the distributed environment. The data location information is maintained in the data dictionary and used by the distributed DBMS to find
the data. The main advantage is that the database may be physically
reorganized by moving relations to different sites, without any impact
on the application programs that access them.

10.3.3 Fragmentation Transparency

The simplest way to store a conceptual object (relation) in a distributed
database is at a single site. However, for performance reasons, it is often
desirable to divide a relation into smaller fragments, each stored at a
different site. A fragment is generally defined by restriction and/or
projection and is therefore another relation. Thus fragmentation is particularly simple in the context of the relational model. Fragmentation
enhances the performance of database queries by increasing the locality
of reference. For example, consider an EMPLOYEE relation in a
database distributed between New York and Paris. The optional fragmentation is probably to store the American employee tuples in New
York and the European employee tuples in Paris. The fragmentation
definition is application dependent.

Fragmentation transparency makes fragmentation transparent to the
user, who sees only nonfragmented relations. Fragmentation information is stored in the data dictionary and used by the distributed DBMS
(DDBMS) to automatically map queries on conceptual relations, called
global queries, into queries on fragments, called fragment queries.

10.3.4 Replication Transparency

Data replication in some form is the single solution to reliability. In a
distributed database, data replication can be used for reliability, avail-

ability, and performance. In general, the unit of fragmentation is the fragment, or the relation if fragmentation is not supported. A fragment is replicated when it is stored as two or more copies, each at a different site. The immediate advantage of replication is high availability. If a site fails, the fragment copy is still available at another site. Furthermore, replication may enhance performance by increasing locality of reference.

The main problems of replication are the complexity and overhead required to keep the copies identical. The update to one copy must be propagated to all its copies. Furthermore, when a site recovers from a failure, all its replicated fragments must reach the same state as the other copies that might have been updated while the site was down. The trade-offs between retrieval and update performance make replication definition a difficult problem, which is highly application dependent.

Replication transparency makes such replication invisible to the user, who sees only nonreplicated relations. Replication information, stored in the data dictionary, is used by the DDBMS for mapping global queries into fragments and to manage copy consistency for update queries and recovery after failure.

10.4 Distributed Database Issues

The database system issues become much more complex in a distributed environment because of specific aspects of distributed databases. First, relations of the same database may reside at more than one site. In addition, a conceptual object can be fragmented and/or replicated. Fragmentation and replication are necessary for performance and availability reasons. They have a strong impact on data dictionary management, data definition, semantic data control, and query processing.

Second, a user transaction that involves data resident at several sites can be executed as several subtransactions, each at a different site. Therefore each site has only partial information to decide whether to commit the subtransaction's updates. Transaction management, in particular concurrency control and commit processing, must ensure synchronization among all participating sites.

Third, since data copies may continue to be updated at various sites while one site is down, the recovery of a failed site requires the cooperation of other sites in order to keep replicated copies identical.

Finally, the support of DBMS transparency adds another translation mechanism between the different models and languages. This translation mechanism must be combined with several other functions, such as data dictionary, data definition and control, and query processing.

10.4.1 Data Dictionary

The data dictionary includes information regarding data descriptions, data placement, and semantic data control. It can be managed as a distributed database. The data dictionary can be centralized on site, fully replicated at each site, or fragmented. Its content can be stored differently according to the kind of information; some information might be fully replicated while other information might be distributed. For example, information that is most useful at query compile time, like security control information, could be duplicated at each site. The implementation of the data dictionary depends on the degree of site autonomy that must be supported. For example, full site autonomy is incompatible with a centralized data dictionary.

10.4.2 Data Definition

Data definition in a distributed database is much more difficult than in a centralized database. Data definition includes the introduction of new database objects and their placement in the network. The way a new object is created depends on the degree of site autonomy and management of the data dictionary. With a centralized data dictionary, the data definition command involves only one site, the one that stores the data dictionary. With a fully replicated data dictionary, all sites of the network must be synchronized to perform the data definition operation. If the data dictionary is fragmented, data definition must be done on a site pair basis whereby two sites, the site at which the object is created and another site, cooperate to exchange data definition information. In this case, only the sites that are aware of the new object definition will be able to access it.

10.4.3 Data Control

Semantic data control typically includes view management, security control, and semantic integrity control. The complexity added by the distributed environment concerns the control definition and enforcement. The problem of managing semantic data control rules is similar to the data definition problem.

In a distributed database, a view can be derived from fragmented relations stored at different sites. The mapping of a query expressed on views into a query expressed on conceptual relations can be done as in centralized systems by query modification. With this technique, the qualification defining the view is found in the data dictionary and merged with the query to provide a query on conceptual relations.

The additional problems of authorization control in a distributed environment stem from the fact that objects and subjects are distributed. These problems are: remote user authentication, management of distributed authorization rules, and handling of user groups.

The main problem of semantic integrity control in a distributed environment is that the cost incurred in communication and local processing for enforcing distributed assertions can be prohibitive.

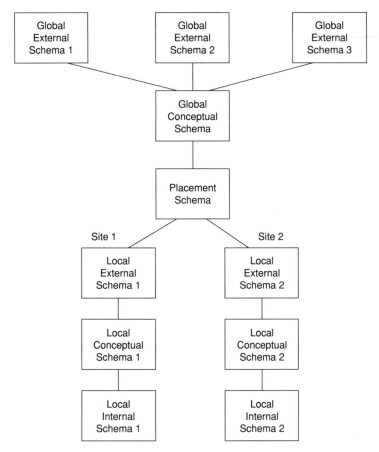

Figure 10.1   Reference architecture for distributed databases.

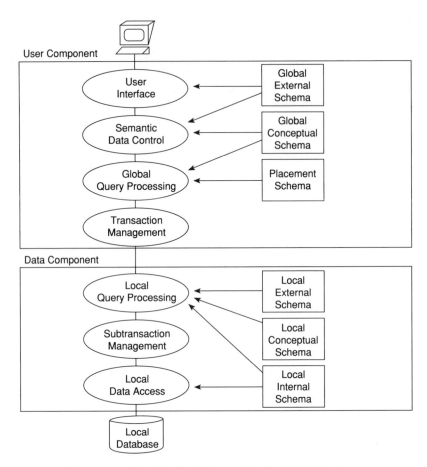

Figure 10.2 Functional architecture for distributed databases.

10.5 Architectures of Distributed DBMSs

Similar to centralized databases, distributed databases may be implemented in many different ways depending on their objective and design choices. However, for our purposes, it is useful to consider a reference architecture and a functional architecture for distributed databases. These architectures are illustrated in Figs. 10.1 and 10.2.

The reference architecture provides an ideal organization of a distributed database that implements all possible levels of transparency. This architecture is given in terms of scheme levels and schema mapping.

The typical functional architecture is grouped into two different components: the user component that handles interaction with the users and the data component that manages the data. A single user query involves the user component at the user site and the data component at one or more sites. The user component consists of four modules while the data component consists of three.

The user interface analyzes user queries and returns the result. Semantic data control performs view, authorization, and semantic integrity controls. Global query processing maps a query enriched with semantic data controls into a set of local queries, each for a different site. Transaction management coordinates the distributed execution of the query.

In the data component, local query processing performs decomposition and optimization of a local query. Subtransaction management cooperates with the user components and other data components to synchronize the execution of the subtransaction of the same transaction. Local data access includes the remaining functions for database management.

CHAPTER 11

Introduction to CASE Tools

Computer-aided software engineering (CASE) has been promoted as the panacea for curing an organization's backlog problems in meeting development schedules, coordinating design efforts, and maintaining its systems. It has also been touted as the tool to increase programmer and systems designer productivity by as much as two to ten times.

This chapter will introduce CASE tools as a design and development aid. It will discuss some selection criteria for deciding on the tool that will best suit a particular environment. Finally, it will list some vendors of CASE tools and the contacts within each vendor.

11.1 Several Definitions of CASE

CASE, although now widely accepted as an acronym, does not yet have a single, widely accepted definition. Perhaps a more appropriate description would be computer-aided systems development, which could be defined as "computers applied to aid in any aspect of systems development."

Because CASE can encompass so many aspects of systems development, the question "When is CASE the right choice?" must be addressed separately for each of three types of CASE tools:

1. Programmer/Project Productivity Tools—These provide support for designers and programmers of software, but only at the back end of the systems development life cycle. These may include tools for natural language programming, project management, and documentation.
2. Systems Development Methodology Tools—Most systems development methodologies are collections of techniques, combined in structures made to minimize redundant effort and maximize coordination between tasks. These methodology tools provide support for and enforce a systems development methodology at any or all stages of the life cycle. They may include any of the systems

development support tools as appropriate for the methodology. In addition, they enforce methodology rules and thus provide systems development expertise to the users.

3. Systems Development Support Tools—These provide support for techniques and tasks of systems development at any or all stages of the life cycle, but do not necessarily enforce a systems development methodology. These may include diagramming tools, data dictionaries and analysis tools, or any of the productivity tools.

11.2 Categories of CASE Tools

An individual CASE tool automates one small, focused step in the life cycle process. Individual tools fall into the following general categories:

- Diagramming tools for pictorially representing system specifications
- Screen and report painters for creating system specifications and for simple prototyping
- Dictionaries, information management systems, and facilities to store, report, and query technical and project management system information
- Specification-checking tools to detect incomplete, syntactically incorrect, and inconsistent system specifications
- Code generators to be able to generate executable code from pictorial system specifications
- Documentation generators to produce technical and user documentation required by structured methodologies

CASE "toolkits" provide integrated tools for developers seeking to automate only one phase of the life cycle process, while "workbenches" provide integrated tools for automating the entire development process. "Frameworks" integrate CASE tools and/or link them with non-CASE software development tools, and "methodology companions" support a particular structured methology and automatically guide developers through the development steps.

11.2.1 Well-Equipped Toolkits

Toolkits can focus on the design of real-time, information, or project management systems. They also can be classified by the hardware and operating system on which they run; by the ease with which they can be integrated into a family of compatible CASE tools; by their architecture, either open, so that it can be used with products from other vendors, or closed; by the structured methodology or methodologies they support; and by development languages, such as ADA, COBOL, FORTRAN, C, and PL/1.

Many CASE toolkits run on an IBM PC or are compatible under DOS. Some run on the Apple Macintosh, Wang PC, or Texas Instruments Professional PC. Others run only on 32-bit workstations, such as Sun, Apollo, or Digital Equipment Corporation (DEC) Vax Station II; on an IBM or Data General mainframe; or across the DEC Vax family. Many open-architecture products are not limited to one specific hardware, operating system, target programming language, or structured methodology.

The analysis toolkit has four basic components: structured diagramming tools, prototyping tools, a repository, and a specification checker.

11.2.2 Structured Diagramming Tools

Structured diagramming tools are computerized tools for drawing, manipulating, and storing structured diagrams such as data-flow and entity–relationship diagrams, which are required documentation for various structured methodologies.

Diagramming tools often reside on PCs or workstations that support graphics manipulation; at the minimum, they draw, update, and store data-flow and entity–relationship diagrams.

11.2.3 Prototyping Tools

Prototyping tools help determine system requirements and predict performance beforehand. Essential to prototyping are user interface painters, screen painters, report painters, and menu builders—that prototype the user interface to give users an advance view of how the system will look and to identify and correct problem areas. Screen dialog and navigation with data entry and edits can be simulated with or without compiles; source code for record, file, screen, and report description can be generated automatically.

Also essential are executable specification languages. These are the most sophisticated prototyping tools, which involve specifying system requirements and executing specifications iteratively to refine, correct, and ensure completeness of the system to meet user requirements.

11.2.4 The CASE Repository

The CASE repository is a design dictionary for storing and organizing all software system data, diagrams, and documentation related to planning, analysis, design, implementation, and project management. Information entered once can be maintained and made available to whomever needs it.

The repository can store more types of systems information, relationships among various information components, and rules for using or processing components than a standard data dictionary used in data management systems. The repository usually has many reporting capabilities that gauge the impact of proposed changes on the system, identify redundant or unneeded data elements, and resolve discrepancies. System diagrams and dictionary entities are linked within the dictionary, and some CASE tools provide automated means of verifying entities for completeness and correctness.

11.2.5 Data Design Toolkits

Data design toolkits support the logical and physical design of databases and files: logical data modeling, automatic conversion of data models to third normal form, automatic generation of database schemas for particular database management systems, and automatic generation of program-code-level file descriptions.

11.2.6 Programming Toolkits

Supported tools include hierarchical tree-structured diagramming tools with a syntax and consistency checker, procedural logic diagrammer and on-line editor, CASE repository with information manager, code generation, test data generator, file comparer, and performance monitor.

A code-generating tool is especially useful because it automatically produces codes from a program design. CASE code generators can generate compiled, structured codes in languages such as COBOL, PL/1, FORTRAN, C, or ADA, manage program specification and design information, generate documentation, and support prototyping.

11.2.7 Maintenance Toolkits

The most useful maintenance tools include documentation analyzers to read source code from existing systems and produce documentation, program analyzers to evaluate execution paths and performance, reverse engineering to identify the model upon which a system is based, and restructures to enforce structured programming and documentation standards.

11.2.8 Project Management Toolkits

Automated project management tools can help project managers to better track, control, and report on software projects, thus improving software development and maintenance. To be most effective, these tools should be able to access the CASE repository in the toolkit or workbench. Besides storing technical system information, the repository should be the central location for current status, estimation, budget, and quality-assurance information.

Some of these toolkits include tools for word processing; interfacing to electronic mail; spreadsheets; project management forms; configuration management for change, version, and access control; project plans; a calendar and task assignment system; and estimation of time tables and scheduling.

11.3 Demonstrated Use of CASE Tools in the SDLC

CASE tools have demonstrated their usefulness in all three components of the CASE environment: planning, systems design, and systems development.

11.3.1 CASE in the Planning Environment

CASE tools gather information about user problems and requirements, setting goals and criteria, and generating alternative solutions. They assist in the budget determinations, project duration and scheduling, manpower planning and scheduling, cost and time estimates, and project control.

11.3.2 CASE in the Systems Design Environment

CASE tools detail the design for a selected solution, including diagrams relating all programs, subroutines, and data flow. They can generate data modeling and relationship diagrams and functional models.

The functional modeling and data modeling processes have tools to construct the appropriate types of design diagrams. Data-flow diagrams, program structure charts, and entity–relationship diagrams are examples.

More detailed tables and text contain the necessary concept descriptions, testable requirements, and data element definitions.

11.3.3 CASE in the Systems Development Environment

CASE tools develop a construct of database information about the physical database scheme and the requirements for building, testing, and checking databases. They produce language codes from definitions of data and processes stored in the data dictionary.

11.3.4 Samples of Deliverables from CASE Tools

This section illustrates the deliverables from the three components of the CASE environment (see Figs. 11.1 and 11.2).
The deliverables illustrated in Figs. 11.3 and 11.4 were produced

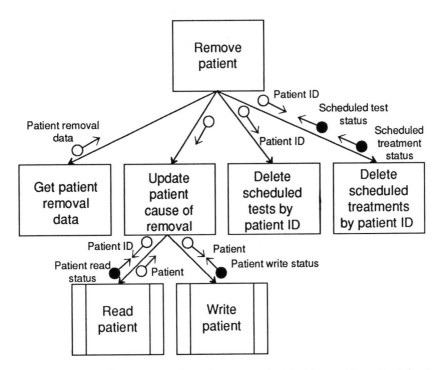

Figure 11.1 Yourdon structure chart. A structure chart is a tree or hierarchical diagram that shows the overall design of the program including program modules and their relationships. This particular structure chart was produced by the Analyst/Designer Toolkit from Yourdon Inc.

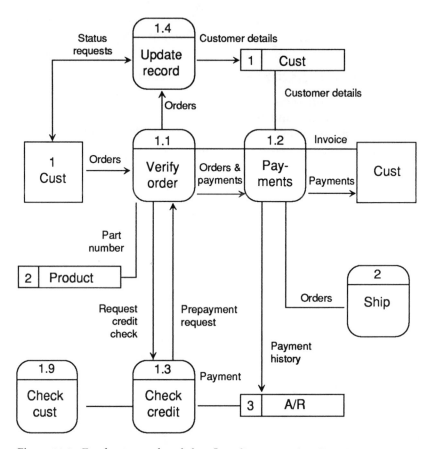

Figure 11.2 Excelerator-produced data-flow diagram. A data-flow diagram traces the flow of data through a system. Data stores are indicated by open-end rectangles, processes by boxes with rounded corners, data flow by arrows, and external entities by squares. This diagram was produced by Excelerator from Index Technology Corp. using the Gene and Sarson technique.

from the following sample problem, which concerns a video rental store with the following elements:

● Customer rents tapes and makes rental payments.
● Customer returns tapes and may pay late charge of $1 per day.
● Time to notify overdue borrowers.
● Time to report rentals.
● Store submits new tape.
● Store submits rate changes in some movie titles.
● Customer changes address.
● Customer requests particular movie title.

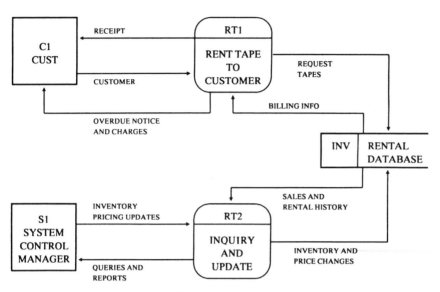

Figure 11.3 Excelerator-produced data-flow diagram.

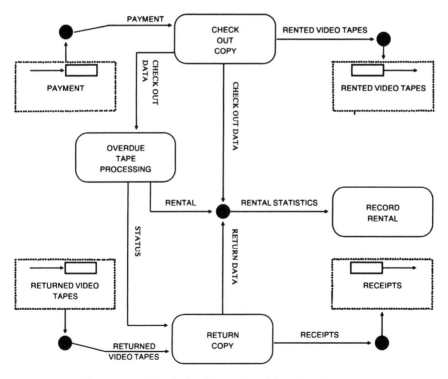

Figure 11.4 Knowledgeable-produced data-flow diagram.

A tape is a cassette of videotape with a prerecorded movie that can be rented. Each tape has a movie title and copy number. All copies of a movie have the same rental rate. Not all movies have the same rental rate.

A rental is the lending of a tape to a person in exchange for cash. A rental has a check-out date, a return date, and a rental charge. If a tape is late, there is a standard $1 per day late charge paid upon return. A customer can rent more than one tape at a time.

A tape can be rented, on the shelf waiting to be rented, or overdue. This video store has no membership plan and does not take American Express. All transactions are in cash on-the-spot, and no deposits are accepted.

The standard time period for a rental is two days after the borrowed tape is rented. If the customer fails to return the tape in time, then a tape overdue notice is sent to the customer address with the title and copy number and past due return date.

11.4 Selection Criteria for CASE Tools

The ever-growing array of CASE tools makes it very difficult to decide on which tool is best suited for a particular environment. This section attempts to ease that uncertainty by posing a list of questions the buyer should try to answer before buying a tool.

- Is the tool a DBMS or dictionary software system? Dictionary and database management systems provide greater integration capabilities. As a result, CASE tools with these underlying structures have a greater capacity for sharing specifications across functions.
- What is the future direction and functionality of the tool? When evaluating CASE tools, remember that CASE systems development is still in its infancy, so do not reject a tool with valuable attributes just because it currently does not have the full capabilities that you want.
- Does the tool's manufacturer have an open-architecture philosophy? A manufacturer's willingness to share file formats with all viable, noncompeting CASE manufacturers means that you can move smoothly from planning to systems development because you will be able to integrate specifications across CASE components. Moreover, you will have a healthy variety of options for CASE software configurations. CASE manufacturers entering into exclusive hierarchical integration agreements with other noncompeting CASE tool manufacturers ultimately limit choice.

- Does the CASE tool produce utility software that will read procedure and source libraries and create CASE component specifications for existing systems? The acquisition of CASE tools in a non-CASE environment creates a potential for inconsistencies in maintenance activities. Design and development specifications for systems designed and implemented before the installation of CASE components will not be consistent with those created after installation of CASE tools. Thus, a multiplicity of maintenance activities will be necessary. Certain CASE tools offer utility software that will prepare procedure and source libraries and create development specifications for existing systems, thereby mitigating the difference between pre-CASE and post-CASE systems documentation.

- Does the tool have an effective interface to other CASE design tools already purchased or under evaluation? Often, several methodologies are used to design a system, so it is important that a CASE tool provide a healthy array of methodological techniques to use in the process. The dictionary entries must be capable of being shared across these methodologies, so the dictionary should be strong and versatile.

- Does the tool have graphical methodologies capable of "exploding" design diagrams and dictionary specifications to a reasonable depth? Most of the CASE design tools provide graphical methodologies for representing proposed systems design. The graphical diagrams and the dictionary entries behind the components of the graphical diagrams must be capable of exploding to a reasonable number of lower, more specific levels.

- Will the tool be capable of executing with windowing capabilities? An advantage of the windowing capability is that multiple portions of the design can be displayed simultaneously and can therefore compensate for weaknesses in embedded explosion capabilities. As a result, the levels of explosion will not be restrictive and the comprehensiveness and integration of CASE design and development specifications should improve.

- Does the planning model in the CASE planning component provide comprehensive coverage of corporate and functional unit strategic planning and systems planning? The planning component contains a model for representing the corporation and for use in determining the direction of the corporation and systems development. The strength of the CASE top-level components lies in the comprehensiveness of this planning model.

- Does the tool provide a thorough means of prototyping? CASE development tools, rather than CASE design tools, provide the strongest prototyping methods. While it is not necessary that both types provide strong prototyping capabilities, at least one must provide this capability.

- Will the tool soon be able to generate automatically first-cut physical design specifications from logical design specifications? The conversion of logical design diagrams into initial physical design diagrams should be automatic because it involves simply the exchange and addition of graphical display table entries. While most CASE design tools currently do not offer this feature, ask your CASE vendor if the tool will offer it in the future.

- Does the CASE design tool provide analysis support for design documentation? This concerns the capacity of the CASE tool to analyze design documentation and determine if the specifications entered by the analyst conform to prescribed methodological rules. The analysis should also indicate where design dictionary entries are incomplete. For example, a data-flow diagram (DFD) with a freestanding block should be highlighted as violating one of the rules of structured methodology. In addition, blocks on a DFD not having a corresponding dictionary entry should be highlighted.

- Does the tool have the capacity to generate design specification reports automatically? The specifications created during logical and physical design activities serve as a source of documentation for the system. While they are permanently stored on disk devices, it is often advisable to get hard-copy printouts of the design specifications for reference. Many CASE tools provide various report formats for this purpose, including the capability of indicating design flaws.

- Does the lower-level CASE development component provide methods for convenience and comprehensive customization of the generated system? The CASE development component can already generate the major portions of the codes systems. Systems development activity using CASE involves providing the customization of the generic code to fit the system. The custom specifications must provide comprehensive coverage of the system requirements. The generated programs must also be able to call on existing routines to prevent the system from "reinventing the wheel."

- Does the tool permit distribution of design/development responsibilities? CASE design and development tools must provide a serviceable means of segregating job responsibilities and interfacing the individual efforts into a single system project.

- Do the CASE design and development tools have the capacity to export portions of the design and development dictionary specifications? This is important, as design and development specifications for one system may be reusable in the design and development of other systems. "Reusable design" will join "reusable code" as a result of this capability.

- Can the tool interface design and development specifications to the functional DBMS be used to maintain the company's data? It is rare to develop systems that are not affected by the database environment, and the development of systems using CASE tools is no exception. Therefore, it is important that the CASE tools can interface design and development specifications of application systems to mainframe DBMSs and database creation or modification.

- Does the tool have word processing capabilities? In addition to built-in word processing capabilities, the tool should have an effective interface with standard word processing systems. An added feature of some tools is the ability to pass documentation to a desktop publishing software system for more professional representation.

- Does the tool enhance project management? The use of CASE tools does not preclude the need for effective project management, in fact, their use can enhance such management. Specifications that are entered using a planning component provide a boundary for design and development activities. This boundary provides a built-in means of determining when design and development activities diverge from originally planned specifications. Some CASE design and development tools can generate reports on the progress of individual project assignments and some can interface to existing project management software systems. Currently, this interface is a temporary exit from the CASE tool into the project management system, but the interface will become much stronger in the future and provide more automatic updating of the project schedule.

- Is it possible to modify the CASE design and development tools relative to your firm's internal or existing methodology? CASE tools are prepackaged systems and may need modifications to make them more suitable for individual installations. Thus, it is important that the system has the ability to add or delete menu options or to modify the style of graphical or dictionary entry screens.

- Can the tool automatically generate design, operations, and end-user documentation? As systems are designed and developed with CASE tools, documentation concerning components and users of the system is entered into the dictionary. Thus, the majority of design, operations, and user documentation required for documentation manuals is available from these dictionary entries. CASE systems should provide this documentation in either on-line or hard-copy form, with little additional work required from the project development team.

- Does the tool have facilities for maintaining design as well as systems? When conditions in business warrant changes in the information systems function, the people responsible for maintenance should be able to effect the required system changes in the system's design specifications automatically. Or, once those changes are made, the development tool should be able to designate where the current systems need changing, as well as indicate which users need to be notified of the changes and what they need to be told. Some development systems already provide some of these capabilities. As the interface between CASE design and development software systems becomes stronger, modifications to design specifications entered into the design software will be able to modify development specifications and, ultimately, the entire system. Since the planning component was the last to emerge, the interface between it and the design component is weak. Subsequently, as the interface between it and the design strengthens, it should have the same effect on those activities as the strengthening of the interface between design and development did.
- Can the tool generate programs that span a range of systems? The hardware and software to create a transparent micro, mini, and mainframe environment are not far off. Consequently, the programs that the CASE tool generates must be able to provide the same execution services on a desktop micro as on a mighty mainframe. Some of today's CASE development systems already offer this.

It goes without saying that the CASE tool manufacturer should be willing to provide a list of installations using its software and grant permission to contact them. This major criterion should govern the purchase of any software system. Should a software vendor refuse to supply this information, you have reason to doubt the validity and comprehensiveness of its product.

11.4.1 Analysis of Selection Criteria

A subset of the foregoing questions was sent to about a dozen vendors of CASE tools. Their responses are recorded in an earlier text (Brathwaite, 1989).

11.5 Vendors of CASE Tools

This section lists some of the major vendors of CASE tools and gives a brief summary of their products.

11.5.1 Vendor List

ADPAC COMPUTING LANGUAGES CORP. Adpac Computing Languages develops, markets, and services technology support tools for the IBM mainframe operating under MVS. Adpac's CASE tools (DPDP and DESIGN) provide a front-end CAD/CAM diagramming technique that assists analysts in drawing any type of diagram and design analysis with the capability to verify the contents of diagrams.

AGS MANAGEMENT SYSTEMS INC. AGS/MS is recognized as the world's leader in systems development methodologies and project management system. MULTI/CAM, the micro-mainframe CASE system created by AGS/MS, integrates software development tools, software design and production models, project management, and any other user-selected CASE tools into a unified, automated work environment.

AMERICAN MANAGEMENT SYSTEMS AMS is a major computer services firm specializing in applications development. AMS's Life-cycle Productivity System (LPS) integrates productivity tools from AMS and other vendors for strategic system planning, design, development, maintenance, and project management. LPS produces all deliverable work products required by most methodologies. Major portions of LPS operate on PCs. Implementation, configuration control, and foundation software modules operate on IBM mainframe.

ANALYSTS INTERNATIONAL CORP. Analysts International, a professional data processing software and services company and a leader in the computer industry for over 22 years, introduced CORVET. CORVET is a graphics-oriented, PC-based, interactive CASE design and development product that generates stand-along COBOL programs and comprehensive documentation for IBM mainframe environments.

ARTHUR ANDERSEN & CO. Arthur Andersen developed FOUNDATION, a computer-integrated environment for software engineering. Covering the entire systems development life cycle, FOUNDATION consists of METHOD/1, a PC LAN-based tool for planning and design, and INSTALL/1, an IBM mainframe-based environment for implementation and support of DB2 applications.

ARTHUR YOUNG & CO.   Arthur Young is an international accounting, tax, and management consulting firm that is working with KnowledgeWare to develop the Information Engineering Workbench (AY/IEW). It markets KnowledgeWare products internationally and uses the AY/IEW and Information Engineering techniques for systems building.

ASYST TECHNOLOGIES, INC.   The DEVELOPER provides multiuser, automated support for the systems development process, through its repository located either at the PC, at the mainframe (using DB2), or at both sites. The DEVELOPER and its CUSTOMIZER module allow the use of any methodology at all levels of compliance and rigor. Repository integrity is maintained through a menu-driven SQL query language and built-in ASYSTants capabilities.

BACHMAN INFORMATION SYSTEMS, INC.   Bachman Information Systems is exhibiting The Bachman Product Set, which supports the development of new applications while supporting existing applications. It provides the powerful maintenance, enhancement, and migration capabilities that MIS departments need to control the largest component of their workload.

CATALYST   CATALYST, an information technology firm of Peat Marwick, presents PATHVU, RETROFIT, ReACT, and DataTEC. PATHVU provides analysis and detailed reporting of program logic and structure. RETROFIT restructures COBOL code. ReACT translates Assembler programs to structured COBOL. DataTEC provides data element analysis, standardization, and migration capabilities. These products make up the reengineering baseline that is necessary to migrate existing systems to advanced technical environments.

CGI SYSTEMS, INC.   PACBASE is a full-cycle CASE product. It integrates mainframe- and PC-based analysis and design workstations for the development and maintenance of application specifications. This is done through active prototypes, a centralized, enterprisewide dictionary that controls and manages all business specifications directly into complete COBOL applications, including all code and documentation.

CHEN & ASSOCIATES, INC.   Chen & Associates provides products, training, and consulting in data-oriented system development. Products (PC-based) are ER-Designer, which defines information requirements in entity–relationship diagrams; SCHEMAGEN, which generates schemata for database systems (from micro-based to mainframe-based); and Normalizer, which normalizes data or words.

support those methods. With more than 250 professionals throughout the world, JMA's teams provide commercial and government clients with technical and management services.

KNOWLEDGEWARE, INC. KnowledgeWare provides a complete Integrated Computer-Aided Software Engineering (I-CASE) environment for the planning, analysis, design, construction, and maintenance of computer-based information systems. The Information Engineering Workbench (IEW) provides enterprise modeling, data modeling, process modeling, systems design, and code generation experts. The "Knowledge-Coordinator/Encyclopedia" team uses state-of-the-art artificial intelligence technology.

LANGUAGE TECHNOLOGY Language Technology provides CASE products to the IBM mainframe market. The company's flagship product, RECODER, is the leading COBOL structuring tool. RECODER automatically transforms difficult to maintain, unstructured COBOL into structured COBOL. Language Technology's INSPECTOR is the only quality-assurance tool based on scientific measurement of COBOL quality and maintainability.

MANAGEMENT SYSTEMS, INC. LBMS presents its PC-based tools, SUPER-MATE and AUTO-MATE PLUS. SUPER-MATE provides a powerful set of automated facilities for strategic planning, including business area/activity analysis, analysis of competitive strategies, the prioritization of applications, and the development of the strategic plan. Results of this plan may be passed to AUTO-MATE PLUS, which provides full support for systems analysis, logical design, and automatic generation of physical designs and data dictionary syntax for ADABAS, DB2, and other DBMSs.

MANAGER SOFTWARE PRODUCTS The MANAGER family of products (PC and mainframe) is dedicated to automating all phases of the systems life cycle, from strategic information planning to the generation of enabled code. MSP will present ManagerVIEW, the intelligent workstation-based graphical information engineering tool driven by the central knowledge base resident on the corporate dictionary. Manager-VIEW is integrated with the mainframe corporate dictionary and also runs on the IBM PC family and PS/2.

MICHAEL JACKSON SYSTEMS, LTD. Jackson CASE tools automate the widely acclaimed Michael Jackson methods of system development and program design. SPEED-BUILDER supports the analysis phases of

development through powerful graphical and text facilities and automates documentation production. The cooperating Program Development Facility (PDF) generates complete, well-structured program code
from Jackson structure charts.

MICRO FOCUS   Micro Focus COBOL/2 Workbench puts a mainframe
programming and testing environment on a PC platform under MS-
DOS or OS/2. It is used by developers of COBOL, CICS DL/I, and IMS
DB/DC applications to improve productivity and cut applications
development backlogs. Micro Focus COBOL compilers and CASE
tools are the choice of IBM, AT&T, Sun Microsystems, Microsoft, and
others.

NASTEC CORP.   Nastec develops tools for commercial, government,
and engineering software developers. CASE 2000 DesignAid is based
on an interactive, multi-user database with features for process modeling, real-time system modeling, and documentation. Operating in the
IBM PC and Digital VAX environment, CASE 2000 also includes tools
for requirements management, project management and control, and
consulting and training in CASE technology.

NETRON INC.   The NETRON/CAP Development Center is a CASE
system for building custom, portable COBOL software using a frame-
based software engineering process called Bassett Frame Technology.
NETRON/CAP unifies the prototyping/development/maintenance life
cycle into an automated specification procedure. The open-design architecture allows unlimited automation of additional application functionality for IBM mainframes and PCs, VAX systems, and Wang VS
minis.

OPTIMA, INC. (formerly Ken Orr & Associates)   Optima integrates the
use of tools and technology with the experience of people. DSSD (Data
Structured Systems Development), the flagship product, is a life cycle
methodology that serves as the base of the product offering. CASE tool
products that automate the methodology are Brackets, for the diagramming process, and DesignMachine, for requirements definition and logical database design.

ON-LINE SOFTWARE INTERNATIONAL   On-Line Software International presents CasePac-Automated Software Development with a
powerful DB2 data dictionary. As the foundation for On-Line Software's CASE platform, CasePac provides a complete, fully active, central repository, software engineering facilities, including a graphics
front end, change management, and maintenance facilities.

PANSOPHIC SYSTEMS, INC. Pansophic Systems presents TELON. The TELON application development system captures design specifications to generate COBOL or DL/I applications. TELON assists the transition from analysis to design by providing interfaces to leading front-end analysis tools. TELON components include directory, data administration, screen/report painters, prototyping, specification facilities, automated documentation, generator, and test facility.

POLYTRON CORP. POLYTRON offers the leading configuration management system for MS/DOSPC and VAX/VMS software development. PVCS maintains versions and revisions of software systems. PolyMake automatically rebuilds any desired version of the system. PolyLibrarian maintains libraries of reusable object modules. The tools work together or independently with ANY language and your existing tools.

POPKIN SOFTWARE & SYSTEMS INC. Popkin Software & Systems offers SYSTEM ARCHITECT, a PC-based CASE tool running under Microsoft Windows. Its set of process- and data-driven methodologies for structured analysis and design include DeMarco/Yourdon, Gane and Sarson, Ward & Mellor (real-time), structure charts, and entity–relationship diagrams. SYSTEM ARCHITECT's Data Dictionary-Encyclopedia utilizes dBase II file format.

READY SYSTEMS Ready Systems presents CARDTools, which supports automatic DoD 2167 documentation generation and specific ADA requirements, including object-oriented design, packages, information hiding, and rendezvous. CARDTools offers real-time performance deadline analysis on multitasking architectures and hardware/software interface specification, including intertasking synchronization and communication designs, allowing for design analysis verification prior to actual implementation.

SAGE SOFTWARE, INC. Sage Software develops, markets, and supports a family of CASE tools for developers of IBM-based information systems. The company's product family (known as the APS Development Center) encompasses the software development cycle and supports the physical design, interactive prototyping, coding, testing, and maintenance of COBOL-based applications software.

SOFTLAB, INC. Softlab presents MAESTRO, the integrated software engineering environment. MAESTRO organizes and manages the software cycle through real-time project management, time accounting, and your standards. MAESTRO integrates customizable tools for design, coding, testing, documentation, and maintenance, is language independent, and fits in numerous hardware and software environments.

TEKTRONIX   TekCASE is a family of automated software development tools that help software engineers and project managers analyze, design, document, manage, and maintain complex real-time systems. Because they support Digital's complete VAX line and integrate with VAXset software, TekCASE products are flexible, extensible, and especially well suited for large projects.

TEXAS INSTRUMENTS   Texas Instruments' integrated CASE product, The Information Engineering Facility, is designed to automate the complete systems development life cycle. It consists of a powerful mainframe encyclopedia and PC-based, graphical toolsets to support analysis and design. TI can demonstrate today the major components of this product, including strategic planning, analysis, design, and COBOL code and database generation.

THE CADWARE GROUP, LTD.   The CADWARE Group designs, produces, and markets rule-based frameworks and modeling tools for development of complex systems. Managers, planners, systems analysts, and designers use these tools to help manage the complexity of defining and evaluating mission-critical business, industrial, and technical systems.

TRANSFORM LOGIC CORP.   Transform addresses the development and maintenance of the entire application life cycle. Using expert system technology, complete COBOL applications are produced for IBM mainframe DBMSs such as DL/I and DB2. The concepts behind automated development, data-driven design architecture, prototyping, and maintenance, are reviewed with examples of user accomplishments.

VISUAL SOFTWARE, INC.   Visual Software markets personal CASE tools for workstations, LAN, and mainframe design environments. The base package, vsDesigner, is a methodology-independent workbench supporting shared access to LAN-based information repositories. Several default design syntaxes come with the product, including those for real-time design. Extensive analysis is supported and an optional SQL interface to the design data is available.

YOURDON INC.   The YOURDON Analyst/Designer Toolkit supports both the traditional and real-time YOURDON Techniques and allows for the creation of all the diagrams associated with the techniques. The diagramming facilities of the Toolkit are integrated with a powerful project dictionary that features dBase III compatibility. The Toolkit provides error checking to ensure the accuracy of diagrams and dictionary entries.

11.6 Getting CASE in Place

There are three basic steps for implementing CASE technology in a software development organization:

● Determine methodology and automation support requirements
● Select a CASE product
● Implement the CASE product

This is a lengthy process involving numerous people, so do not expect major results for a couple of years. Even then, the biggest and longest-term benefits may come in application maintenance. Case tools make it much easier to maintain specifications.

11.6.1 Determine the Methodology

Following agreement on the organization methodology, whether dataflow or entity-relationship diagrams, your next step should be what you need most in automation support. For a larger organization with complex applications, you may want some of the following capabilities:

● Interactive drawing of analysis diagrams
● Automatic date normalization
● Consistency checking
● Initialization of physical design from requirements
● Prototyping tools
● Directory of reusable code modules
● Analysis methodology enforcements
● Interface with application development environment

A second key decision is whether you want a single integrated environment or a CASE front-end to a more classical development environment.

11.6.2 Select a CASE Product

Once you have determined your methodology and decided that CASE capabilities will be useful, you need to select a product. You may decide this on the basis of:

● What environment, PC or mainframe?

- What application does the tool support? Some tools support a specific database or language, for example, DB2 or ADA.
- Does the tool support your methodology?
- Is the vendor financially secure?

You may want to talk to people who have experience using the vendor's CASE tool.

11.6.3 Implement the CASE product

An aggressive strategy for CASE implementation in smaller organizations is to automate many software engineering techniques simultaneously on a small trial project. The basic steps are:

- Select a new development project to be used for the CASE trial situation
- Staff the trial project with your best requirements and design analysts
- Assign a full-time CASE administrator to learn the tool, make detailed methodology decisions, enter information, run analysis reports, and generate specifications

A large organization with thousands of users nationwide must take a different approach. Most such organizations find it physically impossible to decide on a complete automated methodology and then train hundreds of people in a short time period. In this circumstance, a method or support group acts as change agent, introducing a few techniques at a time and supporting them with automation.

11.7 Summary

This chapter introduced a tool that has literally "taken the software development world by storm." CASE tools are making a big impact on software development and will continue to do so for years to come.

The chapter introduced and described various CASE tools and showed how they could be selected and used in small or large organizations.

CHAPTER 12

Introduction to DB2 and SQL/DS

12.1 Introduction

DB2 and SQL/DS have become the flagships of relational database management systems. The universal acceptance of these two products coupled with the strong support of IBM has made them the DBMSs of the future.

The vendor, IBM, has indicated that these two DBMSs are compatible database engines and differ only in the operating system that supports them. DB2 is supported by MVS, whereas SQL/DS is supported by DOS/VSE and VM/CMS. With this in mind, the coverage in this chapter will treat them as one and will only differentiate between them when the differences are significant enough to merit discussion.

12.2 Background of DB2

DB2 (Database 2) was announced in June 1983. Delivery was said to be 15 months away, so IBM was again executing its normal gambit to discourage customers from defecting to third parties, or giving sites the opportunity to plan ahead depending on one's viewpoint. The new product was intended to run under MVS/370 and MVS/XA, though it was clearly intended to cooperate with the latter and could be seen as another incentive to opt for this operating environment. DOS/VSE users already had their own relational database management system, SQL/DS, and the new product was very similar to it. The main differences were that DB2 supported much larger databases, DB2's IMS interface, and, of course, the fact that DB2 is tightly coupled with MVS/XA.

Two packages were also announced to provide support for DB2 in the MVS environment. Query Management Facility (QMF) uses Structured

Query Language (SQL) and QBE to provide interactive extraction, manipulation, and generation.

Data Extract (DXT) uses ISPF menu-driven panels to enable data to be extracted from IMS/VS and DL/1 databases, and from VSAM and SAM data sets in readiness for loading into DB2. The intriguing thing about DXT, apart from the fact that it was scheduled to be available three months before DB2, is the implication that MVS users were expected to run both IMS and DB2. This makes business sense from IBM's point of view, however, IMS was supposed to be the corporate DBMS, and one of the primary reasons for implementing a DBMS, particularly a corporate one, is to reduce data redundancy. Issues such as data integrity, support, security, DASD requirements, and programmer productivity also arise.

In April 1985, IBM announced that DB2 was generally available, and at the same time IBM extended its data dictionary to give support to DB2. DD-DB2's main objective was to improve system and application programmer productivity. Interestingly, IBM was already beginning to suggest that DB2 was not entirely unsuitable for production applications. IBM also started to produce throughput figures for DB2, which suggested that it might be suitable as a general-purpose DBMS, and to push IMS into a more specialized high-throughput role.

In February 1986, Release 2 of DB2 was announced, with the stated intention of giving the product a large-scale production role, as well as an Information Center one. This message was reinforced by the introduction of the DB2 Performance Monitor (DB2PM) and a more flexible version of DXT.

12.3 A DB2 Perspective

Before discussing techniques for development under DB2, it is useful to step back for a perspective on what makes up a DB2 development environment. This section discusses the various components of IBM's environment for DB2 development and the relative strengths and weaknesses of that environment. This will lay the basis for later discussion of the techniques needed to supplement that environment.

A useful paradigm for the evaluation of DB2 is called a Comprehensive Information Management System (CIMS). Such a system provides a fully integrated environment revolving around a repository. Closely tied to the repository are a distributed DBMS, a systems designer system, a systems implementor system, and interactive end-user access.

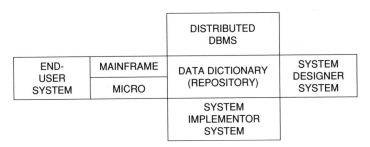

Figure 12.1 CIMS components.

A CIMS environment enhances and simultaneously constrains the development of systems. It constrains development because it provides the structures and architectures that are vital to a highly productive environment. At the same time, it enhances development by allowing designers and implementors to concentrate their efforts on creative and responsive solutions to business problems rather than to reinventing interfaces to the technical environment.

True integration in a CIMS environment means that systems will be built in new and more rigorous ways.

The CIMS components are shown in Fig. 12.1. The integration between them will be developed later. This section will simply summarize the features of each component as a basis for describing the DB2 environment.

12.3.1 Repository

The repository is the heart of the CIMS environment. The dictionary provides the descriptions of the processing that is required and the data that are required for the processing. It provides common definitions for all users of the same data item, whether it be screens, reports, databases, or other file types, or program processing.

The repository allows the DBMS to do more than just identify its objects. It contains information about all data that are of interest to the enterprise. Therefore, it includes database elements, screens, reports, programs, and systems. To provide the level of functionality required, a repository must provide both a standard set of entities, which are useful in most environments, and an extensibility feature that allows individual enterprises to include entities of unique interest to that organization.

12.3.2 Distributed DBMS

The CIMS environment provides a powerful DBMS, which services data in a fashion analogous to that provided by the repository for metadata. All master information of interest to the organization resides under the control of the DBMS. It ensures integrity and security of the data while providing access to authorized users. In today's world of far-flung enterprises, the DBMS must be distributed if it is to achieve its objective. The definition of distributed DBMS is still evolving, however, it is clear that a distributed DBMS must provide location transparency, partitioning, and replication around the network with full integrity and location independence.

12.3.3 System Designer System

System designer systems are commonly called CASE tools, and such tools provide facilities to improve designer productivity by automating designer tasks. These include word processing integrated with graphics, functional prototyping, data modeling, database design, and performance prototyping. A critical aspect of CASE tools is that they must provide multi-user access to a central design dictionary to ensure vital cross-team communication.

12.3.4 System Implementor System

System implementor systems are increasingly being labeled as CASE tools. More recognizable labels include 4GLs and workbenches. Facilities of a truly complete system implementor would include:

- A standardized architecture for on-line and batch processes, incorporating standard interfaces to the technical environment
- Code generation
- Screen and report generation
- Database generation
- Test data generation
- Test data management and testing management
- Configuration management for systems moving through unit testing, system testing, and production

12.3.5 End-User Systems

End-user systems require a wide variety of options. For high-volume systems, such as order processing or reservations, a high-performance

TP monitor such as CICS or IMS/DC is needed. For simple ad hoc requirements, a query tool that has a short learning curve for nondedicated users is necessary. For complex ad hoc requirements, a powerful decision support product is required. In today's world of microcomputers, interface software to download and/or upload between micro and mainframe is increasingly necessary.

12.4 DB2 as a Database Management System

As described earlier, DB2 is a powerful DBMS. Its primary weakness under the CIMS model is its lack of distributed capabilities. In this section, we discuss DB2's capabilities in more detail.

Today, we expect a DBMS to be relational and to provide all the advantages promised by relational theory. First and foremost, the advantage expected from relational theory is that of programmer productivity. The characteristics of a fully relational system may be summarized as follows:

- Data are always presented to users as tables consisting of rows and columns.
- The DBMS provides the functions of the relational algebra, especially SELECT, PROJECT, and JOIN.
- The DBMS enforces the integrity of primary keys and foreign keys.
- The databases are managed strictly through relational capabilities of the DBMS.

DB2 maintains data integrity during multiple-user accesses; it provides security against unauthorized access from programs or end users; it provides roll-back in the event of program or system failure and roll-forward in the event of medium failure; and it provides that functionality at a speed suitable for most on-line transaction processing systems.

DB2 has two weaknesses when viewed from a traditional perspective. For batch processing, DB2 seems to ignore the typical situation of batch posting to master files while creating audit trail records for a batch report. The DB2 integrity features do not encompass sequential files of the type typically used for report records. Therefore, there is an integrity exposure if a batch program fails and is subsequently restarted. The state of the sequential file may not match the state of the master files. Techniques for overcoming this weakness tend to require one of the following:

- Use of Assembler programming, which is increasingly unacceptable to today's data processing management
- Use of DB2 for report records, which leads to significant performance degradation when the volume of report records is large

The second weakness in DB2 is the structure of the security system. The system is inherently hierarchical, assuming that the system administrator should have full authority to manipulate all DB2 objects. In fact, security has been implemented for many decades under the principle of separation of duties, so that no one individual has full access to sensitive assets. Within data processing, someone in operations typically needs enough authority to fix problem programs in the middle of the night and put them back into production. Ensuring that this same individual does not also have the authority to dynamically change sensitive production data can be problematic under DB2. The difficulty is heightened by the fact that DB2 does not provide any audit trails of interactive changes.

12.5 Application Development Using DB2

The major advantage of a relational DBMS is application programmer productivity gains, which have been reported as two to four times better than with a traditional DBMS. The author's experience with relational databases supports these claims. Not only are these gains found when writing new applications, but they are even greater when modifying existing relational DBMS applications.

There is absolutely no question that the application programmer productivity gains of a relational DBMS are significant. These productivity gains are possible because of two fundamental differences between a relational DBMS and a traditional DBMS.

The first difference is that a relational DBMS uses the values in the data fields themselves to relate data items, rather than using physical pointers or indices to connect data items. In fact, a relationship can be made dynamically between two data items. When you ask for data, you do not have to know whether or not there are predefined access paths. This truly separates the application program from having to know about the physical structure of the data, unlike a traditional DBMS. Thus, the application programmer can focus on building applications and does not have to waste time working out how to navigate through the database. Usually, changes to data structures and changes to applications are independent of each other; this rarely happens in a traditional DBMS. Although using the values in the data fields to connect the data items does introduce more data redundancy than a traditional database, it can be dealt with by the application.

The second difference is that, unlike a traditional DBMS, which deals with data one record at a time, a relational database is set or multi-record oriented. When you ask for data from a relational DBMS, you do not have to know how many records, if any, satisfy the criteria. With one single statement you get all the data to satisfy your request. You do not have to write application program statements to determine if and when you have all the data. When you ask for data from a traditional DBMS, you get only one record at a time.

This is why a relational database, like DB2, is ideal for ad hoc query and report writing applications, which are sometimes called Information Center or decision support applications. Ad hoc query and report applications typically have the following attributes:

- Cannot be preplanned
- Create data relationships dynamically
- Require rapid turnaround
- Tend to be run infrequently

Since a relationship between two data items can be made dynamically, and predefined access paths are not required, ad hoc query and report applications are ideal for implementation under DB2.

Conversely, with a traditional DBMS, data can only be retrieved using predefined access paths. You might not even be able to write a particular query or report application until the database administrator builds the particular predefined access path required by that application. This can take days or even weeks to accomplish.

12.5.1 CICS-DB2 Transaction Processing

Implementing a new CICS transaction processing application for DB2 is easier than doing the same for a traditional DBMS. To obtain good performance in a relational DBMS, it is mandatory that the application deal with sets of records at a time, not single records. This section describes some of the problems that can occur when implementing CICS transactions that use DB2.

To process a CICS transaction under DB2, you issue SQL "select" statements in your application program and pass control to DB2. DB2 then involves the optimizer to determine how the request will be handled.

Having a predefined index available does not necessarily mean that DB2 will use it. DB2 searches for the records that meet the selecting criteria and puts the records in DB2 virtual memory and transfers control back to the application program. If the data must be reordered, the answer set must be sorted before control is returned to the user. This can take a long time.

The application program will issue "fetches" for as many records as it can deal with, typically a screenfull. After it gets them, it writes to the screen. Writing to the screen is end-of-transaction, which means CICS will release all those records you just found. Your selection criteria should be very specific, so all the selected records can fit on one screen.

But what if one screen could only hold 20 records and the selection criteria found 100 records? The application program has to remember the key of the last record found and save that key in the transaction work area. Then you must reissue the "select" statement with a "where" clause asking for records with a higher key value. This is passed to DB2, which does the entire search over again and stores the records in virtual memory, although not all the records, just 21 to 100. Your application then must process 20 more records and you have to repeat the entire process again for records 41 to 60. This continues until you process the hundredth record. Note that you have read records 81 to 100 five times and only displayed them once.

12.6 Logical Database Design for DB2

There are three parts to database design under DB2:

- Data normalization
- Logical database design
- Physical database design

12.6.1 Data Normalization

Over the last decade, data normalization techniques have demonstrated their value. Normalized data structures survive corporate growth and reorganization, and this stability in data structure brings commensurate stability to the applications that use the data while allowing development of new applications using the old data.

There are many texts on data normalization, so we will not attempt to define techniques for normalization here. Suffice it to say that a rigorous approach to data normalization is strongly encouraged. Researchers need not be in third normal form; first normal form is all that is required.

However, there is no substitute for rigorous data analysis for understanding the business relationships of data elements. Therefore, we recommend that the first stage of database design should take the data to third normal form at a minimum. Fourth or fifth normal form may be preferable where data relationships are complex.

12.6.2 Logical Database Design

Logical database design has four steps:

- Define tables
- Define referential integrity requirements
- Denormalize the table designs
- Define views

Table definitions begin by assuming that each normalized entity from the data analysis will become a DB2 table. The first step is to define all columns that will be contained in the table, recognizing that additional columns will typically be identified during programming.

DB2 column names may contain 18 characters, including the 26 letters of the alphabet, the 10 digits, the special COBOL characters, and the underscore ___. It is helpful to use COBOL data name for the column names.

The data characteristics of each column must be identified at this stage. This includes defining alphabetic versus numeric format, as well as the use of nulls or variable-length fields. When there are frequent opportunities to conserve at least 20 bytes by making the field length variable, and the field will not increase in size during the life of any specific row occurrence, VARCHAR is appropriate. For example, when four address lines are allowed, but normally only two are used, it is appropriate to use VARCHAR for lines 3 and 4. However, if a long text field is normally omitted at the time of entry, but keyed into the system at some subsequent time, it is not appropriate to use VARCHAR. There are four types of fields available for defining numeric fields in DB2:

- Integer (half-word or full-word)
- Decimal (packed decimal)
- Float (full-word or double-word)
- Calendar (date, time, or timestamp)

Nulls are occasionally used for numeric data. They are appropriate when functions need to know a minimum, nonempty value, but empty values are permissible. For example, it may be necessary to know the smallest salary, excluding unknown salaries. Nulls are also appropriate when the function must compute an average by excluding empty values. Once you have defined the data types of all columns, the next step is to define the primary keys of all DB2 tables. Generally, these will be the primary keys defined during data analysis. Primary keys should guarantee uniqueness of each row of the table and should also be acceptable as the primary means for accessing the data. DB2 can always retrieve data, regardless of what criteria are defined. As a practical matter, though, only one access path will give better performance than any other, and transaction processing systems should maximize use of that path. All columns included in primary keys should be defined as NOT NULL. Default values should never be acceptable.

Once the initial table designs are complete, it is necessary to identify the relationships between tables that must be maintained by the applications. For example, in a Receivable System, it will be important to ensure that the customer numbers are always valid and that no customers are deleted from the customer file while they still have outstanding receivables in the Receivable file. This is called "referential integrity."

Referential integrity is enforced by identifying columns that contain data that serve as a primary key to another table. For example, the Receivables table will contain customer number, which is the primary key to the Customer table. Therefore, customer number is called a foreign key in the Receivables table. Referential integrity says that all foreign keys must be valid.

Rows may not be inserted to the secondary table if the related row does not exist on the primary table. If a key is updated on the primary table, all occurrences of that value on secondary tables are updated as well. A value cannot be changed on a primary table if there are any occurrences of that value in secondary tables. The matching values in the secondary tables are set to null and the primary is then updated. A foreign key cannot be changed to a value that does not exist on the primary tables. If a primary key is deleted on the primary table, all occurrences of that value on secondary tables are deleted as well.

The third step of logical database design is to denormalize the data. During this phase of denormalization, look for opportunities to minimize the number of tables that must be accessed to complete a single application. Typically, this will be made possible by creating redundant data in certain tables to avoid accessing other tables for those columns. The reduction in accesses for the application must be balanced with the cost of maintaining redundant data. Therefore, it is desirable to replicate only stable data that will not require maintenance.

Another common technique for reducing the number of tables accessed is the compaction of two or more tables into a single table. This is particularly useful when tables have a one-to-one relationship. It is also useful when only few data must be replicated if tables are combined. For example, if data analysis defines a very narrow order header table and a wide (many columns) order line table, the two tables can be combined at relatively little cost. Typically, the order header data would appear on every associated table, and the order header table would disappear.

Data analysis, when completed to third normal form, can produce too many tables to be supported effectively. Comparison of third normal form data structures to first normal form structures may suggest additional denormalization that will improve performance.

12.6.3 Physical Database Design

During the physical database design task, there are seven steps for DB2:

- Group tables into databases
- Group tables into tablespaces
- Analyze requirements for partitioning large tablespaces
- Define unique indexes
- Create a project storage group
- Create databases, tablespaces, tables, and primary indexes
- Identify additional indexes

Begin with the data model of the logical database that was developed during the logical database design. Each such grouping of tables defines a database. Typically, databases hold 6 to 10 tables. These databases are typically defined along traditional database lines, that is, Customer, Product, Order, and Inventory.

You may expect a one-to-one correlation between tablespaces and tables. The only exceptions are small tables that can more easily be grouped together and managed as a single unit. It is possible to load several related tables into a single tablespace so as to force the clustering of related rows from different tables into common data pages.

Large tablespaces are typically partitioned by key range. Partitioning allows faster backup, reorganization, and recovery of large tablespaces. It also allows key ranges that are accessed frequently to be placed on faster devices. I/O bottlenecks may be reduced by placing partitions of frequently accessed tables on different devices and/or different controllers.

However, partitioning has its disadvantages. It prevents programmers from updating the columns that are used as the basis of partitioning. For example, if a table is partitioned by region ID, region ID cannot be updated. The row must be deleted and inserted with the new ID.

The final step in physical database design is to define unique indexes. Usually, the primary keys defined during normalization will be the unique indexes. It is very important that each table has a unique key. Because of the set processing nature of DB2, it is impossible to delete a single erroneous row of a table unless uniqueness of the key can be assured.

Indexes should be smaller than 40 bytes. Eight to 12 bytes is the preferred range of index sizes. In addition to the unique indexes, it is necessary to define the partitioning index at this time. This is the index that DB2 will use to create the tablespace partitions.

The partitioning indexes have two special features:

- They define the physical sequence of the data in the table.
- The data columns used for partitioning indexes cannot be updated.

There are several parameters that should be specified when defining tablespaces. These include:

- Database that holds the tablespace
- Patitioning
- CLOSE—whether the tablespace should be closed when the program using it terminates
- PRIQTY—primary space allocation in kilobytes
- SECQTY—secondary space allocation in kilobytes
- ERASE—whether to rewrite DASD space with binary zeros whenever the tablespace is dropped
- Locking level
- Buffer pools
- Password

12.7 The DB2 Catalog

DB2 as a database manager is required to manage data that are defined to it. DB2 uses tables to manage the data that it keeps. In addition to keeping track of every object defined in the relational system, information is recorded pertaining to who can create new objects or access the existing ones. All of these tables are grouped into what is known as the DB2 Catalog or the DB2 System Catalog. The DB2 Catalog contains approximately 30 tables.

Let us identify some of these objects that have to be managed by the database management system. These objects include buffer pools, storage groups, databases, tablespaces, tables, indexes, views, synonyms, and plans. DB2 keeps track of not only the just mentioned objects in the Catalog, but also who has access and control over these objects.

Execution of various DB2 utilities, such as COPY, RECOVERY, REORGANIZATION, LOAD, RUNSTATS, and STOSPACE, will either retrieve or update information contained in columns in one or more of the DB2 Catalog tables. This information is valuable to DB2 when determining data access strategies and recovering tables. The DB2 Catalog tables are unlike normal tables in that SQL operations to perform inserts, updates, or deletes are not allowed. Instead, the DB2 Catalog is updated indirectly through special SQL data definition statements, such as create, alter, and drop.

DB2 uses buffer pools when building temporary tables to store data resulting from sorts and joins. There are only four buffer pools available: PF0, BP1, BP2, and BP32K. DB2 uses DP0 to store its data pages. Performance-critical applications can process in their own buffer pools such as BP1 and BP2.

CHAPTER 13

Introduction to SQL

13.1 Introduction

The standard language for handling data stored in relational databases is called Structured Query Language (SQL). SQL commands can be entered directly from display terminals, used as DBS utility program input, or embedded in application programs written in COBOL, PL/1, FORTRAN, C, or assembler language. Any operation that can be done with SQL commands from a terminal can be done with SQL commands embedded in an application program. Some SQL commands can be used only in application programs.

Relational databases present all data as tables in a simple row and column format. The table in Fig. 13.1 has three rows and four columns. The data value in row 1 and column 2 is 06/06/1988.

SQL commands can perform many common data processing tasks, such as:

● Selecting and updating some items
● Sorting data
● Calculating values using stored data
● Copying data from one table into another
● Combining tables based on values in the tables themselves

CHECK	DATE	RECIPIENT	AMOUNT
101	06/06/1988	C. Clark	262.00
102	06/07/1989	M. Bass	40.50
103	06/08/1990	M. Cook	478.35

Figure 13.1   SQL table.

	DATA MANIPULATION COMMANDS
SELECT	Retrieves data from one or more tables
INSERT	Places one or more rows into a table
UPDATE	Changes field level data in one or more
	rows of a table
DELETE	Removes one or more rows from table
	DATA DEFINITION COMMANDS
CREATE TABLE	Defines a new table and its columns and
	optionally specifies a primary key and
	referential constraints
DROP TABLE	Drops or deletes a table
ALTER TABLE	Adds a new column to a table; it may
	also add or drop a primary key, and
	add, drop, deactivate, or activate
	referential constraints
DROP INDEX	Drops or deletes an index
CREATE INDEX	Defines an index that enables accessing
	the rows of a table in specific
	sequence; a table can have many indexes
CREATE VIEW	Defines a logical table from one or more
	tables or views in terms of a SELECT
	command
DROP VIEW	Drops or deletes a view definition

Figure 13.2   Classification of SQL commands.

13.2 SQL Data Types

SQL supports 13 types of data as listed in Fig. 13.2. All the field values of a column must be exactly the same.

13.2.1 Date/Time Data Type Formats

The following table describes the available date/time data type formats: where

- ISO is the International Standards Organization
- JIS is the Japanese Industrial Standard
- EUR is the European IBM Standard
- USA is the USA IBM Standard

DATA TYPE	DESCRIPTION	FORMAT
DATE	ISO JIS EUR USA LOCAL	yyyy-mm-dd yyyy-mm-dd dd.mm.yyyy mm/dd/yyyy user defined
TIME	ISO JIS EUR USA LOCAL	hh.mm.ss hh:mm.ss hh.mm.ss hh:mmxm user defined
TIMESTAMP		yy-mm-dd- hh.mm.ss (nnnnn)

and

- yyy is the year
- mm is the month
- dd is the day
- hh is the hour
- mm is the minute
- ss is the second
- nnnnn is the microsecond
- xm is AM or PM

13.3 Classification of SQL Commands

SQL commands consist of command verbs, one or more optional clauses, language keywords, and parameter operands. The structured use of verbs and keywords in SQL syntax permits exact specification of data requests in a readable fashion. The language allows single-bye characters and double-bye characters to be used in identifiers and character string constants and variables.

SQL commands have many types. Some are for handling the data itself and others are for controlling administrative matters, such as who can access what data. The most commonly used commands are shown in Fig. 13.2.

SCHEDULE 1

CO	FLT	Origin	Dest	Depart	Arrive	Stops
A	100	New York	LA	12.30.00	16.40.00	0
A	101	New York	LA	09.00.00	16.00.00	2
B	978	New York	LA	18.30.00	22.30.00	1
C	50B	New York	LA	08.00.00	12.00.00	0

Figure 13.3 Table of flight and destination.

13.4 Structure of SELECT Command

The SELECT command is used to retrieve data from a table. The basic
form of the SELECT command is:

- SELECT some data
- FROM some table
- WHERE specific conditions are met.

13.4.1 Examples of SELECT Command

Using the data in Fig. 13.3, we can illustrate the following examples of
the SELECT statement.

EXAMPLE 1

SELECT * FROM SCHEDULE1

In this example, all the data shown in Fig. 13.3 will be selected and
returned.

EXAMPLE 2

SELECT * FROM SCHEDULE1
WHERE ORIGIN = 'NEW YORK' AND
DEST = 'L.A.'

In this example, the following data will be returned:

A   100   New York   LA   12.30.00   16.40.00   0
A   101   New York   LA   09.00.00   16.00.00   2

EXAMPLE 3

```
SELECT CO, FLT, DEPART, ARRIVE
FROM SCHEDULE1
WHERE ORIGIN = 'NEW YORK'
AND DEST = 'S.F'
AND DEPART BETWEEN '08.00.00' AND '10.00.00'
AND STOP = 0
```

In this example, the following data will be returned:

```
C   50B   08.00.00   12.00.00
```

The BETWEEN keyword in this example is one keyword used in SQL to denote a special type of qualifying phrase. Some other keywords are IN, LIKE, IS NULL, and EXISTS. IN tests for values from a user-specified list of values. LIKE searches for character string data that fully or partially match a user-specified character string. IS NULL looks for NULL values. EXISTS tests for the existence of a row.

EXAMPLE 4

```
SELECT COUNT (*)
FROM SCHEDULE1
WHERE ORIGIN = 'NEW YORK'
AND DEST = 'L.A.'
```

In this example, 2 will be returned. The expression COUNT(*) means count all the rows that satisfy the selection rules given in the WHERE clauses of the "select" command. COUNT is one of the SQL's column functions. Others are MAX, MIN, AVG, and SUM.

EXAMPLE 5

```
SELECT ORIGIN, COUNT(*)
FROM SCHEDULE1
WHERE DEST = 'L.A.'
GROUP BY ORIGIN
ORDER BY ORIGIN
```

In this example, the following data will be returned:

ORIGIN	COUNT
New York	2

The WHERE clause determines the rows of the table that are to be counted. The GROUP BY clause causes the counting to be done for each group of rows that have a common ORIGIN value. The ORDER BY clause presents the results in alphabetic order by ORIGIN. The data for ORDER BY are in either ascending or descending order. Ascending order is the default. The keyword DESC can be appended to one or more of the columns referred to in the ORDER BY clause.

13.5 Structure of INSERT Command

The SQL INSERT command lets the user put a row of values into a table.

13.5.1 Examples of INSERT Command

EXAMPLE 1

    INSERT INTO SCHEDULE1
    VALUES ('A', '100', 'New York', 'Chicago',
        '12.30.00', '16.00.00', 0)

The preceding INSERT command would be entered into the table of Fig. 13.3 in the order in which they appear in the command. Values that go into columns that hold character, graphic, date, or time data are enclosed in single quote marks.

EXAMPLE 2

    INSERT INTO SCHEDULE1
    SELECT * FROM SCHEDULE2

This example will copy all the rows from SCHEDULE2 and add them to SCHEDULE1.

13.6 Structure of UPDATE Command

The SQL UPDATE command lets you specify the columns to be updated and the rows on which the updating should be done.

13.6.1 Examples of UPDATE Command

EXAMPLE 1

UPDATE SCHEDULE1 SET FLT = '602'
WHERE CO = 'A'
AND FLT = '101'

This UPDATE command would cause the second row of Fig. 13.3 to be changed as follows:

CO	FLT	Origin	Dest	Depart	Arrive	Stops
A	602	New York	LA	12.30.00	16.40.00	0

EXAMPLE 2

UPDATE SCHEDULE1 SET DEPART = '09.15.00'
WHERE CO = 'A'
AND FLT = '101'
AND ORIGIN = 'NEW YORK'

This UPDATE command will affect more than one row in Fig. 13.3. The updating affects the table in such a way as to change it as follows:

CO	FLT	Origin	Dest	Depart	Arrive	Stops
A	101	New York	LA	09.15.00	16.00.00	2

This UPDATE command will change the table of Fig. 13.3 as follows:

CO	FLT	Origin	Dest	Depart	Arrive	Stops
B	97A	New York	S.F.	18.30.00	22.30.00	0

13.7 Structure of DELETE Command

The SQL DELETE command lets the user drop a row of values from a table.

13.7.1 Examples of DELETE Command

EXAMPLE 1

DELETE FROM SCHEDULE1

WHERE FLT = '50B'
AND CO = 'B'

In this example, all rows of Fig. 13.3 that satisfy the WHERE clause criteria will be deleted.

13.8 Structure of CREATE Command

The CREATE command defines the format of a table, but it does not put any data into the table.

13.8.1 Examples of CREATE Command

EXAMPLE 1

CREATE TABLE SCHEDULE1
(CO CHAR(1) NOT NULL,
FLT CHAR(3) NOT NULL,
ORIGIN VARCHAR(11),
DEST VARCHAR(11),
DEPART TIME,
ARRIVE TIME,
STOPS SMALLINT)

This example will create a table of the format shown in Fig. 13.3. However, no data will exist in the table. To put data into the table, one must use the INSERT command.

EXAMPLE 2

CREATE INDEX SICOFLT
ON SCHEDULE1
(CO, FLT)

This example will create an index SICOFLT and specify the columns to be used for the data access path.

13.9 Structure of ALTER Command

The ALTER command allows the users to add columns to a table.

13.9.1 Examples of ALTER Command

EXAMPLE 1

ALTER TABLE SCHEDULE1
ADD FOOD CHAR(1)

This example will add a new column to the table of Fig. 13.3. The new table looks like:

<u>CO</u> <u>FLT</u> <u>ORIGIN</u> <u>DEST</u> <u>DEPART</u> <u>ARRIVE</u> <u>STOPS</u> <u>FOOD</u>

It should be noted that there are no data entered into the FOOD column. One would use the UPDATE command to add data to the FOOD column.

13.10 Referential Integrity

Two tables are joined or related through columns that have equal values in the columns of both tables. That is, every value of one column in one table must be the same as the value in the other table. To ensure referential integrity, one must follow several rules:

- Do not add a row to one table unless one column matches one of the columns in the other table.
- If a row is deleted from one table, set the dependent rows in the other table to null values.
- If a value is changed in one row of one table, no row in the next table can contain the old value of the other table.

13.11 Interactive SQL (ISQL) Facility

Users of SQL/DS can access and manipulate data directly from display terminals. This capability is provided through the Interactive SQL (ISQL) facility of SQL/DS.

ISQL runs as a CMS application in multiple-user mode. The ISQL facility is controlled by CMS in the VM system and works with a variety of display terminals, including the larger screen sizes offered by some models of IBM 3270 and 3279 devices.

ISQL enables users to:

- Enter SQL commands and observe the results on the display screen
- Obtain an estimate of the processing resources needed to run a query
- Control for display screen
- Write data from query results
- Enter data into tables in bulk
- Display on-line reference information (HELP)
- Create and run stored SQL commands
- Create and run stored routines
- Control logical units of work
- Cancel commands in progress
- Use the SHOW and COUNTER operator commands

13.12 Embedded SQL Commands

Languages such as COBOL, PL/1, FORTRAN, C, or Assembler allow SQL statements to be embedded in their languages. These embedded statements are executed as part of the language and produce identical results as stand-alone SQL.

The reader should refer to the numerous books on the subject to see how the host language is altered to accommodate the SQL statements.

CHAPTER 14

Introduction to QMF

14.1 Introduction

The Query Management Facility (QMF) is a licensed interactive product offered by IBM to supplement DB2 in the TSO environment. QMF is a must because it allows each user to manage his or her SQL statements. To many users, QMF is inseparable from DB2. QMF provides the user-friendly interface to DB2 that is necessary to make DB2 usable by non-professionals and professionals alike.

The user can develop, test, and store SQL queries for future use. QMF displays the rows retrieved in reports and charts. The user can then modify the report to suit his or her own needs. Not only will QMF allow users to execute stored queries, but it also allows users to share queries with others.

Queries can be developed to serve multiple functions by allowing the development of SQL statements in such a manner that the user is prompted for variables to complete the query. One query could serve the needs of many users, thus reducing redundant development. Through QMF variables, different tables can be accessed by the same stored query. QMF allows a person to select a subset of rows from a large table, save the selected rows in a new table, and proceed to analyze the new table. QMF is also suitable for ad hoc user requests.

14.2 QMF System Tables

QMF contains several system tables. Availability of the system tables will vary according to the controls placed by the installation. The content and use of these tables are outlined below:

- Q.COMMAND_SYNONYMS allows the installation to make additional commands available to users. Commands such as SAVE and ERASE allow users to save and remove their stored queries.
- Q.ERROR_LOG is used automatically by QMF to record informa-

tion when a user encounters resource, system, or QMF program errors.
- Q.OBJECT_DATA contains information describing the item stored. A stored item could be a procedure, form, or query.
- Q.OBJECT_DIRECTORY describes what kind of object is being stored and whether others are allowed to access the stored object.
- Q.OBJECT_REMARKS gives the individual saving the query the ability to record comments about the stored object.
- Q.PROFILES contains information about how an individual's QMF session is structured.
- Q.RESOURCE_TABLE is a table that provides individuals responsible for QMF administration with a method of treating QMF users differently.

14.3 Issuing QMF Commands

There are four ways to issue QMF commands:

- On the COMMAND line
- On a PROMPT panel
- By pressing a PF key
- From a Procedure

14.4 The Program Function (PF) Keys

The following PF keys are used in QMF processing:

- PF1—HELP
- PF2—RUN
- PF3—END
- PF4
- PF5
- PF6—QUERY
- PF7
- PF8
- PF9—FORM
- PF10—PROC
- PF11—PROFILE
- PF12—REPORT

```
┌──────────────────────────────────────────────────────────────────────┐
│                                                                        │
│   SQL QUERY                                                    LINE 1  │
│                                                                        │
│                                                                        │
│                                                                        │
│                                                                        │
│                                                                        │
│   ------ END -----                                                     │
│   1-HELP       2-RUN      3-END     4-PRINT      5 – 6-DRAW            │
│   7-BACK       8-FORWARD  9-FORM    10-INSERT       11-DEL            │
│   12-REPORT                                                            │
│                                                                        │
│   COMMAND ------>                              SCROLL ------> PAGE     │
│                                                                        │
└──────────────────────────────────────────────────────────────────────┘
```

Figure 14.1   QMF screen image.

14.5 Creating and Entering an SQL Query

The following scenario of panels illustrates some of the potential uses of QMF. To begin, let us enter the command DISPLAY QUERY on the Command Line and Press ENTER. Pressing PF6 will also execute the DISPLAY QUERY command. The panel in Fig. 14.1 shows an empty SQL QUERY work area. On this panel, SQL statements are constructed within QMF.

14.5.1 Entering a SELECT Statement in QMF

The panel in Fig. 4.2 shows how a SELECT statement is processed in QMF. To execute this SELECT statement, press PF2.

14.5.2 Interrupting a Query

To interrupt a query, do the following:

● Press PA1
● Press CLEAR
● Press ENTER
● Do one of the following:
  1. Type CONT to continue the query
  2. Type CANCEL to cancel the query
  3. Type DEBUG to display the query

```
┌─────────────────────────────────────────────────────────────┐
│  SQL QUERY                                          LINE 1    │
│     SELECT NAME, YEARS, SALARY, DEPT                          │
│     FROM Q STAFF                                              │
│     ORDER BY NAME                                             │
│                                                               │
│                                                               │
│                                                               │
│  ------ END -----                                             │
│  1-HELP       2-RUN     3-END     4-PRINT    5 - 6-DRAW       │
│  7-BACK       8-FORWARD 9-FORM    10-INSERT       11-DEL      │
│  12-REPORT                                                    │
│                                                               │
│  COMMAND ------>                         SCROLL ------> PAGE  │
└─────────────────────────────────────────────────────────────┘
```

Figure 14.2 Panel showing SELECT statement.

14.5.3 Changing and Running an SQL Query

To change a query, do the following:

- Press PF6
- Type your changes
- Press PF2 to run your query

14.6 Using FORM to Change Report Formats

QMF uses what is called a FORM to format a report for the data retrieved. To display the FORM and optionally change the report layout, press PF9. You will then see the default FORM placed in the FORM work area. The FORM.MAIN PANEL in the FORM work area is displayed in Fig. 14.3 and the FORM.COLUMNS in Fig. 14.4.

14.6.1 The FORM.COLUMNS Panel

The FORM.COLUMNS panel of Fig. 14.4 shows the following:

- NUM shows the number of each column (cannot change)
- COLUMN HEADING shows the column name selected (can change)
- USAGE
- IDENT shows the number of blank spaces from the left margin (column)

```
FORM. MAIN
COLUMNS:                      Total Width of Report Columns:   82

NUM    COLUMN HEADING              USAGE   INDENT   WIDTH   EDIT

 1     EMPLOYEE_NO                           2       11      L
 2     EMPLOYEE_NAME                         2       16      C
 3     ADDRESS_STATE                         2        7      C
 4     DEPT                                  2        4      C
 5     SALARY                                2       10      L2


         PAGE:    HEADING  ------->
                  FOOTING  ------->
         FINAL:   TEST  ------->
         BREAK1:  NEW PAGE FOR BREAK?  ---------> NO
                  FOOTING  ------->
         BREAK2:  NEW PAGE FOR BREAK?  ---------> NO
                  FOOTING  ------->
         OPTIONS: OUTLINE?  -------> YES    DEFAULT BREAK TEST  --------> YES


         1-HELP      2-RUN     3-END     4-PRINT    5 - 6-DRAW
         7-BACK      8-FORWARD 9-FORM    10-INSERT     11-DEL
         12-REPORT

         COMMAND  ----->                              SCROLL  -----> PAGE
```

Figure 14.3   The FORM.MAIN panel.

- WIDTH shows column width (can change)
- EDIT shows how the column is punctuated (can change)
- REPORT WIDTH shows number of characters in line of report (cannot change)

14.6.2   Changing the Column Headings

In this example, we want to replace the column heading DEPT with DEPT_NUMBER. In this case the underscore ___ character splits the column heading between two lines. Figures 14.5 and 14.6 illustrate the splitting of the column heading.

14.6.3   Indenting the Column Headings

We can control the spacing between columns by showing the required number of spaces to the left of each column on the report. We can accomplish this in Figs. 14.5 and 14.6 by changing the 2 to 4. The results are shown in Figs. 14.7 and 14.8.

```
FORM. COLUMNS
                              Report Width is Now:      64


NUM     COLUMN HEADING            USAGE    INDENT    WIDTH    EDIT

 1      DEPT                                  2        6       L
 2      JOB                                   2        5       C
 3      NAME                                  2        9       C
 4      SALARY                                2        10      L2
 5      COMM                                  2        10      L2
 6      EXPRESSION 1                          2        10      L2


***  END  ***


1-HELP       2-CHECK     3-END      4-FORM. MAIN        5-FORM. OPTIONS
6-QUERY      7-BACKWARD      8-FORWARD      9-FORM. PAGE
10-FORM. FINAL      11-FORM. BREAK1      12-REPORT

OK, FORM. COLUMNS IS DISPLAYED

COMMAND------>
                                          SCROLL------> PAGE
```

Figure 14.4   The FORM.COLUMNS panel.

```
)RM. COLUMNS        ENTMS099.QMF083_0

                         REPORT WIDTH IS NOW: 64
JM    COLUMN HEADING                          USAGE    INDENT    WIDTH    EDIT

 1    DEPT._NUMBER                               2        6        L
 2    JOB                                        2        5        C
 3    EMPLOYEE_NAME                              2        9        C
 4    SALARY                                     2        10       L2
 5    COMMISSIONS                                2        10       L2
 6    TOTAL_EARNINGS                             2        12       L2
      *** END ***
=HELP        2=CHECK      3=END         4=FORM.MAIN     5=FORM.OPTIONS    6=QUERY
=BACKWARD   8=FORWARD    9=FORM.PAGE   10=FORM.FINAL   11=FORM.BREAK1   12=REPORT
<, FORM. COLUMNS IS DISPLAYED.
)MMAND →                                                      SCROLL → PAGE
```

Figure 14.5   Splitting of column headings.

```
REPORT                                          LINE 1      POS 1      7
    DEPT.              EMPLOYEE                        TOTAL
    NUMBER    JOB       NAME        SALARY   COMMISSION   EARNINGS
++ ─────── ++ ──── ++ ──────── ++ ─────── ++ ────────── ++ ──────── ++++─

    DEPT.              EMPLOYEE                         TOTAL
    NUMBER    JOB       NAME        SALARY   COMMISSION   EARNINGS
   ───────   ────     ────────     ───────   ──────────  ────────

       15    SALES    ROTHMAN      16502.83     1152.00   17654.83
       15    CLERK    KERMISCH     12258.50      110.10   12368.60
       15    CLERK    NGAN         12508.20      206.60   12714.80
       20    SALES    PERNAL       18171.25      612.45   18783.70
       20    CLERK    JAMES        13504.60      128.20   13632.80
       20    CLERK    SNEIDER      14252.75      126.50   14379.25
       38    SALES    O'BRIEN      18006.00      846.55   18852.55
       38    SALES    QUIGLEY      16808.30      650.25   17458.55
       38    CLERK    ABRAHAMS     12009.75      236.50   12246.25
       38    CLERK    NAUGHTON     12954.75      180.00   13134.75
1 = HELP        2 =           3 = END      4 = PRINT   5 =          6 = QUERY
7 = BACKWARD    8 = FORWARD   9 = FORM    10 = LEFT    11 = RIGHT   12 =
OK, REPORT IS DISPLAYED.
COMMAND →                                              SCROLL → PAG
```

Figure 14.6   Results of splitting of column headings.

```
FORM. COLUMNS        ENTMS099.QMF084_0

                          REPORT WIDTH IS NOW: 69
NUM    COLUMN HEADING                        USAGE   INDENT   WIDTH   EDI
 ───   ──────────────                        ─────   ──────   ─────   ───

 1     DEPT._NUMBER                            2        6       L
 2     JOB                                     4        5       C
 3     EMPLOYEE_NAME                           4        9       C
 4     SALARY                                  2       10       L2
 5     COMMISSIONS                             2       11       L2
 6     TOTAL_EARNINGS                          2       12       L2
       *** END ***
1=HELP      2=CHECK      3=END        4=FORM.MAIN    5=FORM.OPTIONS   6=QUERY
7=BACKWARD  8=FORWARD    9=FORM.PAGE  10=FORM.FINAL  11=FORM.BREAK1   12=REPOR
OK, FORM.COLUMNS IS DISPLAYED.
COMMAND →                                               SCROLL → PAG
```

Figure 14.7   Controlling spacing between columns.

```
EPORT                                              LINE 1      POS 1      79
   DEPT.                    EMPLOYEE                          TOTAL
   NUMBER       JOB           NAME      SALARY   COMMISSIONS   EARNINGS
+ + ———————+ + + +————————+ + + +————— + + ——————— + + ——————— + + ——————+ + + + +

   DEPT.                    EMPLOYEE                          TOTAL
   NUMBER  /  JOB     /       NAME      SALARY   COMMISSIONS   EARNINGS
          √         √                  —————    ——————————    ————————

       15     SALES       ROTHMAN      16502.83      1152.00    17654.83
       15     CLERK       KERMISCH     12258.50       110.10    12368.60
       15     CLERK       NGAN         12508.20       206.60    12714.80
       20     SALES       PERNAL       18171.25       612.45    18783.70
       20     CLERK       JAMES        13504.60       128.20    13632.80
       20     CLERK       SNEIDER      14252.75       126.50    14379.25
       38     SALES       O'BRIEN      18006.00       846.55    18852.55
       38     SALES       QUIGLEY      16808.30       650.25    17458.55
       38     CLERK       ABRAHAMS     12009.75       236.50    12246.25
       38     CLERK       NAUGHTON     12954.75       180.00    13134.75
 = HELP          2 =            3 = END      4 = PRINT      5 =              6 = QUERY
 = BACKWARD      8 = FORWARD    9 = FORM    10 = LEFT      11 = RIGHT       12 =
K, REPORT IS DISPLAYED.
OMMAND →                                                   SCROLL → PAGE
```

Figure 14.8   Results of controlling spacing between columns.

14.6.4   Editing the Column Headings

We can edit the column headings by using the following codes to change the EDIT column on the FORM panel:

CODE	DEFINITION
C	CHARACTER
L	NUMERIC, NO DECIMAL
L1	NUMERIC, ONE DECIMAL
D	DOLLAR AMOUNT, NO CENTS
D2	DOLLAR AMOUNT, WITH
P	CENTS
P1	PERCENT, NO DECIMAL
	PERCENT, ONE DECIMAL

Figures 14.9 and 14.10 illustrate the editing of columns.

```
FORM. COLUMNS        ENTMS099.QMF085_0

                        REPORT WIDTH IS NOW: 69
NUM    COLUMN HEADING                         USAGE   INDENT   WIDTH   EDIT

 1     DEPT._NUMBER                                     2        6      L
 2     JOB                                              4        5      C
 3     EMPLOYEE_NAME                                    4        9      C
 4     SALARY                                           2       10      D2
 5     COMMISSIONS                                      2       10      D2
 6     TOTAL_EARNINGS                                   2       12      D2
       *** END ***
1=HELP        2=CHECK      3=END        4=FORM.MAIN    5=FORM.OPTIONS   6=QUERY
7=BACKWARD    8=FORWARD    9=FORM.PAGE  10=FORM.FINAL  11=FORM.BREAK1   12=REPORT
OK, FORM.COLUMNS IS DISPLAYED.
COMMAND →                                                    SCROLL → PAGE
```

Figure 14.9 Editing of columns.

```
REPORT                                       LINE 1     POS 1      79
      DEPT.              EMPLOYEE                        TOTAL
      NUMBER     JOB       NAME      SALARY  COMMISSIONS EARNINGS
++ ———————++++———————++++——————— ++ ——————— ++ ——————————— ++ ——————— — — —

      DEPT.              EMPLOYEE                        TOTAL
      NUMBER     JOB       NAME      SALARY  COMMISSIONS  EARNINGS

        15      SALES    ROTHMAN    ********   $1152.00   $17,654.83
        15      CLERK    KERMISCH   ********    $110.10   $12,368.60
        15      CLERK    NGAN       ********    $206.60   $12,714.80
        20      SALES    PERNAL     ********    $612.45   $18,783.70
        20      CLERK    JAMES      ********    $128.20   $13,632.80
        20      CLERK    SNEIDER    ********    $126.50   $14,379.25
        38      SALES    O'BRIEN    ********    $846.55   $18,852.55
        38      SALES    QUIGLEY    ********    $650.25   $17,458.55
        38      CLERK    ABRAHAMS   ********    $236.50   $12,246.25
        38      CLERK    NAUGHTON   ********    $180.00   $13,134.75
1 = HELP       2 =           3 = END    4 = PRINT    5 =            6 = QUERY
7 = BACKWARD   8 = FORWARD   9 = FORM   10 = LEFT    11 = RIGHT     12 =
OK, REPORT IS DISPLAYED.
COMMAND →                                                    SCROLL → PAGE
```

Figure 14.10 Results of editing of columns.

14.6.5 The USAGE Code

The USAGE code shows how a column is used. The following table lists the codes and their meanings.

USAGE CODE	MEANING
BLANK	Display or Print the column
OMIT	Do not display the column
SUM	To display the column and add it to the total at the bottom of the column
CSUM	To show the cumulative total for each line of the report
AVERAGE	To average the values in a column
MAXIMUM	To choose the maximum value in a column
MINIMUM	To choose the minimum value in a column
COUNT	To count the non-null values in a column
PCT	To show the percent that each line represents of the total for the column in the report

The results of the USAGE code in a column are shown in Figs. 14.11 and 14.12.

```
'ORM. COLUMNS        ENTMS099.QMF086_0

                          REPORT WIDTH IS NOW: 70
JUM    COLUMN HEADING                        USAGE    INDENT   WIDTH    EDIT

 1     DEPT._NUMBER                                     2        6       L
 2     JOB                                              4        5       C
 3     EMPLOYEE_NAME                                    4        9       C
 4     SALARY                            ─→ SUM         2        11      D2
 5     COMMISSIONS                       ─→ SUM         2        11      D2
 6     TOTAL_EARNINGS                    ─→ SUM         2        12      D2
       *** END ***
=HELP       2=CHECK       3=END        4=FORM.MAIN    5=FORM.OPTIONS   6=QUERY
=BACKWARD  8=FORWARD   9=FORM.PAGE  10=FORM.FINAL  11=FORM.BREAK1   12=REPORT
)K, FORM.COLUMNS IS DISPLAYED.
:OMMAND →                                            SCROLL → PAGE
```

Figure 14.11   The USAGE code.

```
REPORT                                          LINE 1      POS 1      79
     DEPT.              EMPLOYEE                               TOTAL
     NUMBER     JOB      NAME        SALARY    COMMISSIONS    EARNINGS
++ ————————++++————————++++———————— ++ ————————— ++ ————————— ++ —————————


     DEPT.              EMPLOYEE                               TOTAL
     NUMBER     JOB      NAME        SALARY    COMMISSIONS    EARNINGS
    ————————            ————————    —————————  —————————     —————————
         15    SALES    ROTHMAN     $16,502.83   $1,152.00   $17,654.83
         15    CLERK    KERMISCH    $12,258.50     $110.10   $12,368.60
         15    CLERK    NGAN        $12,508.20     $206.60   $12,714.80
         20    SALES    PERNAL      $18,171.25     $612.45   $18,783.70
         20    CLERK    JAMES       $13,504.60     $128.20   $13,632.80
         20    CLERK    SNEIDER     $14,252.75     $126.50   $14,379.25
         38    SALES    O'BRIEN     $18,006.00     $846.55   $18,852.55
         38    SALES    QUIGLEY     $16,808.30     $650.25   $17,458.55
         38    CLERK    ABRAHAMS    $12,009.75     $236.50   $12,246.25
         38    CLERK    NAUGHTON    $12,954.75     $180.00   $13,134.75
 1 = HELP       2 =           3 = END      4 = PRINT    5 =          6 = QUERY
 7 = BACKWARD   8 = FORWARD   9 = FORM    10 = LEFT    11 = RIGHT   12 =
OK, REPORT IS DISPLAYED.
COMMAND →                                               SCROLL → PAGE

REPORT                                          LINE 1      POS 1      79
     DEPT.              EMPLOYEE                               TOTAL
     NUMBER     JOB      NAME        SALARY    COMMISSIONS    EARNINGS
++ ————————  ++  ————————  ++  ———————— ++ ————————— ++ ————————— ++ —————————

                                     =========   =========    =========
                          →        $146,976.93   $4,249.15  $151,226.08
*** END ***
```

Figure 14.12 Results of the USAGE code.

```
FORM.COLUMNS        ENTMS099.QMF088_0

                         REPORT WIDTH IS NOW: 70
NUM     COLUMN HEADING                      USAGE    INDENT   WIDTH    EDIT
  ——    ——————————————                      —————    ——————   —————    ————
  1     DEPT._NUMBER                    →    BREAK1     2        6       L
  2     JOB                                             4        5       C
  3     EMPLOYEE_NAME                                   4        9       C
  4     SALARY                               SUM        2       11       D2
  5     COMMISSIONS                          SUM        2       11       D2
  6     TOTAL_EARNINGS                       SUM        2       12       D2
        *** END ***
1=HELP        2=CHECK      3=END        4=FORM.MAIN    5=FORM.OPTIONS   6=QUERY
7=BACKWARD    8=FORWARD    9=FORM.PAGE  10=FORM.FINAL  11=FORM.BREAK1   12=REPORT
OK, FORM.COLUMNS IS DISPLAYED.
COMMAND →                                               SCROLL → PAGE
```

Figure 14.13 Formatting by USAGE code.

14.6.6 Formatting with the USAGE Code

The USAGE code determines where subtotals are taken in the report. In this instance, the control column is used to control the display of results from another column. Control columns that are used as breaks must appear in the ORDER BY clause in the sequence in which the breaks are taken. The sequence of the breaks is:

- BREAK1 the major sort key
- BREAK2 the minor sort key
- BREAK6 the lowest-level sort key

Figures 14.13 and 14.14 illustrate formatting by the USAGE code.

```
REPORT                                              LINE 1      POS 1      79
   DEPT.                    EMPLOYEE                             TOTAL
   NUMBER       JOB           NAME        SALARY   COMMISSIONS   EARNINGS
++ ———————— ++++ ———————— ++++ ———————— ++ ———————— ++ ———————— ++ ————————

   DEPT.                    EMPLOYEE                             TOTAL
   NUMBER       JOB           NAME        SALARY   COMMISSIONS   EARNINGS
   ————————      ————          ————       ————————  ———————————   ————————
      15       SALES        ROTHMAN     $16,502.83   $1,152.00   $17,654.83
               CLERK        KERMISCH    $12,258.50     $110.10   $12,368.60
               CLERK        NGAN        $12,508.20     $206.60   $12,714.80
                              ——→ *     $41,269.53   $1,468.70   $42,738.23
      20       SALES        PERNAL      $18,171.25     $612.45   $18,783.70
               CLERK        JAMES       $13,504.60     $128.20   $13,632.80
               CLERK        SNEIDER     $14,252.75     $126.50   $14,379.25
1 = HELP        2 =          3 = END       4 = PRINT    5 =         6 = QUERY
7 = BACKWARD    8 = FORWARD  9 = FORM     10 = LEFT    11 = RIGHT  12 =
OK, REPORT IS DISPLAYED.
COMMAND →                                                  SCROLL → PAGE
```

```
REPORT                                              LINE 16     POS 1
   DEPT.                    EMPLOYEE                             TOTAL
   NUMBER       JOB           NAME        SALARY   COMMISSIONS   EARNINGS
++ ———————— ++++ ———————— ++++ ———————— ++ ———————— ++ ———————— ++ ————————
                              ——→ *     $45,928.60     $867.15   $46,795.75

      38       SALES        O'BRIEN     $18,006.00     $846.55   $18,852.55
               SALES        QUIGLEY     $16,808.30     $650.25   $17,458.55
               CLERK        ABRAHAMS    $12,009.75     $236.50   $12,246.25
               CLERK        NAUGHTON    $12,954.75     $180.00   $13,134.75
                              ——→ *     $59,778.80   $1,913.30   $61,692.10


                                       $146,976.93   $4,249.15  $151,226.08
*** END ***
```

Figure 14.14 Results of formatting by the USAGE code.

```
FORM. MAIN       ENTMS099. QMF089_0

COLUMNS:                         REPORT WIDTH IS NOW:  70
NUM     COLUMN HEADING                        USAGE     INDENT     WIDTH     EDIT

  1     DEPT._NUMBER                          BREAK1      2          6         L
  2     JOB                                               4          5         C
  3     EMPLOYEE_NAME                                     4          9         C
  4     SALARY                                SUM         2         11         D2
  5     COMMISSIONS                           SUM         2         11         D2
PAGE:     HEADING → DIVISION EARNINGS REPORT  ←——
          FOOTING → COMPANY CONFIDENTIAL ←——
FINAL:    TEXT → TOTALS ←——
BREAK1:    NEW PAGE FOR BREAK? → NO
              FOOTING →
BREAK2:    NEW PAGE FOR BREAK? → NO
              FOOTING →
OPTIONS:      OUTLINE? → YES            DEFAULT BREAK TEXT? → YES
1=HELP       2=CHECK      3=END        4=FORM. COLUMNS   5=FORM. OPTIONS   6=QUERY
7=BACKWARD   8=FORWARD  9=FORM. PAGE  10=FORM. FINAL     11=FORM. BREAK1   12=REPORT
OK, FORM. MAIN IS DISPLAYED.
COMMAND →                                                   SCROLL → PAGE
```

Figure 14.15   Entries to FORM.MAIN panel.

14.6.7   Adding Subheadings to a Report

Subheadings are added to a report by using HEADING, FOOTING, and
TEXT entries of the FORM.MAIN panel. For example, if we wanted to
add Division Earnings Report, Company Confidential, and Totals to the
following report, we would make the entries to the FORM.MAIN panel
as shown in Fig. 14.15. The results of those entries are shown in Fig.
14.16.

```
REPORT                                           LINE 1      POS 1      79
    DEPT.                      EMPLOYEE                      TOTAL
    NUMBER      JOB              NAME         SALARY    COMMISSIONS    EARNINGS
++ ─────── ++++ ─────── ++++ ─────── ++ ─────── ++ ─────── ++ ───────
                              DIVISION EARNINGS REPORT ⟵──

    DEPT.                      EMPLOYEE                                 TOTAL
    NUMBER      JOB              NAME         SALARY    COMMISSIONS    EARNINGS
                              ──────          ──────    ──────         ──────

      15       SALES          ROTHMAN       $16,502.83   $1,152.00    $17,654.83
               CLERK          KERMISCH      $12,258.50     $110.10    $12,368.60
               CLERK          NGAN          $12,508.20     $206.60    $12,714.80
                                       *    $41,269.53   $1,468.70    $42,738.23
      20       SALES          PERNAL        $18,171.25     $612.45    $18,783.70
               CLERK          JAMES         $13,504.60     $128.20    $13,632.80
               CLERK          SNEIDER       $14,252.75     $126.50    $14,379.25
1 = HELP           2 =              3 = END        4 = PRINT       5 =          6 = QUERY
7 = BACKWARD       8 = FORWARD      9 = FORM      10 = LEFT       11 = RIGHT    12 =
OK, REPORT IS DISPLAYED.
COMMAND →                                                        SCROLL → PAGE
```

```
REPORT                                           LINE 16     POS 1      79
    DEPT.                      EMPLOYEE                       TOTAL
    NUMBER      JOB              NAME         SALARY    COMMISSIONS    EARNINGS
++ ─────── ++ ─────── ++ ─────── ++ ─────── ++ ─────── ++ ───────

                                       *    $45,928.60     $867.15    $46,795.75
      38       SALES          O'BRIEN       $18,006.00     $846.55    $18,852.55
               SALES          QUIGLEY       $16,808.30     $650.25    $17,458.55
               CLERK          ABRAHAMS      $12,009.75     $236.50    $12,246.25
               CLERK          NAUGHTON      $12,954.75     $180.00    $13,134.75
                                       *    $59,778.80   $1,913.30    $61,692.10
                    ──⟶ TOTALS
                                            $146,976.93   $4,249.15   $151,226.08

                    ──⟶ COMPANY CONFIDENTIAL
1 = HELP           2 =              3 = END        4 = PRINT       5 =          6 = QUERY
7 = BACKWARD       8 = FORWARD      9 = FORM      10 = LEFT       11 = RIGHT    12 =
OK, FORWARD PERFORMED. PLEASE PROCEED.
COMMAND →                                                        SCROLL → PAGE
```

Figure 14.16   Results of entries to FORM.MAIN panel.

CHAPTER 15

Introduction to ORACLE

15.1 Introduction

At the heart of ORACLE is a set of fourth-generation environment (4GE) tools. These include:

- ORACLE RDBMS
- SQL*PLUS
- SQL*FORMS
- CASE*METHOD
- CASE*DESIGNER
- SQL*MENU
- SQL*REPORT WRITER
- SQL
- PRECOMPILERS

At the heart of ORACLE's 4GE toolset is SQL*FORMS, the high-level screen painter and forms application generator. Via a menu-driven interface, the designer uses SQL*FORMS to automatically generate the basic functionality, or "primitives," for any application—the end-user interface, appropriate field attributes, validation rules to ensure accurate data entry, cursor navigation to control application flow, and the screen manager to direct the flow of data traffic between the screen and the database.

SQL*FORMS is extensible. For more robust application, the default logic supplied by SQL*FORMS can be augmented. SQL*FORMS lets the designer embed SQL statements at various event points in the application to do unique validation checking, perform complex field computations, or retrieve related information from the database. SQL*FORMS provides a macro language for reprogramming function keys, customizing the keyboard layout, calling other forms, performing if-then-else logic on field variables, and passing variable strings between forms with the application.

The other major 4GE tools are:

- SQL*Report Writer—A nonprocedural report written for controlling a range of report output formats.
- SQL*MENU—A nonprocedural menuing system with a choice of menu styles for application integration.
- CASE*Method—A proven, structured design methodology that provides application designers with practical techniques for analyzing users' requirements and then developing systems that fully satisfy those requirements.
- CASE*Designer—A multi-user design dictionary to capture application information for system documentation. Information stored in the dictionary can also be used as source input for automatically generating the table design and the application code.

15.2 Querying the Database

SQL is the main query language used by ORACLE to query the database. SQL processes entire groups or sets of records at a time, in contrast to procedural languages, which perform repetitive processing on single records.

Though powerful, SQL does not offer as much flexibility or programming control as procedural languages offer. SQL is not a full programming language; it is a database access and manipulation language.

15.2.1 The SELECT Command

As in all other relational database management systems, ORACLE supports the high usage of the SELECT command. SQL*PLUS is the 4GE tool used by ORACLE to display the results of a SELECT command.

SQL*PLUS displays column names as defined when the table you want to query is created, and truncates them according to column width. When issuing a query, you can change the name of the column on the fly by adding a new name, often called an alias name, after the column name.

Although you can change the name of a column in a query, the new name lives only for the life of the query. An alternative approach is to use the COLUMN format command, an SQL*PLUS command that is far more flexible and enduring. The COLUMN format command lets you alter the format of the column and heading, including the column name, its width, and its justification position, and whether to wrap or truncate text. The new format endures for the duration of your SQL*PLUS session. A changed column displays the new format any time the column is referred to by any query until it is redefined or until you exit SQL*PLUS.

The COLUMN format command is issued at the SQL> prompt and would look similar to the following example:

> SQL > COLUMN TITLE FORMAT A25 HEADING 'Film Title'

The format parameter controls the column width. Different format models are available for character, number, and data fields. As in the preceding example, the width of a character field is defined with an 'a', followed by the new width of the column; the width of a number field is defined by the digit 9, repeated once for each digit of the new width.

The HEADING parameter controls the displayed column name. If the new heading contains blanks or punctuation, it must be enclosed in single quotes.

You can reset a column to its default format, the format originally defined when the table was created, by using the DEFAULT parameter as follows:

> SQL > COLUMN title DEFAULT

To view the column format for a given column, simply enter the COL-UMN command followed by the column name as follows:

> SQL > COLUMN title

15.2.2   Editing SQL Commands

SQL*PLUS temporarily stores SQL commands that you enter in a buffer. The commands remain in the buffer until you enter a new SQL command or explicitly clear the buffer. With the aid of several SQL edit commands, you can examine, modify, or rerun the current SQL command without reentering it.

The SQL edit commands are line-oriented, allowing you to manipulate—change, append, delete, and add—a single SQL command line at a time. They are handy when constructing a query that is constantly being modified and reexecuted. However, when working with longer queries or highly formatted reports composed of multiple queries, you must use a text editor. The SQL edit commands are listed in Table 15.1.

Table 15.1. SQL Edit Commands

Command	Abbreviation	Purpose
APPEND	A text	Add text at the end of a line
CHANGE	C/old/new	Change old text to new
CHANGE	c/text/	Delete text from a line
CLEAR BUFFER	CL BUFF	Delete everything in a buffer
INPUT	I	Add an indefinite number of lines
INPUT	I text	Add a line of text
LIST	L	List all lines in SQL buffer
LIST n	Ln	List one line
LIST mn	Lmn	List range of lines (m to n)
RUN	R	Run the current SQL command

15.2.3 Building an SQL Command File

When working with longer queries or designing highly formatted reports, you may want to work with a text editor and build SQL command files. However, while constructing a query on-line, you can save it to a text file. You can save the contents of the current SQL buffer to disk with the SAVE command, which can be recalled or run directly from the command file. ORACLE appends the suffix .SQL to the saved file unless you specify a different suffix.

The operative commands for working with script files within SQL*PLUS are shown in Table 15.2.

15.3 Advanced SQL Capabilities

Character values, such as products, titles, customers, addresses, and other text, are normally displayed in the same form as they were entered into the database. If you enter a title code in uppercase, for example, it will be displayed in uppercase, unless you use one of the many

Table 15.2. Command File Commands

Command	Purpose
SAVE File	Saves current SQL buffer to the named file
GET File	Retrieves named file to the current SQL buffer
START File	Retrieves the named file and runs it automatically
HOST dir*.sql	Lists the SQL script files stored in the operating system directory

SQL*PLUS character expressions of functions that can transform the way character values appear when displayed.

SQL*PLUS lets you combine character columns and constraints into character expressions. A character express can be manipulated and selected as though it were a single column.

15.3.1 Field Concentration

One prevalent use of character expressions is to string two or more columns together and display them as a single column. This is called field concatenation. To concatenate fields, you use the concatenate operator (: :) in a query as follows:

```
SELECT category :: description
FROM category
```

This would result in, for example:

CATEGORY :: DESCRIPTION
```
100   ADVENTURE
120   COMEDY
135   CLASSICS
140   MUSICALS
165   HORROR
899   SLASHER
```

When concentrating fields, SQL*PLUS removes any trailing blanks in the first column that you specify. To fix the appearance of the display, you might separate the values with literal blanks enclosed in single quotes and perhaps add an alias as follows:

```
SELECT category :: ' ' description "film category"
FROM category
```

The result will be:

FILM CATEGORY
CATEGORY :: DESCRIPTION
```
100   ADVENTURE
120   COMEDY
135   CLASSICS
```

140   MUSICALS
165   HORROR
899   SLASHER

15.3.2 Date Functions

SQL*PLUS offers many functions to empower date arithmetic expressions. You can use numbers to add or subtract calendar days to and from dates. With the ADD_MONTHS function, you can manipulate calendar months in arithmetic expressions as well. For example, you can pinpoint the exact date six months from April 1, 1988, by entering:

    SELECT ADD_MONTH ('01-APR-88', +6)
    FROM Table

This returns:

    ADD_MONTH
    01-OCT-88

Instead of using a constant you can plug in the pseudocolumn "sysdate." To find the exact date 15 months from today, if today's date is "15-APR-88," enter:

    SELECT ADD_MONTHS (sysdate, +15)
    FROM table

This returns:

    ADD_MONTH
    15-JUL-89

15.4 The SQL*FORMS Design Program

SQL*FORMS contains two parts: SQL*FORMS (Design) used to design and create forms and SQL*FORMS (Runform) to execute forms built with the Design program. The ability to run a form from the Design program cuts down debugging time because you do not need to log out of the program to generate and execute the form, and then log back when you are finished.

SQL*FORMS lets you design a form on the screen and modify it interactively until you are satisfied with it. There are essentially three levels of form design:

1. Creating the blocks and fields—The simplest form is merely a window on the base tables without any special validation or functionality.
2. Defining the blocks and fields—Once the form is laid out, you can enhance it by adding validation and functionality.
3. Defining triggers—At this advanced level, you take the foundation of the form and mold it into a robust application. You provide complex validation by writing "triggers." These are SQL statements.

15.5 Generating Reports

SQL*PLUS's reporting extensions let you easily control the output format of ad hoc reports, including header and foot titles, line positioning, page size, and page numbering controls. SQL*PLUS provides much finer control of page formatting, margin, spacing, and column layout of the printed output than is offered by SQL. With SQL*PLUS, you can design complex tabular reports, organizing groups of rows in the report on column, row, page, or report breaks, and computing subtotals on any combination of breaks.

15.5.1 Specifying Report Breaks

You can organize rows of a report into groups with the BREAK command, and you can dictate special actions that a query should take when the report "breaks" on these rows. For example, you can skip a line when the break occurs, start a new page, or compute subtotals on the rows organized by the break.

SQL*PLUS lets you organize rows at the following BREAK points:

On a single column	BREAK on column
On more than one column	BREAK on column
Whenever a row is retrieved	BREAK on Page
At the end of the report	BREAK on Report

15.5.2 SQL*PLUS Reportwriter

SQL*Reporterwriter is a comprehensive reporting tool that meets virtually all your production reporting needs. With SQL*Reportwriter, you can develop a full range of business reports, including:

- Versatile tabular and control break reports
- Multisection reports
- Matrix reports, such as crosstabs with cross-tabulation of data laid out in a spreadsheet format
- Wide reports with repeated columns, and so spread reports that are wider than a page onto multiple pages

15.6 SQL*MENU

SQL*MENU is based on SQL*FORMS technology and allows you to build a menu that lets you point to and select the menu choices—using the [UP] or [DOWN ARROW] keys to highlight choices—or simply enter the number of the menu choice. The menuing environment can be customized for different groups of users, and several menu commands and macros are available to control menu navigation. SQL*MENU can be linked with SQL*PLUS and SQL*FORMS tools for fast execution of forms and reports.

15.7 ORACLE-Supported Hardware Platforms

The following is a list of ORACLE-supported hardware platforms:

COMPANY	OPERATING SYSTEM
AT&T	UNIX SYSTEM V
ALTOS	UNIX SYSTEM V
AMDAHL	MVS/SP, MVS/XA
APOLLO	AEGIS-DOMAIN/1X
COMPAREX	MVS/SP, MVS/XA
CONTROL DATA	NOS/VE
CONVERGENT TECHNOLOGIES	CTIX
DANSK DATA	UNIX SYSTEM V

COMPANY	OPERATING SYSTEM
DDE	UNIX
DEC	VMS, ULTRIX
EDGE	UNIX
ENCORE	UNIX
GOULD	UNIX
HARRIS	VOS, UNIX SYSTEM V
HEWLETT-PACKARD	HP-VX
HONEYWELL-BULL	GCOS, UNIX SYSTEM V
IBM	MVS/SP, MVS/XA, VM/CMS
ICL	UNIX SYSTEM V, VME
MOTOROLA	UNIX
NAS	MVS/SP, MVS/XA, VM/CMS
NCR	UNIX SYSTEM V
NIXDORF	OSx
NORSK	SINTRAN
PCS	UNIX SYSTEM V
PLEXUS	UNIX SYSTEM V
PRIME	PRIME, UNIX
PYRAMID	OSx
SEQUENT	DYNIX
SIEMENS	BS2000, SINIX
STRATUS	VOS
SUN	SUNOS 3X
UNISYS	UNIX SYSTEM V
WANG	VS

CHAPTER 16

Performance Issues and Standards

16.1 Introduction

There are very few subjects in the database environment that are more controversial, yet more ambiguous, than the subjects of performance and standards. The issue of performance of a particular database management system is so important that failure to address it very often results in the lack of commercial acceptance of that DBMS. Information technology will succeed as a business endeavor only when that technology is standardized and the tools that drive the technology can be evaluated against a common set of guidelines.

This chapter looks at some of the most important issues in database performance and standardization and discusses how these two important aspects can be monitored.

16.2 The Database Management System Functions

It is generally accepted that all DBMSs should provide most or all of the following nine functions, items, and services:

- Storage, retrieval, and updating of data
- Integrity services to enforce database constraints
- A user-accessible catalog of definitions
- Control of concurrent processing
- Support of logical transactions
- Failure recovery
- Complete security provisions
- An interface to communications control programs
- Utility services

The performance of a database management system, whether relational or nonrelational, must be measured against these nine items.

16.2.1 Controlling Integrity with a DBMS

Application programs that maintain database contents by adding, deleting, and updating data typically have a very high percentage of their logic devoted to ensuring that these operations are valid and the content of the database is not corrupted. This may include code for validating that:

- Certain associated master data are present in the database before a new detail is added. For example, the program may check to ensure that a valid customer exists in the database before recording an order against that customer.
- An input value is placed in more than one location in the database. For example, the program may check to ensure that when the quantity on hand for a particular item is updated, that update is carried to all redundant occurrences of that value.
- Data are not still referencing or depending on data to be deleted from the database. For example, the program may check to ensure that a customer with outstanding orders is not inadvertently deleted from the database.

These integrity constraints should be controlled by the DBMS, not by the application program.

16.2.2 Relational Data Integrity Rules

The primary key provides guaranteed access to a single, unique tuple within a relation. In fact, if the name of the relation, the value of the primary key, and the name of the attribute are known, every attribute value in a relational database is directly addressable. This helps to identify one of the most important properties in electing a primary key from among several candidate keys: the primary key should be one that will definitely remain unique over time. Its important identification role is supported by the first of two relational data integrity rules: no part of the primary key value may be null.

Associations between tuples that occur in the organization, whose data are being modeled by the database, must also be represented. In a relational data model, these associations are represented by storing the referenced tuple's primary key in the referencing tuple. These foreign occurrences of primary key values are called foreign keys. The referencing role played by the foreign occurrences of primary keys is supported by the second of the two relational data integrity rules: the value of a foreign key must reference a valid existing tuple where that value is the primary key.

Relations in a relational database must be normalized. There are multiple levels of normalization, from first normal form, through second, third, Boyce–Codd, fourth, and fifth normal forms. When to stop in the normalization process is a matter of judgment for the designer, but a relational database must be in at least first normal form.

Domains are also central to the enforcement of the integrity of foreign key values. Regardless of the role name of the foreign key attributes, the foreign key's existence can be identified through the knowledge that the domain is the same as an existing primary key. The knowledge of which domains are represented by the attributes of the primary key makes this possible.

Entity integrity ensures that a value is provided for the attributes whenever a new tuple is added to this relation. Domain definition ensures that that value represents a read product for the organization.

Referential integrity ensures that any value provided for an attribute not only is valid for the domain definition but also appears as the primary key value to some tuple in the main relation. The ability to define domains directly and associate every attribute with a domain is a cornerstone component of the relational data model.

16.2.3 Relational DBMS Performance Issues

A relational database system is termed fully relational if it supports:

- Relational databases including the concepts of domain and key and the two integrity rules
- A language that is at least as powerful as the relational algebra and that would remain so even if all facilities for loops and recursions were to be deleted

The combination of the three concepts of fully relational (i.e., relational structure, manipulation, and integrity), a three-schema architecture, and full DBMS capability results in a basic definition of what a relational DBMS should be: a system that functions as a full capability DBMS, based on a three-schema architecture, and that supports relational databases and a powerful relational language.

Because applications are not tied to any one data structuring technique, an organization can use any number of data structures, for example, indexing, hashing, chaining, clustering, sequential, flat, or coded. The flexibility to choose the most effective data structuring technique for each application translates into improved performance. However, some relational systems require the use of only one data structuring technique, which can yield ineffective performance.

In the absence of a three-schema relational DBMS, many organizations have had to follow a two-database strategy. To improve performance, a nonrelational DBMS typically controls the production environment and a relational DBMS supports end-user and information center needs.

Another way to improve performance in any DBMS is to provide tools for reducing the number of I/O's needed to access data. As the database is tuned, I/O's should always be minimized. In the relational system, the key is the optimizer and how well it translates relational operations on the conceptual schema into efficient physical file access.

Designing and tuning the database in the internal schema without changing the definition of views used by applications increase performance. The three-schema architecture used with relational technology and an efficient optimizer provides the performance required in heavy transaction-oriented data processing environments.

16.3 Improving SQL/DS Performance

As with any data access method, the proper tuning of the database management system is essential for the efficient operation of the system. The place to start tuning SQL/DS is on the system level. First, be sure that the Directory data set is located on a DASD device that contains no other SQL/DS data sets. The Directory is constantly being accessed by SQL/DS, so isolating it will speed access times by decreasing DASD contention. Isolation also helps to protect the Directory from DASD failures.

The next step is to look at your log data sets. As with the Directory, the log data set should be placed on a DASD device that contains no other SQL/DS data sets. The data sets on the DASD device with the log should also be ones that are not heavily accessed.

If you are using dual logging, you are probably doing twice as much I/O for logging than is needed. If you have isolated your log data set from the rest of the database, you are fairly safe using a single log data set. If you lose the data, you have the log to recover from. If you lose the log, you have the data and can initialize a new log data set to restart the system.

If you are using a log archiving (LOG MODE = L), then automatic log archives will be initiated when the percentage of log space used equals the value of the initialization parameter ARCHPCT. To keep automatic logs from starting, set ARCHPCT at about 90. Also, be sure to regularly take log archives during a time period when the database is not heavily accessed.

16.3.1   Buffer Pool Tuning

SQL/DS operates with two buffer pools to increase I/O efficiency. The buffer pools are the Directory block pool and the data page pool, the number of which are specified at initialization time by the parameters NDIRBUF and NPAGBUF, respectively. The 512-byte Directory block buffers contain the most recently used Directory blocks and the 4096-byte buffers of the data page buffers contain the most recently accessed data pages. The tuning of these pools can be one of the most important performance factors and one of the easiest to change.

To determine how effective these values are at reducing DASD I/O in your current system, use the COUNTER* operator command. Calculate the hit ratio for each pool by dividing LPAGBUF by PAGEREAD and LDIRBUF by DIRREAD. This ratio shows you how often the I/O request was able to be satisfied by data already in the buffers. For example, a page pool ratio of five means that for every five requests for database page data, only one needed to go to the DASD device for the data.

Deciding how large to make the buffer pools can be difficult and is affected by the amount of virtual and real memory available. The default value for both pools is 14 buffers in each. Since Directory blocks are only an eighth the size of page pools, begin by increasing the Directory block buffers by two to three times. Repeat the process for page pool and observe the LDIRBUF/DIRREAD ratio. If it has increased, you have improved the Directory block buffer performance.

16.3.2   Concurrent Users Tuning

The number of concurrent users (NCUSERS) that the system can handle is another important performance consideration. Each user link requires a minimum of 16K of real storage and a minimum of 54K for each ISQL user. The value of NCUSERS might be high enough to allow for the average number of concurrent on-line users that you will have, plus at least one batch user. To determine if your NCUSERS value is appropriate, use the SHOW ACTIVE operator command. If at peak usage times the number of active users tends to be significantly lower than the value of NCUSERS, lower the value of NCUSERS. On the other hand, if the number of users tends to be constantly close to the NCUSERS value, you may need to increase the value of NCUSERS if real storage is available.

Again using the COUNTER* command, look at the checkpoint interval, CHKINTVL. For a system with a small database or a large database that is infrequently modified, CHKINTVL should be between 200 and 300. For a large volatile database, the value should be between 50 and 100. The number represents how many log data-set pages may be filled before a checkpoint is taken.

There are two advantages to increasing the checkpoint interval. First, the overhead involved in the checkpointing process may be considerably reduced. Second, the frequency of checkpoint delays is reduced by reducing the number of times checkpoints must be taken.

There are also disadvantages to increasing the checkpoint interval. First, the length of time needed to restart SQL/DS after a system failure will increase. Second, though the number of times the checkpoint needs to be taken decreases, the length of time the checkpoint will take to complete will increase.

16.4 Database-Level Considerations

Indexing tables, data clustering, placement of tables in DBSPACES, nonrecoverable storage pools, and maintaining table statistics can be done on the database level to improve performance.

Every table should have at least one index, preferably one that is clustered and reflects the method by which the data will most frequently be accessed. If the table does not, do a DBSPACE scan to locate the requested data.

There are several techniques that can be used to increase the efficiency of an index. If possible, make the index unique so that each index entry points to only one data row. Also, the index should be clustered. Clustering is simply loading the data so that rows with similar values are located near each other. A large table should be placed in its own DBSPACE. This prevents DBSPACE scans from searching data from other tables.

Tables that are read-only or are "work tables" should be placed in nonrecoverable storage pools. This eliminates the overhead of logging and checkpoint processing for these tables.

16.5 Performance Tuning for Applications

If no other users are accessing the table during a program's execution, consider issuing the lock table statement to reduce CPU consumption caused by page locks.

Avoid using subroutines for I/O if possible. It is difficult to construct a query that meets the needs of many applications. As a result, there is a tendency to transfer more data, which also means more cross-memory calls. You may find that changing the SQL statements is more desirable than having application programs contain logic to discard unwanted columns and rows.

The parameters specified during the BIND process can have a major impact on the performance of your application program. VALIDATE at BIND time is preferred over VALIDATE at RUN time. The tables and columns will be checked for existence and the individual binder is checked to determine if he or she has the authority to execute SQL statements contained in the program being prepared for execution. Validation at RUN time causes the validation process to be delayed until the first time the plan is accessed. The first user will experience delays while the validation process is performed.

Use static SQL over dynamic SQL whenever possible. Dynamic SQL has to go through the same BIND functions associated with static SQL for every execution. It has to be read, verified, prepared for execution, checked for authorization of binder, and then executed. There is significant cost for the SQL flexibility associated with dynamic SQL. If you have to use dynamic SQL, avoid views if possible because SYSIBM.SYSTABLES and SYSIBM.SYS-COLUMNS are accessed once for the view and again for the base table.

Declaring a SELECT . . . FOR UPDATE OF avoids potential deadlocks with other applications that are processing concurrently, which would not be the case if you issued independent of the select. In performing multiple row updates and deletes, issuing queries to do set processing is the most efficient; then cursors will be the next choice; followed finally by multiple update and delete statements. If the column you are updating is contained in an index you may want to consider deleting the row and reinserting it. Unless the update can use another index, a scan would be required.

16.6 Performance Monitoring

Monitoring the applications running on a DB2 system can require the use of many different tools. The first such tool is the DISPLAY command. The DISPLAY THREAD command can be used to display the status of a thread or connection to DB2. Coupled with the DISPLAY DATABASE command, you can determine what plan a particular user is executing and the kind of locks held on the tablespace and index space data sets. For monitoring utilities, the DISPLAY UNTIL command is very useful in following the progress of a large load or REORG. It provides information on which of the several phases are currently being executed. In the UNLOAD and RELOAD phases, the number of rows processed is recorded and made available to the DB2 command processor.

The EXPLAIN statement is an excellent tool to analyze a query prior to execution. It displays the access method to be used, what indexes if any will be used, the order in which tables and composite tables are accessed, the order in which multiple tables will be joined, which of the join methods will be used, whether sort needs to be invoked, and the type of locks to be issued. All queries where index usage is expected should be explained.

16.7 DB2 Standards for Performance

The database world is still struggling to decide on standards for a data dictionary, measurement of productivity, and even performance. Here we are not attempting to establish any elaborate standards, but merely to list a few statements regarding what should be in place in various areas of DB2 processing. The following table lists performance areas and recommendations.

AREAS	RECOMMENDATION
Denormalization	Denormalize tables if there is a requirement to update joined tables
Vertical partitioning	Consider vertical partitioning on tables with a large number of columns
Pre-Join tables	When data items from two or more tables are nearly always accessed together, create a single table rather than multiple separate tables
Allocation of DASD space	Use 4096 page size for DB2 data sets

AREAS	RECOMMENDATION
Create free space	It is better to increase PCTFREE and leave FREEPAGE at the default of zero
Locking	If row level locking is desired, consider specifying PCTFREE of 90
Table spaces	Use partitioned table spaces for very large tables
Null columns	Specify NOT NULL WITH DEFAULT OR NOT NULL when defining columns that have no specific need for nullable columns
VARCHAR	Only use VARCHAR when the field is at least 32 bytes in length and there is a 30% savings per row length; the use of variable-length columns should be avoided unless there is a potential savings of at least 20 bytes per column
Variable-length columns	Place variable-length columns at the end of a row

CHAPTER 17

Auditing the DB2 Environment

17.1 Introduction

The introduction of databases and on-line systems in many businesses has offered several new opportunities as well as new control issues for internal auditors. Some of these control issues of databases in general and DB2 in particular are identified in this chapter, as are traditional controls for less complex data processing environments.

17.2 Auditing the Database Environment

The internal auditor must become involved in the following activities of the database environment:

- Planning for the database
- System design consideration
- Administration and coordination of the database effort
- Documentation of the database

Planning is a staff function and ensures that top management is involved in the decision to enter the database era and committed to continued support throughout the life of the database. Planning is also useful in determining the initial cost of going to a database environment and the operating cost thereafter. The internal auditor should be actively involved in this phase of the database design because it allows him or her to monitor the cost performance of the database and the application in relation to the planned cost.

One of the major failures of the database environment is neither the technology nor the supporting software, but the conflict that results from the need to share data in an integrated environment. The cause of these conflicts is very often the lack of planning for data sharing in the new environment. The internal auditors should be involved in the coordination of the data-sharing effort.

The internal auditor must now assess the corporation's ability to deal with contingencies and review the plans for recovery and backup of the database, as well as attest to its adequacy. Now that the organization's whole data resource is concentrated in one collection and is more vulnerable to accidental as well as intentional threats, the need for adequate contingency measures is greater. The internal auditor must be an integral part of the team that plans for these contingencies.

Database technology has affected the role of the internal auditor more than that of any other single individual. It has now become extremely difficult to audit "around the computer," so the auditor has to develop even greater breadth of data processing expertise than the increasingly specialized systems professional. The internal auditor must now be in a position to monitor the effective and efficient utilization of the new database technology.

The success of the database environment depends on the discipline introduced by a formal development life cycle that describes the deliverable for each phase of development, clear and well-understood responsibilities, and the role that each individual plays in the organization.

The internal auditor must become increasingly involved in systems development, preferably as part of the development team; she must review each phase of the development for proper controls, provision for audit trails, backup and recovery plans, and effective testing; and she must participate in developing those aspects of data administration planning that involve control and auditability, particularly the data dictionary plan. Internal auditors should understand that their support is essential and can lead to a more efficient, less complex, better-controlled database environment.

The internal auditor must be familiar with the commonly implemented controls that now migrate to the DBMS. Some of these controls include:

- Uniqueness checking
- Structure/semantic integrity
- Concurrency control
- Access control
- Restart/recovery
- Audit trail

The access control should include password, sign-on, and user identification verification and authentication. They should include automatic lock-out of users after at least three attempts to log on to the system and the creation of facilities to log those attempts. Access control should also include terminal security, logical terminal name usage, and the ability of security terminals to list, audit, and monitor security violations.

The auditor in the database environment consults with the user on the requirements for edit and validation rules, partial acceptance or rejection of errors, and responsibility for correctness. The auditor consults with the database administrator on the implementation plan and ensures the existence of procedures for edit and validation maintenance. He determines if the edit and validation rules are sufficient and examines the procedures for adding new data elements.

The auditor also specifies what checking of initial content of the database is carried out and may use statistical methods when appropriate to carry out these checks. He sets objectives for auditing, assessing the environment, and verifying the existence of controls.

The environment control objectives in the database environment should include:

- Adequate documentation
- Recovery and restart procedures
- Adequate security and accessibility
- Complete, accurate, and authorized data

17.3 Auditing of On-Line Systems

The control issues that are inherent in on-line systems are categorized into the following basic types:

- Unauthorized access
- Data file controls
- Transmission line controls
- Audit trial considerations
- Output controls
- Failure and recovery considerations

17.3.1 Unauthorized Access

Prevention of unauthorized access to the various stages of the on-line system is critical to the overall security and accuracy of operations. The controls against unauthorized access fall into two categories: physical and logical.

Physical controls are measures taken to prevent entry or access to installations. The standard safeguards needed in most installations will be security guards, locks, and keys, and personal identification.

Logical controls are measures taken to prevent access to the stored data, including:

- Passwords
- Verification routines
- Audit or management control log
- Restriction on the level or types of access by users

To ensure that logical controls are effectively utilized, a monitoring or review function should also be in existence. A cyclical review of the proper procedures performed each day is usually sufficient and should include the proper sign-on and sign-off procedures, unsuccessful attempts, and attempts to override or patch controls and programs during operations.

17.3.2 Data File Controls

As the transaction process continues from data entry to transmission, the next area of concern is data file protection and controls. The relationship between transaction and programs is reversed in on-line applications in that it is the transaction that uses a particular program or programs as opposed to the converse in batch systems.

In addition, multiple users may need a particular data file at or near the same time, which could lead to a conflict over priorities or errors due to incomplete or inaccurate updating. A supervisory program is usually employed to prevent application programs from getting to the database. This exclusive control function is responsible for granting permission for such access. While one program is using a file, others are prevented or locked out until control is passed back to the supervisory continue. This locking mechanism, present in DB2, eliminates the possibility of two programs becoming deadlocked when each has one file or record or rows and needs a second that the other program has, while waiting for the first.

17.3.3 Evaluation of Controls

In the on-line environment, a proper evaluation of the controls that should be in place as well as those that are in operation is necessary as a basis for any reliance on their use.

Proper documentation is one important element required for auditors to understand how and why the system operates as it does. With the loss of many conventional audit procedures inherent in such advanced systems, adequate description of the steps and stages of processing and record keeping will be the basis for choosing how the subsequent compliance and substantive testing will be done.

17.4 Inherent DB2 Control Features and Functions

The internal auditor who must audit the DB2 environment must be familiar with some of the environment control features. These features include:

- Provide effective protection of system resources and data from unauthorized intruders of a distributed database processing network
- Provide protection against unauthorized modifications to programs or system code by those responsible for installing and maintaining the system
- Execution of SQL operations, DB2 utilities, or commands requires the executor to hold specific authorities
- Properly capturing and reporting on authorization violations and security breaches
- Allow for the definition and enforcement of primary keys and entity integrity constraints
- Maintain an internal catalog integrity control mechanism that does not allow data structure definitions to be at variance or inconsistent with previously defined data objects
- Provide utilities and service aids to verify DB2 internal data structure integrity
- Provide performance monitoring and tuning facilities to ensure continuous, reliable DBMS operation and maintenance of service levels
- Provide data relationships by value instead of by pointer

17.5 Auditability of DB2

Auditability may be defined as the measures and provisions taken to facilitate the tracking and recording of significant processing events and system changes so that the controls in place can be effectively reviewed and assessed. DB2 has provision for auditability since it provides several of the features necessary for maintaining data integrity and security.

17.5.1 Evidence of Auditability in DB2

Auditability is established by the existence of and consistent use of audit trails. Auditability in DB2 should be established in the following areas:

- Transaction   Verify the complete, correct, and accurate processing transactions as intended.
- System   Record and track DB2 and application processing events, authorization activity, access attempts, and access denials.
- Recovery   Record DB2 system events and data changes in the event that a failure occurs and the DB2 system and/or its data need to be restored.
- Program change   Record and track changes to program or DB2 system code, definitions, and installation parameters.

17.5.2 DB2 Audit Objectives

The internal auditor who is auditing the DB2 environment must establish some audit objectives for his study and report. The following objectives are suggested:

- To examine the trail of DB2 system activity to alert management of potential or real: (a) security penetrations and authorization procedure breaches, (b) data integrity problems, and (c) duty segregation issues
- To assess the control techniques utilized to be reasonably assured that the database environment is conducive to the reliable, complete, and accurate processing of data used to prepare and report information

17.5.3 DB2 Audit Resources

DB2 provides a host of loop, catalogs, utilities, and reports that assist the internal auditor in conducting an audit of the environment. Some of these are:

- DB2 operating environment profile
- DB2 standards and procedures
- DB2 utilities

- DB2 Audit Trace Facility
- DBMAUI reports
- SQL EXPLAIN output
- DB2 display command output
- DB2PM reports and displays

Comparison of Relational DBMSs

This appendix covers the basic qualifications a product must have to be considered a relational database management system. It then looks at the more detailed list of facilities to be expected in such a system.

Does the product include the following features?

- Database definition separate from programs
- Multiple views possible against same database
- Facilities for administration of shared data
- Access control facilities (i.e., restriction of rights to see or change particular data to those authorized to do so)
- Concurrency control facilities (i.e., prevention of undesirable results or interaction in cases of simultaneous access to data)

Some products may be marketed under the "database" flag while failing to offer the basic facilities for sharing of data. The concept of a single-user database is really a contradiction in terms. Unless this is what you require, you will probably need some facilities under all the preceding headings.

Does the product include the following features?

- All commands are independent of the existence of any access path support (e.g., indexes)
- All data are viewed in third normal form (TNF) relations
- Command language includes functional capabilities equivalent to SELECT, PROJECT, and JOIN of relational algebra
- Data resulting from any command on existing relations are another relation (i.e., the system is "closed")
- Restructuring commands (ADD/DROP a table or column) are included and are executable interactively

	Database definition separate from programs	Multiple views	Administration of shared data	Access control	Concurrency control
ADABAS:	x	x	x	x	x
BL700:	x	x	x	x	x
CA-UNIVERSE:	x	x	x	x	x
CRESTA/DB:	x	x	x	x	x
DATACOM/DB:	x	x	x	x	x
DB2:	x	x	x	x	x
FOCUS:	x	x	x	x	x
IDMS/R:	x	x	x	x	x
Model 204:	x	x	x	x	x
ORACLE:	x	x	x	x	x
SQL/DS:	x	x	x	x	x
SUPRA:	x	x	x	x	x
Sybase:	x	x	x	x	x

These qualifications re-present the discussion in the introduction to this volume. A product that falls seriously short here should not be considered truly relational.

Mitigating circumstances might include the following:

1. A product with which hierarchical or network structures are possible, but where a "relational only" subset can be enforced.
2. A product that allows "export" of data to other systems may have facilities to create nonrelational data (this is an extension of the concept of printing a result relation in some report format).

A product with no JOIN functionality (see later question) should not be considered as a serious relational DBMS candidate.

In conclusion, one is forced to say that the products in the list fall into two classes:

● Those that are "relational" in the sense that they can *only* be used in a relational manner
● Those that are "relational" in the sense that they *can* limit usage to being in a relational manner by not using certain facilities or by masking them out by front ends

If the vendors of products in the second group claim to be flying the "relational" flag but then offer instructions to user staff that involve use of the product in a nonrelational manner (i.e., other than in the preceding questions), then they are not selling a relational DBMS!

Does the product permit the use of predefined access path support at the physical level? If so, which types of support are permitted?

- Primary key index
- Secondary indexes (including bit maps, etc.)
- Pointer arrays (index tables listing addresses or keys of records of type B that are related to each instance of record type A)
- Record chains

The existence of predefined access path support at the physical level does not necessarily disqualify a product from the "relational" club, as long as it is invisible to programs and DBA utilities (except for tuning purposes).

	Primary key index	Secondary indexes	Pointer arrays	Pointer chains	Other
ADABAS:	x	x	–	–	$
BL700:	x	x	–	–	–
CA-UNIVERSE:	x	x	–	–	–
CRESTA/DB:	x	x	x	–	–
DATACOM/DB:	x	x	x	–	–
DB2:	x	x	–	–	–
FOCUS:	x	x	–	x	*
IDMS/R:	x	x	–	x	–
Model 204:	–	x	x	–	–
ORACLE:	x	x	–	–	x!
SQL/DS:	x	x	–	–	–
SUPRA:	x	x	x	–	–
Sybase:	x	x	–	–	@

* Choice of above may be program defined
! Table clustering
+ Hash random and clustering
@ Clustered index
$ Hash random

Does the product provide the following relational features?

- Enforcement of referential integrity (i.e., allowing specification of constraints on "foreign keys")

- Enforcement of entity integrity (i.e., null values not allowed in primary keys)
- Definition of named VIEWS (i.e., virtual relations desirable by normal commands from stored relations or other VIEWS)
- "Outer" joins
- "Greater-than" and "less-than" joins as well as joins based on equality of corresponding attributes

These features are considered part of the mainstream relational theory but are not always included in relational DBMS products.

Referential integrity is important because it expresses how things work in many practical situations. For example, if one is adding orders to an order relation, then one should check that the customer number on the order already appears in the customer relation. Likewise, when deleting customers, one should ensure that there are no orders in the order relation with the same customer number as that being deleted. Customer number is a "foreign key" of the order relation, and the referential integrity constraint needed is that the customer number for any order must exist in the customer relation for some customer. In addition, null (i.e., unknown) foreign key values may or may not be permitted. Some older (i.e., prerelational) products allowed more here than the orthodox products like SQL, though sometimes integrity is forced on insertion but not on deletion.

Views have many uses, including access control and increased data independence. Some products offer a macro facility in the language that defines a view, but this is not to be considered equivalent as there is then no named virtual relation that can be treated as the object of further commands.

Outer joins also express the functionality required for many practical instances. When making a join, one often wishes to keep the information about the rows that do not have any match in the other relation. Instead of dropping this information, an outer join creates a row in the joined relation with null values for the attributes of the "other" relation.

Some of the positive answers to the first two questions may have been based on specifying the conditions within a command language rather than as a constraint embedded within the data definition. Another possibility is that those DBMSs allowing nonrelational structures may be enforcing referential integrity through their linkage mechanisms (e.g., hierarchies or Codasyl sets).

Commands independent of access path support
| Data viewed in TNF relations
| | SELECT, PROJECT, JOIN capabilities
| | | Closed system
| | | | Restructuring commands

	Commands independent of access path support	Data viewed in TNF relations	SELECT, PROJECT, JOIN capabilities	Closed system	Restructuring commands
ADABAS:	x	x	x	—	x
BL700:	x	x*	x	x	x
CA-UNIVERSE:	x	x	x	x	x
CRESTA/DB:	x	x	x	—	x
DATACOM/DB:	x	x	x	x	x
DB2:	x	x	x	x	x!
FOCUS:	x	x	x	x+	—
IDMS/R:	x	x	x	x	x
Model 204:	x	—	x	—	x
ORACLE:	x	x	x	x	x
SQL/DS:	x	x@	x	x	x^
SUPRA:	x	x	x	x	x
Sybase:	x	x	x	x	x

* This is possible but not required
! Yes; except "dropping" a column from an existing table is not possible
+ Optional under program control
@ Optional
^ Cannot drop a column

Referential integrity
| Entity integrity
| | Definition of named VIEWS
| | | Outer joins
| | | | Greater-than & less-than joins

	Referential integrity	Entity integrity	Definition of named VIEWS	Outer joins	Greater-than & less-than joins
ADABAS:	x	x	x	x	x
BL700:	—	x	x	x	x
CA-UNIVERSE:	x	x	x	x	x
CRESTA/DB:	—*	x	—	x	—
DATACOM/DB:	x	x	x	x	x
DB2:	x	x	x	—+	x
FOCUS:	x	x	—	x	—
IDMS/R:	x	x	x	x	x
Model 204:	x	x	x	x	x
ORACLE:	—	x	x	x	x
SQL/DS:	x	x	x	—	x
SUPRA:	x	x	x	x	x
Sybase:	x	x	x	x	x

* Partially
+ Except by Program Offering DB2 Outer Join

Does the product provide a freestanding "user language" in which the database can be accessed and updated without the use of a normal programming language? If so, does it conform to any of the following prospective or de facto standards?

- SQL (as ANSI X3 H2 draft standard)
- SQL superset
- QUEL (Berkeley-type RDBMS language)
- Vendor's own syntax

Whereas previous DBMSs were very often primarily host-language based, the norm with relational DBMSs is to base most access on a "user language," which may or may not be very suitable for naive users. Such a user language would be regarded as a requirement, and use of one of the de facto standards (SQL, QUEL) is desirable.

	SQL	SQL superset	QUEL	Vendor's own syntax	Other
ADABAS:	x	–	–	x	–
BL700:	x	–	x	–	–
CA-UNIVERSE:	–	x	x	–	–
CRESTA/DB:	–	–	–	x	–
DATACOM/DB:	x	x	–	x	–
DB2:	x	x	–	–	–
FOCUS:	x	–	–	x	–
IDMS/R:	x*	–	–	x	–
Model 204:	–	–	–	x	–
ORACLE:	x	x	–	–	–
SQL/DS:	x	x	–	–	–
SUPRA:	x	x	–	–	–
Sybase:	x!	x	–	–	–

*   SQL is retrieval only in current release
!   Transact SQL

Does the user language (if provided) include the following commands or their equivalent?

- SELECT (WHERE condition)
- PROJECT (all columns, named columns only, all except named columns)
- JOIN ?

- DIVIDE (join followed by project of first relation's columns only)
- ORDER (by sort key)
- INSERT (new rows)
- DELETE (on selected rows)
- UPDATE (on selected rows)
- UNION (set operations on compatible tables)
- INTERSECTION (set operations on compatible tables)
- DIFFERENCE (set operations on compatible tables)
- GROUP BY (merge rows with same values of the specified attribute)
- HAVING (condition on aggregate value of an attribute in a relation undergoing GROUP BY)

	SELECT	PROJECT	JOIN	DIVIDE	ORDER	INSERT	DELETE	UPDATE	UNION	INTERSECTION	DIFFERENCE	GROUP BY	HAVING
ADABAS:	x	x	x	x	x	x	x	x	x	x	x	–	–
BL700:	x	x	x	x	x	x	x	x	–	–	–	x	x
CA-UNIVERSE:	x	x	x	x	x	x	x	x	x	x	x	x	x
CRESTA/DB:	x	x	x	x	x	x	x	x	x	x	x	x	x
DATACOM/DB:	x	x	x	x	x	x	x	x	x	–	–	x	x
DB2:	x	x	x	x	x	x	x	x	x	x	–	x	x
FOCUS:	x	x	x	x	x	x	x	x	x	x	x	x	x
IDMS/R:	x	x	x	x	x	x	x	x	x	x	x	x	x
Model 204:	x	x	x	x	x	x	x	x	x	x	x	x	x
ORACLE:	x	x	x	x	x	x	x	x	x	x	x	x	x
SQL/DS:	x	x	x	x	x	x	x	x	x	x	–	x	x
SUPRA:	x	x	x	x	x	x	x	x	x	x	x*	x	x
Sybase:	x	x	x	x	x	x	x	x	–	–	–	x	x

* Not directly with SQL

These commands are essentially the "full range" of an orthodox RDBMS user language with respect to data manipulation. One would expect all systems claiming to be relational either to have these verbs explicitly or to be able to give the same effect with a fairly brief combination of other commands. The difficulty in reading any significance into the differences in the table is in knowing how complex the formulation is in cases where the direct verb is not used.

If the product provides a user language, which data definition/ restructuring commands are included? The more orthodox RDBMSs will include these commands in the same user language, but some have separate facilities and possibly provide just as adequate functionality.

	CREATE TABLE	ALTER TABLE	ADD attribute	DROP attribute	DROP TABLE	CREATE VIEW	DROP VIEW	NULL VALUE of attribute
ADABAS:	x	x	x	x	x	x	x	x
BL700:	x	x	–	–	x	x	x	–
CA-UNIVERSE:	x	x	x	x	x	x	x	–
CRESTA/DB:	x	x	x	x	x	x	x	x
DATACOM/DB:	x	x	x	x	x	x	x	x
DB2:	x	x*	x	–	x	x	x	x
FOCUS:	x	x	x	x	x	–	–	–
IDMS/R:	x	x	x	x	x	x	x	–
Model 204:	x	x	x	x	x	x	x	x
ORACLE:	x	x	x	x	x	x	x	x
SQL/DS:	x	x	x	–	x	x	x	x
SUPRA:	x	x	x	x	x	x	x	x
Sybase:	x	x	x	–	x	x	x	x

* The SQL ALTER statement allows changes to be made to indexes, tables, storagegroups, and tablespaces. Not all properties may be changed using the ALTER statement; some changes may require objects to be dropped and recreated.

What is involved in modifying the data definition?

ADABAS:	Use of PREDICT on-line data dictionary.
BL700:	Copying table over. This requires one command.
CA-UNIVERSE:	Change made to active data dictionary using ALTER command or through the data modeling facility; the rest is automatic.

CRESTA/DB: Not difficult.

DATACOM/DB: Execution of the command that
                  is processed by DATACOM/DB
                  and recorded in DATADIC-
                  TIONARY automatically.

DB2:   Some modifications can be
                  done via the ALTER statement;
                  others might require DROP and
                  RECREATE.

FOCUS: Changes are made to a
                  keyword-
                  driven data definition file.
                  Changes are actively reflected
                  in applications

IDMS/R: —

Model 204:   —

ORACLE: The data definition held in the
                  data dictionary is updated auto-
                  matically whenever a data defi-
                  nition statement is executed.

SQL/DS: Fully interactive and dynam-
                  ically executed. However, for
                  performance reasons tables may
                  need unload/reload.

SUPRA: Alter statement, either interac-
                  tive or in batch. No table reload
                  necessary. All views adjusted
                  automatically.

Sybase: Issuing new command.

Does the user language (if provided) include the following options on the JOIN function?

- Nested join syntax (e.g., SQLs IN)
- Symmetric linking condition (e.g., WHERE C. CUSTNUM = O. CUSTNUM)
- Recursive join (i.e., on two attributes in the same relation)
- Outer join (see Question 4)
- Greater-than, less-than joins
- Full Cartesian product

The second option of JOIN is generally regarded as more elegant than the first, although, especially where SQL is an option, both may be provided. Recursive JOIN is very desirable. The more complex types are useful to have to avoid what might otherwise be very long-winded circumlocutions. The trend is for more RDBMSs to offer them or to be working toward their early implementation.

	Nested join syntax	Symmetric linking condition	Recursive join	Outer join	Greater-than, less-than joins	Full Cartesian product
ADABAS:	x	x	x	x	x	x
BL700:	x	x	x	x	x	x
CA-UNIVERSE:	x	x	x	x	x	x
CRESTA/DB:	x	−	x	x	−	−
DATACOM/DB:	x	x	x	x	x	−
DB2:	x	x	x	−*	x	x
FOCUS:	x	x	x	x	−	−
IDMS/R:	−	x	x	x	x	−
Model 204:	x	x	x	x	x	x
ORACLE:	x	x	x	x	x	x
SQL/DS:	x	x	x	−	x	x
SUPRA:	x	x	x	x	x	x
Sybase:	x	x	x	x	x	x

* No, except by Program Offering DB2 Outer Join

Does the user language (if provided) include facilities to support the following requirements?

- Save a result relation into a temporary name
- Derived attributes within a row
- Aggregation (over all rows by attribute/column)
- Transaction control (e.g., LOCK, FREE)
- Update transaction control (e.g., COMMIT, ROLLBACK)

These facilities are not classic relational DBMS language features but are desirable for practical purposes. For any multi-user situation, the last two can be regarded as essential—though in some packages they are provided in the "embedded" forms rather than in the user language.

	Save a result relation	Derived attributes within a row	Aggregation	Transaction control	Update transaction control
ADABAS:	x	x	x	x	x
BL700:	x	x	x	–	x
CA-UNIVERSE:	x	x	x	x	x
CRESTA/DB:	x	–	x	–	–
DATACOM/DB:	x	x	x	x	x
DB2:	–*	x	x	x!	x
FOCUS:	x	x	x	x	x
IDMS/R:	x	x	x	x	x
Model 204:	x	x	x	x	x
ORACLE:	x	x	x	x	x
SQL/DS:	x+	x	x	x^	x
SUPRA:	x	x	x	x@	x@
Sybase:	x	x	x	x	x

*   Not within SQL, but QMF provides this function
!   At tablespace level
+   Format 2 insert or QMF only
^   Automatically handled except locktable
@   Automatic

Does the user language (if provided) support access to data in a different DBMS by allowing relational views to be defined on top of a possibly nonrelational structure? If so, what DBMSs/files can be handled? The need for bridges to existing data held in other DBMSs is obvious when one considers that the relational product is often acquired by an organization as a "second" DBMS.

ADABAS:	Yes, ADABAS, DB2, DL/I, VSAM, OS data sets.
BL700:	No.
CA-UNIVERSE:	No.
CRESTA/DB:	Not yet.
DATACOM/DB:	No.
DB2:	Yes. VSAM through DB/2 VSAM Transparency Program Offering.
FOCUS:	Yes, SQL/DS, DB2 (Read/Write), SQL/DS, DB2, IMS, ADABAS, IDMS/R, TOTAL/TIS/SUPRA, DATACOM DB, Model 204 (read only).
IDMS/R:	Yes, VSAM.

Model 204:   Yes, through Imagine/204: DB2,
             VSAM, DL/I, and others.
ORACLE: Yes, DB2, SQL/DS, others
             planned.
SQL/DS: Yes. VSAM through SQL/DS
             Application Interface for VSAM
             Feature under CICS/VM.
SUPRA: VSAM, RMS, DB2, DL/I and
             Rdb planned.
Sybase: Oracle, RDB, IMS, Ingres, DB2,
             flat files. Sybase provides an
             open server environment that
             gives the user the tools to set
             up links with any DBMS or flat
             file system.

Does the relational DBMS include an "embedded" language that can be used within a "host" programming language? It is generally a requirement that there are some cases of application logic that will be better written using a "3GL" host programming language, and one would expect an RDBMS to support such a facility.

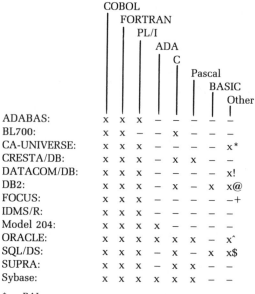

	COBOL	FORTRAN	PL/I	ADA	C	Pascal	BASIC	Other
ADABAS:	x	x	x	−	−	−	−	−
BL700:	x	x	−	−	x	−	−	−
CA-UNIVERSE:	x	x	x	−	−	−	−	x*
CRESTA/DB:	x	x	x	−	x	x	−	−
DATACOM/DB:	x	x	x	−	−	−	−	x!
DB2:	x	x	x	−	x	−	x	x@
FOCUS:	x	x	x	−	−	−	−	−+
IDMS/R:	x	x	x	−	−	−	−	−
Model 204:	x	x	x	x	−	−	−	−
ORACLE:	x	x	x	x	x	x	−	x^
SQL/DS:	x	x	x	−	x	−	x	x$
SUPRA:	x	x	x	−	x	x	−	−
Sybase:	x	x	x	x	x	x	−	−

*	BAL
!	RPGII, BAL
@	Assembler, APL2
+	BAL
^	Assembler
$	Assembler, APL2, REXX

What facilities does the embedded language offer? The embedded language should be functionally equivalent to the user language. It may also be the means by which applications involving concurrency control are implemented. Another frequent reason for using an embedded language is for record-by-record processing, where a row cursor is appropriate.

Again the answers reveal different approaches, with some of the "prerelational" DBMSs offering concurrency and cursor functions through their old-style DML or HLI.

	All facilities provided in user language	LOCK, COMMIT, ROLLBACK, etc.	CURSOR functions (i.e., individual row functions)
ADABAS:	x	x	x
BL700:	x	x	−
CA-UNIVERSE:	x	x	x
CRESTA/DB:	x	−	x
DATACOM/DB:	x	x	x
DB2:	x	x	x
FOCUS:	−	−	x
IDMS/R:	x	x	x
Model 204:	x	x	x
ORACLE:	x	x	x
SQL/DS:	x	x	x
SUPRA:	x	x	x
Sybase:	x	x	x

Which access control facilities are provided?

● DBA granting of access permissions
● Granting of access permissions can be delegated by authorized users
● Separate read and write access control
● Access control by table
● Access control by view
● Access control by specified columns
● Access control by rows (specified instances)
● Revoking of access permissions

Access control is clearly vital in any DBMS, since by definition it is concerned with the sharing of data. Therefore, most, if not all, of the preceding facilities are essential. Access control by views is a particularly valuable feature, since it provides an easy mechanism to introduce controls by both rows and columns.

	Access permissions granted by DBA	Access permissions granted by users	Separate read and write	By table	By view	By specified columns	By rows	Revoking of permissions
ADABAS:	x	x	x	x	x	x	x	x
BL700:	x	–	x	x	x	x	x	x
CA-UNIVERSE:	x	–	x	x	–	x	x	x
CRESTA/DB:	–	–	–	x	x	–	–	–
DATACOM/DB:	x	x	x	x	x	x	x	x
DB2:	x	x	x	x	x	x!	x!	x
FOCUS:	x	–	x	x	x	x	x	x
IDMS/R:	x	x	x	x	x	x	x	x
Model 204:	x	x	x	x	x	x	x	x
ORACLE:	x	x	x	x	x	x@	x!	x
SQL/DS:	x	x	x	x	x	x!	x!	x
SUPRA:	x	x	x	x	x	x	x*	x
Sybase:	x	x	x	x	x	x	x	x

!   Using VIEWS
@   Update access by column, rest by view

What integrity checks may be defined for the data?   Because of their use as end-user as well as production tools, relational databases have a greater requirement for good integrity checking then "traditional" databases. Few relational databases are well endowed in this respect.

ADABAS:	Domain integrity via PREDICT Dictionary (including unique values).
BL700:	Macros can be created to test for existence and valid data ranges.
CA-UNIVERSE:	Full referential and entity integrity is supported.

CRESTA/DB:	Input validation. Check "Reports" defined by user.
DATACOM/DB:	Full entity and referential integrity checking.
DB2:	Check utility, check index integrity (DB2 V2 includes Check Data utility to check referential integrity). The CHECK utility can check the integrity of an index against the table it is defined for. Three data exits are provided which may be invoked to perform various functions against the data, including checking validity, etc. DB2 V2 includes referential integrity. All the existing DB2 utilities have been modified, as appropriate, to handle referential integrity. There is a new utility CHECK DATA that will check that no referential constraints are violated by data in the tables.
FOCUS:	Range and existence checks plus referential integrity checks.
IDMS/R:	Edit tables, referential integrity, value lists.
Model 204:	—
ORACLE:	Views may be created with "check option" such that any updates or insertions must satisfy the WHERE criterion specified.
SQL/DS:	Referential integrity. Data must match data type. No domain integrity.
SUPRA:	Entity, referential, domain validation.
Sybase:	Full referential and domain integrity plus user defined.

Of the following criteria for a fully relational RDBMS (which are attributed to Dr. E. F. Codd), which does your RDBMS satisfy? Ted Codd is widely recognized as the man who created the relational database market. He has drawn up a list of criteria that can be used to specify the degree of adherence to the relational model. Some of Codd's criteria may be considered to be of academic interest only; the following list shows the criteria that will be of interest to practical users.

- Every value can be accessed via a combination of table name, primary key, and column name.
- The database description can be represented at the logical level in the same way as ordinary data.
- The RDBMS must support at least one language that includes data definition, view definition, data manipulation, integrity constraints, authorization, and transaction begin, commit, and rollback.
- It must be possible to update all views that can be updated in theory.
- Applications and terminal activity must have physical independence from the data.
- Applications and terminal activity must have logical independence from the data.
- The integrity constraints must be definable in the relational sublanguage and stored in the catalog, not in the application programs.
- It must not be possible to use any low-level language supported by the DBMS to subvert or bypass the integrity rules and constraints expressed in the high-level relational language.

Access by combination
| Database description at logical level
| | Language support
| | | Update of all views
| | | | Physical independence
| | | | | Logical independence
| | | | | | Definable integrity constraints
| | | | | | | Prevention of subversion

	Access by combination	Database description at logical level	Language support	Update of all views	Physical independence	Logical independence	Definable integrity constraints	Prevention of subversion
ADABAS:	x	x	x	x	x	–	x	–
BL700:	x	x	x	–*	x	x	–	–
CA-UNIVERSE:	x	x	x	x	x	x	x	x
CRESTA/DB:	x	–	–	x	x	x	x	–
DATACOM/DB:	x	x	x	x	x	x	x	x
DB2:	x	x!	x	–@	x	x	x	x
FOCUS:	x	x	x	–	x	x	x	x
IDMS/R:	x	x	x	x	x	–	x	–
Model 204:	x	x	x	x	x	x	–	x
ORACLE:	x	x	x	–	x	x	–	x
SQL/DS:	x	x+	x	x^	x	x	x	x
SUPRA:	x	x	x	x	x	x	x	x
Sybase:	x	x	x	x	x	x	x	x

* Most but not all
! Information about all DB2 objects is stored within DB2 tables (the Catalog)
@ Some but not all
+ System catalogs are tables themselves
^ Only views derived from a single table

BIBLIOGRAPHY

Atre, S. "Data Base: Structured Techniques for Design, Performance, and Management." J. Wiley & Sons, 1988, New York.

Brathwaite, K. S. "Analysis, Design, and Implementation of Data Dictionaries." McGraw-Hill, 1988, New York.

Braithwaite, K. S. "Data Administration." J. Wiley & Sons, 1985, New York.

Braithwaite, K. S. Management involvement in data security, integrity, and privacy. *AGT Tech.* Memo, No. 15, 1980, Edmonton, Alberta.

Braithwaite, K. S. A study of data base security, integrity and privacy in a large public utility. *AGT Tech.* Memo, No. 20, 1980, Edmonton, Alberta.

Brown, D. RACF a program to enhance security and control. *EDPACS*, **6:**12, Institute of Internal Auditors, June 1979, Washington, D.C.

Brown, P.S. Computer security a survey. NCC, 1976 AFIPS Press, Washington, D.C.

Brown, P. S. "Security: Checklist for Computer Center Self-Audits." AFIPS Press, 1979, Washington, D.C.

Chen, P. P. "Proceedings of the International Conference on the Entity–Relationship Approach to Systems Analysis and Design." North-Holland Publishing, 1979, New York.

Chen, P. P. "Proceedings of the International Conference on the Entity–Relationship Approach to Information Modeling and Analysis." North-Holland Publishing, 1981, New York.

Courtney, R. H. Security risk assessment in electronic data processing systems. *AFIPS Conf. Proc.* 46, 1979, NCC 97-104, AFIPS Press, 1977, Washington, D.C.

Davenport, R.A. Data analysis for database design. *The Australian Computer Journal*, **10:**4, 122–137, 1979.

Dinardo, C. T. "Computer and Security." AFIPS Press, 1978, Washington, D.C.

Durell, W. R. "Data Administration." McGraw-Hill, 1985, New York.

Engelman, C. Audit and surveillance of multi-level computing systems. MTR-3207, The Mitre Corporation, June 1975, Tyson Corner, Virginia.

Fernandez, E. B. "Database Security and Integrity." Addison-Wesley, 1981, Reading, Massachusetts.

Fisher, A. S. "Case Using Software Development Tools." Wiley, 1988, New York.

Fosdick, H. "Using IBM's ISPF Dialog Manager." Van Nostrand Reinhold, 1987, New York.

Gillenson, M. "Database: Step-by-Step." Wiley & sons, 1985, New York.

Gillenson, M. and Goldberg, R. "Strategic Planning Systems Analysis and Data Base Design." Wiley & Sons, 1984, New York.

Grady, R. "Software Metrics." Prentice-Hall, 1987, Englewood Cliffs, New Jersey.

Hoffman, L. J. The formulary model for access control and privacy in computer system. SCAC Report No. 119, May 1970, Palo Alto, California.

Hsiao, D. K. "Computer Security." Academic Press, 1979, New York.

Hubbard, G. "Computer-Assisted Data Base Design." Van Nostrand Reinhold, 1981, New York.

Kahn, B. K. A method for describing the information required by the data base design process. *Proc. Int. ACM Sigmod Conf. Management of Data*, 1976, ACM Press, New York.

Katzan, H. "Computer Data Security." Van Nostrand Reinhold, 1973, New York.

Korth, H. F. and Silbersehatz, R. "Database System Concepts." McGraw-Hill, 1986, New York.

Larson, B. "The Database Expert's Guide to DB2." McGraw-Hill, 1988, New York.

Lusardi, F. "The Database Expert's Guide to SQL." McGraw-Hill, 1988, New York.

Lusk, E. L. A practical design methodology for the implementation of IMS database using the E–R model. *ACM* **4**, 9–21, 1980, ACM Press, New York.

Martin, J. "Information Engineering." Prentice-Hall, 1989, Englewood Cliffs, New Jersey.

Martin, J. and McClure, C. "Structured Techniques: The Basis for CASE." Prentice-Hall, 1988, Englewood Cliffs, New Jersey.

McClure, C. "CASE Is Software Automation." Prentice-Hall, 1989, Englewood Cliffs, New Jersey.

Novak, D. and Fry, J. The state of the art of logical database design. *Proc. 5th Texas Conf. Computing Systems (IEEE)*, Long Beach, California, 1976.

Stratland, N. Data security and its impact on EDP auditing. *EDPACS*, **3**:4, Institute of internal Auditors, October, 1979, Washington, D.C.

Weldon, J. L. "Database Administration." Plenum Press, 1981, New York.

Whitemore, J. C. Design for multics security enhancements. EDS-TR-74-176, Honeywell Information Systems, 1974, Palo Alto, California.

Whiten, N. "Managing Software Projects." Wiley & Sons, 1990, New York.

Yao, S. B. An integrated approach to logical database design. NYU Symposium on Database Design, May 18–19, 1978, New York University, New York.

INDEX